Professional Struts Applications
Building Web Sites with Struts, ObjectRelationalBridge, Lucene, and Velocity

John Carnell

Jeff Linwood

Maciej Zawadzki

Wrox Press Ltd. ®

Professional Struts Applications
Building Web Sites with Struts, ObjectRelationalBridge, Lucene, and Velocity

© 2003 Wrox Press

First Printed in March 2003

Published by Wrox Press Ltd,
Arden House, 1102 Warwick Road, Acocks Green,
Birmingham, B27 6BH, UK
Printed in the United States
ISBN 1-86100-781-7

Trademark Acknowledgments

Wrox has endeavored to provide trademark information about all the companies and products mentioned in this book by the appropriate use of capitals. However, Wrox cannot guarantee the accuracy of this information.

Credits

Authors
John Carnell
Jeff Linwood
Maciej Zawadzki

Commissioning Editor
Craig A. Berry

Technical Editors
Victoria Hudgson
Unnati Umesh Kulkarni

Project Managers
Cilmara Lion
Abbas Saifuddin Rangwala

Managing Editors
Matthew Cumberlidge
Kalpana Garde

Proof Reader
Chris Smith

Technical Reviewers
Cosmo Difazio Jr.
Stephen Foster
Benjamin Galbraith
Bjarki Holm
George Kowalski
Vinay Menon
Arthur Skip Walker

Production Coordinators
Sarah Hall
Santosh Haware
Manjiri Karande

Cover Design
Natalie O'Donnell

Indexer
Adrian Axinte
Andrew Criddle
Vinod Shenoy

About the Authors

John Carnell

John Carnell is a Principal Architect for NetChange, LLC (http://www.netchange.us). NetChange, LLC is an IT management consulting firm specialized in enterprise application design and implementation. John is also an adjunct facility member of the Waukesha County Technical College's (WCTC) School of Business. In addition, John is a prolific speaker and writer. He has spoken at national conferences, such as Internet Expo, the Data Warehousing Institute, and the CompleteProgrammer's Network Software Symposiums.

John has authored, co-authored, and has been a technical reviewer for a number of technical books and industry publications. Some of his previous works include:

- ❑ *J2EE Design Patterns Applied*, Wrox Press (2002)
- ❑ *Oracle 9i Java Programming*, Wrox Press (2002)
- ❑ *Beginning Java Databases*, Wrox Press (2001)
- ❑ *Professional Oracle 8i Application Programming*, Wrox Press (2001)

John is always open to queries and if you need to contact him about book-related questions or about training or consulting engagements, he can be reached at john.carnell@netchange.us.

The amount of work and effort that goes into writing a book cannot be understated. However, it is not the author's efforts alone and I think it important to recognize the people who often contribute directly and indirectly to the writing effort.

First, I would like to give thanks to my wife Janet and my son Christopher. Both of you are my inspiration. Janet, you are always there when I need strength and that is why I will always love Mia. Christopher, for being only 9 months old, you have an amazing ability to make me smile. Every time you make me laugh, I realize how precious you are and what you sacrifice when your "DA" is away writing.

Second, I would like to thank my mother, Deborah: Mom, you always pushed me. You sometimes questioned whether I was doing the right thing, but when I look in the mirror I see the reflection of your love and patience staring back at me.

To my father Salvatore: Dad, you passed on a long time ago but I can still feel your presence and your compassion have always served as a model to live my life.

Finally, the Wrox staff: Wrox editors work insane hours and they have to put up with neurotic and flaky writers (I am one of them). However, in the end, no matter what kind of pressure or deadlines they face, they always come in a cool and calm manner. Thanks Craig for this book and thanks Tony for our previous efforts! I always appreciate your time and effort.

John contributed Chapters 1-5 in this book.

Jeff Linwood

Jeff Linwood has been in software programming since he had a 286 in high school. He got caught up with the Internet when he got access to a Unix shell account and it has been downhill ever since. Jeff has published articles on several Jakarta Apache open source projects in *Dr. Dobb's Journal* and *JavaWorld*.

Jeff has a Bachelors of Science degree in Chemical Engineering from Carnegie Mellon University. He enjoys hiking, road trips, biking, and reading *Slashdot*. Jeff currently works for the Gossamer Group in Austin, Texas, on content management and web application syndication systems. He gets to play with all the latest open source projects there.

Jeff can be reached at jlinwood@yahoo.com.

I'd like to thank my family (Nancy, Gary, Judy, Rob, and Beth), my friends Don and Cherise in Arizona, Dave, Brandon, and all of my friends and co-workers in Austin. Special thanks to Skip Walker for reviewing the book. I'd also like to acknowledge the hard work and long hours that all of the volunteers on the Jakarta Apache projects put in.

Jeff contributed Chapters 6 and 7 to this book.

Maciej Zawadzki

Maciej Zawadzki is the President of Urbancode Software Development, Inc., a firm of software experts that offers custom development, developer training, and mentoring, as well as architecture and design evaluation services. Maciej is the original author of the open source Anthill Build Management Server and Urbancode's EJB Benchmark. He has over a decade of experience in the software industry, with the last six years focused on the development of enterprise-level server-side Java applications.

Maciej contributed Chapter 8 to this book.

Table of Contents

Table of Contents

Table of Contents

Table of Contents

Introduction

Software developers often have to spend a good 30-40% of their effort writing code that deals with such mundane tasks as screen navigation, validation, and business rule management. All of this "infrastructure" code distracts the development team from what is really important: writing application code that adds value to the organization they work for.

This book explores several Java open source development frameworks that have been built and made available from the Apache Software Foundation's Jakarta group. The Jakarta group is a collection of volunteers spread across the globe who contribute their time, energy, and intellect to building high-quality Java-based open source software. We chose to the use the Jakarta group's technology because they have become the de facto standard of excellence in the area of open source software.

Java open source development frameworks can significantly reduce the amount of time needed to build an application by providing a development team with a set of core services that take care of this application scaffolding. In the last three years the software development community has seen an explosion in the number of development frameworks available for writing applications.

While these frameworks are powerful they can sometimes be intimidating to use. They offer a lot of features, but often have haphazard documentation. The documentation for Java open source frameworks tends to be very detailed, but often fails to do what is needed by a developer learning how to use the framework.

> **That is, provide a straightforward explanation of the different pieces of the framework and demonstrate through code examples how to use the framework to start building applications.**

The Goal of This Book

With that being said, individuals who are looking at this book should realize that they will not get a detailed examination of every aspect of the frameworks we are covering. To cover each of these frameworks in full detail would require several books. Instead, the authors' goal in writing this book is to:

❏ **Introduce each of the different frameworks with enough detail so that the reader can begin working with them immediately**
The reality is that most people only gain a true mastery of a technology by using it. This book was written to help a developer gain enough insight to "jumpstart" their use of these technologies.

❏ **Use code as our roadmap**
Code is the language all developers speak, so this book places a heavy emphasis on code examples. The examples are straightforward and can easily be applied to your own projects.

❏ **Share our personal experiences**
Being successful with open source development frameworks goes beyond just the technology. The authors have blended their own experiences together to provide insights in how to build a business case for using open source technologies within your organization. In addition, the authors explore some common mistakes developers make when using open source development frameworks for this first time.

Who Should Use This Book?

This book was written for the intermediate to advanced Java developer who is looking at using open source development frameworks for their own projects. The authors did not spend a lot of time on introductory material regarding the Java programming language or web-based application development. This is a professional-level book that tries to address problems encountered by the software development professional in their work place.

The reader should be familiar with building web applications using Java technology. In addition, a basic knowledge of design patterns is helpful.

Technologies Used in This Book

This book is going to cover how to use and integrate the following Jakarta technologies:

❏ The Struts development framework

❏ The Lucene search engine

❏ The Velocity templating framework

❏ The ObjectRelationalBridge persistence tool

❏ The Ant build utility

All of these development tools and frameworks are available for download from the Jakarta web site (http://jakarta.apache.org).

All of the code examples were built and tested using JDK 1.3+ and were deployed running on the Jakarta group's Tomcat Servlet/JSP engine (version 4.0 higher). All J2EE examples were built using the J2EE 1.3 specification and were deployed on the JBoss application server (http://www.jboss.org).

The database used for the application code was deployed using version 3.23 of the MySQL database (http://mysql.org).

Conventions

To help you get the most from the text and keep track of what's happening, we've used a number of conventions throughout the book.

For instance:

> **These boxes hold important, not-to-be-forgotten information, which is directly relevant to the surrounding text.**

While the background style is used for asides to the current discussion.

As for styles in the text:

❑　When we introduce them, we **highlight** important words

❑　We show keyboard strokes like this: *Ctrl-K*

❑　We show filenames and code within the text like so: `<element>`

❑　Text on user interfaces and URLs are shown as: Menu

We present code in two different ways:

```
In our code examples, the code foreground style shows new, important,
    pertinent code
while code background shows code that is less important in the present
    context or has been seen before.
```

Customer Support

We always value hearing from our readers and we want to know what you think about this book: what you liked, what you didn't like, and what you think we can do better next time. You can send us your comments, either by returning the reply card in the back of the book, or by e-mail to feedback@wrox.com. Please be sure to mention the book title in your message.

Errata

We've made every effort to make sure that there are no errors in the text or in the code. However, no one is perfect and mistakes do occur. If you find an error in one of our books, like a spelling mistake or faulty piece of code, we would be very grateful for your feedback. By sending in errata you may save other readers hours of frustration, and of course, you will be helping us provide even higher quality information. Simply e-mail the information to support@wrox.com; your information will be checked and if, appropriate, posted to the errata page for that title or used in subsequent editions of the book.

To find errata on the web site, go to http://www.wrox.com/books/1861007817.htm. Click on the View errata link, which is below the cover graphic on the book's detail page.

E-Mail Support

If you wish to directly query a problem in the book with an expert who knows the book in detail then e-mail support@wrox.com. A typical e-mail should include the following things:

- ❏ The **title of the book**, **last four digits of the ISBN (7817)**, and **page number** of the problem in the Subject field.

- ❏ Your **name**, **contact information**, and the **problem** in the body of the message.

We won't send you junk mail. We need the details to save your time and ours. When you send an e-mail message, it will go through the following chain of support:

- ❏ Customer Support – Your message will be delivered to our customer support staff, and they will be the first people to read it. They have files on the most frequently asked questions and will answer anything general about the book or the web site immediately.

- ❏ Editorial – Deeper queries are forwarded to the technical editor responsible for that book. They have experience with the programming language or a particular product, and are able to answer detailed technical questions on the subject.

- ❏ The Authors – Finally, in the unlikely event that the technical editor cannot answer your problem, they will forward the request to the author. We do try to protect the authors from any distractions to their writing; however, we are quite happy to forward specific requests to them. All Wrox authors help with the support on their books. They will e-mail the customer and the editor with their response, and again all readers should benefit.

The Wrox support process can only offer help on issues directly pertinent to the content of our published title. Answers to questions that fall outside the scope of normal book support may be obtained through the community lists of our http://p2p.wrox.com/ forum.

p2p.wrox.com

For author and peer discussion, join the P2P mailing lists. Our unique system provides **Programmer to Programmer**™ contact on mailing lists, forums, and newsgroups, all in addition to our one-to-one e-mail support system. If you post a query to P2P, you can be confident that many Wrox authors and other industry experts on our mailing lists are examining it. At p2p.wrox.com you will find a number of different lists to help you, not only while you read this book, but also as you develop your applications.

To subscribe to a mailing list just follow these steps:

1. Go to http://p2p.wrox.com/

2. Choose the appropriate category from the left menu bar

3. Click on the mailing list you wish to join

4. Follow the instructions to subscribe and fill in your e-mail address and password

5. Reply to the confirmation e-mail you receive

1

The Challenges of Web
Application Development

This book will demonstrate the use of freely available **Java Open Source (JOS)** development frameworks for building and deploying applications. Specifically, we will focus on the JOS development frameworks available from the Apache Software Foundation's Jakarta group (http://jakarta.apache.org).

While most books are heavy on explanation and light on actual code demonstration, this book emphasizes approachable code examples. The authors of this book want to provide a roadmap of JOS development tools to build your applications. Our intent in this book is not to present each of the frameworks in minute detail. Frankly, many of the development frameworks presented in this book could have entire books written about them.

This book will build a simple application using the following Jakarta technologies:

- ❑ **Struts Web Development Framework**:
    A Model-View-Controller-based development framework that enables developers to quickly assemble applications in a pluggable and extensible manner.

- ❑ **Lucene**:
    A powerful indexing and search tool that can be used to implement a search engine for any web-based application.

- ❑ **Velocity**:
    A templating framework that allows a development team to easily build "skinnable" applications, whose "look and feel" can be easily modified and changed.

❑   **Ant**:
    An industry-accepted Java build utility that allows you to create sophisticated application and deployment scripts.

This chapter will not go into the details of the technologies listed above. Instead, it will highlight some of the common challenges in building web applications and explore some common design mistakes and flaws that creep into web-based application development efforts.

The truth is that, while all developers would like to write new applications from scratch, most of their time is spent in performing maintenance work on existing software. Identifying design flaws, referred to as antipatterns throughout this book, and learning to use JOS development frameworks to refactor or fix these flaws can be an invaluable tool.

Specifically, the chapter will explore how the following web-based antipatterns contribute to entropy within an application:

❑   Concern Slush
❑   Tier Leakage
❑   Hardwire
❑   Validation Confusion
❑   Tight-skins
❑   Data Madness

The chapter will end with a discussion of the cost savings associated with building your own application development framework vs. using JOS development framework.

Challenges of Web Application Development

In the mid-nineties, the field of software development was at its peak. The importance of using the Internet was quickly recognized as a revolutionary means for companies to communicate their data and processes not only to their employees but also to their customers.

Fueling the Internet explosion was the World Wide Web and the web browser. Web browsers offered an easy-to-use graphical interface that was based on standards and allowed easy to access to data on a remote server. Originally, the web browser was viewed as a means of allowing end-users to access static content of a web server. Early web applications were often nothing more than "brochures" that provided users browsing information about a company and the products and services it offered.

However, many software developers realized that the web browser was a new application development platform. The web browser could be used to build applications that provided customers with direct and easy access to corporate applications and data sources. This was a revolutionary concept because for many businesses, it eliminated the need to have a large customer service department to handle routine customer requests. It allowed them to make their processes more efficient and develop a more intimate relationship with their customers.

The 'thin' nature of the web browser meant that software could be quickly written, deployed, and maintained without ever touching the end user's desktop. Moreover, the web browser had a naturally intuitive interface that most end users could use with very little training. Thus, the Internet and the web browser have become a ubiquitous part of our computing lives and a primary application development platform for many of today's applications.

However, the transition of the web from being an electronic brochureware to an application development platform has not been without growing pains. Writing anything more than a small web application often requires a significant amount of application architecture before even a single line of real business logic is written.

The additional overhead for implementing a solid web application is the result of several factors, such as:

❑   The stateless nature of the web: **HyperText Transport Protocol (HTTP)**, the communication protocol for the web, was built around a request/response model. The stateless nature means a user would make a request and the web server would process the request. But the web server would not remember who the user was between any two requests.

❑   The limited functionality of a web browser-based user interface: The web originally started as a means to share content and not perform business logic. The **HyperText Markup Language (HTML)** used for writing most web pages only offers limited capabilities in terms of presentation. A web-based interface basically consists of HTML forms with a very limited number of controls available for capturing user data.

❑   The large number of users that the web application would have to support: Often a web application has thousands of concurrent users, all hitting the application using different computing and networking technologies.

❑   The amount of content and functionality present in the web application: In equal proportion to the number of end users to be supported, the amount of content and navigability of a web-based application is staggering. Many companies have web-based applications where the number of screens the user can interact with and navigate to, is in the thousands. Web developers often have to worry about presenting the same content to diverse audiences (also known as internationalization).

❑   The number of systems that must be integrated so that a web application can give its end-user a seamless, friction-free experience: Most people assume that the front-end application that a user interacts with is where the majority of development work takes place. This is not true. Most web application development involves the integration of back-office applications, built on heterogeneous software and hardware platforms and distributed throughout the enterprise. Furthermore, extra care must be taken in securing these back-end systems so that web-based users do not inadvertently get access to sensitive corporate assets.

❑   The availability of web-based applications: Web-based applications have forced enterprises to shift from a batch-process mentality to one in which in their applications and the data they use must be available 365 days a year.

Early web-based development was often chaotic and free flowing. Little thought was given to building web applications based on application frameworks that abstracted away many of the "uglier" aspects of web development. The emphasis was on the first-to-market with their functionality. However, the size and complexity of web-applications grew with time, and many web developers found it increasingly difficult to maintain and add additional functionality to their applications.

Most experienced software developers deal with this complexity, by abstracting various pieces of the application's functionality into small manageable pieces of code. These small pieces of code capture a single piece of functionality and when taken together, as a whole, form the basis for an application development framework.

An application development framework can be defined as:

> **A collection of services that provides a development team with common set of functionality, which can be reused and leveraged across multiple applications.**

For web applications these services can be broken down into two broad categories:

- ❑ Enterprise Services
- ❑ Application Services

Enterprise Services

Enterprise services consist of the traditional "plumbing" code needed to build applications. These services are extremely difficult to implement and are outside the ability of most corporate developers.

Some examples of enterprise services include:

- ❑ Transaction management, to make sure any data changes made to an application are consistently saved or rolled back across all the systems connected to the application. This is extremely important in a web application that might have to process the updates across half a dozen systems to complete an end-user's request.

- ❑ Resource pooling of expensive resources like database connections, threads, and network sockets. Web applications often have to support thousands of users with a limited amount of computing resources. Managing the resources, like those named above, is essential to have a scalable application.

- ❑ Load balancing and clustering to ensure that the web application can scale gracefully, as the number of users using the application increases. This functionality also ensures that an application can continue to function even if one of the servers running the application fails.

- ❑ Security to ensure the validation of the users (authentication) and that they are allowed to carry out the action they have requested (authorization). While security is often considered an administrative function, there are times when application developers need to be able to access security services to authenticate and authorize an action requested by a developer.

Fortunately, the widespread acceptance of building applications based on application servers has taken the responsibility for implementing these services out of the hands of corporate developers. Enterprise-level development platforms, like Sun's J2EE specification and Microsoft's .NET, offer all of the functionalities listed above as ready-to-use services that developers can use in their applications. Application servers have minimized the amount of plumbing code that an application developer has to write.

This book will not be focusing on the services provided by J2EE and .NET application servers, rather it will be focusing heavily on the next topic, that is application services.

Application Services

The enterprise-level development platforms, such as J2EE or .NET, simplify many of the basic and core development tasks. While the services offered solve many of the enterprise issues (security, transaction management, etc.), they do not help the application architect with the often daunting task of building web applications that are maintainable and extensible. To achieve the goals of maintainability and extensibility, several challenges need to be overcome. These challenges include:

- **Application navigation**
  How does the end user move from one screen to the next? Is the navigation logic embedded directly in the business logic of the application? Web applications, having a primitive user interface, can allow users to access and navigate through thousands of pages of the content and functionality.

- **Screen layout and personalization**
  As web applications run in a thin client environment (with a web browser) the screen layout can be personalized to each user. Since user requirements are constantly changing, web developers need to adapt the look and feel of the application quickly and efficiently. Design decisions made early in the application design process can have a significant impact on the level of personalization that can be built into the application at a later date.

- **Data validation and error handling**
  Very few web development teams have a consistent mechanism for collecting data, validating it, and indicating to the end user that there is an error. An inconsistent interface for data validation and error handling decreases the maintainability of the application and makes it difficult for one developer to support another developer's code.

- **Reuse of business logic**
  This is one of the most problematic areas of the web application development. The reason being that the development team does not have a disciplined approach for building their business logic into discrete components that can be shared across applications. The developers couple the business logic too tightly to the web application, and resort to the oldest method of reuse, cut and paste, when they want to use that code in another application. This makes it difficult to maintain the business rules in a consistent fashion across all of the web applications in the organization.

- **Data abstraction services**
  The majority of web application development efforts involve integrating the front-end web application with back-office data stores. However, data retrieval and manipulation logic is tedious code to write, and when poorly implemented, ties the front-end application to the physical structure of the back-office data stores.

Unfortunately, most developers either do not have the expertise, or are not given the time to properly address these issues *before* they begin application development. With the pressure to deliver the application, they are forced to "design on the fly" and begin writing code with little thought to what the long-term implications of their actions are. This may result in antipatterns being formed within their applications.

These antipatterns contribute to the overall complexity of the application and ultimately increase the presence of entropy within the code base. Often, they do not realize the impact of these antipatterns until they have implemented several web applications and are now trying to support these applications while developing new code.

In the following sections, we are going to introduce the concept of patterns and antipatterns. We will then identify some common antipatterns in web application development, based on the discussion above.

An Introduction to Patterns and Antipatterns

One cannot open a software development journal or go to the bookstore without seeing some reference to the software design patterns. While many software architects love to enshroud patterns in a cloak of tribal mysticsm, the concept of a software development pattern is really quite simple.

Design patterns capture software development patterns in a written form. The idea behind design patterns is to identify and articulate these best practices so as to help other developers avoid spending significant amount of time re-inventing the wheel. The notion of the design pattern did not originate in the field of software development.

Design patterns originated in the field of architecture. In 1977, an architect by the name of Christopher Alexander was looking for method to identify common practices in the field of architecture that could be used to teach others. The concept of design patterns was first applied in 1987 by Kent Beck and Ward Cunningham (http://c2.com/doc/oopsla87.html).

However, the embracing of the software development design patterns really occurred with the publishing of the now famous Gang of Four (GOF) book, *Design Patterns: Elements of Reusable Object Oriented Software* (Gamma, Helm, Johnson, Vlissides), Addison-Wesley, ISBN 0-201-63361-2. First published in 1995, this classic book identified 23 common design patterns used in building software applications.

The concept of the antipattern was first introduced in the groundbreaking text, *AntiPatterns: Refactoring Software, Architectures, and Projects in Crisis,* John Wiley (ISBN 0-471-19713-0). The book examined common patterns of misbehavior in system architecture and project management. As we are going to explore various antipatterns associated with web application development, it is useful to look at the original definition (from the aforementioned book) of the antipattern:

> *"An antipattern is a literary form that describes a commonly occurring solution to a problem that generates decidedly negative consequences. The antipattern might be the result of a manager or developer not knowing any better; not having sufficient knowledge or experience in solving a particular type of problem, or having applied a perfectly good pattern in the wrong context."*

An antipattern is a means of establishing a common language for identifying poor design decisions and implementations within your application. Antipattens help identify poor design decisions and help give suggestions on how to refactor or improve the software. However, the suggestions associated with the antipattern are only that. There is no right or wrong way of refactoring any antipattern, because every instance of an antipattern is different. Each instance of an antipattern will often have a unique set of circumstances that caused the pattern to form. Web antipatterns focus on poor design decisions made in web-based applications.

It is not an uncommon experience for a developer studying an antipattern to stop and say: "I have seen this before" or to feel a sense of guilt and think, "I have done this before". Antipatterns capture common development mistakes and provide suggestions on how to refactor these mistakes into workable solutions. However, there is no single way to refactor an antipattern. There are dozens of solutions. In this book, we merely offer guidance and advice, not dogmatic principles.

The web development antipatterns that are identified and discussed throughout this book are not purely invented by the authors. They are based on their experience working with lots of development teams on a wide variety of projects.

Web Application Antipatterns

For the purpose of this book, we have identified six basic antipatterns that most Java developers will encounter while building web-based applications. The web development antipatterns to be discussed are:

- ❑   Concern Slush
- ❑   Tier Leakage
- ❑   Hardwired
- ❑   Validation Confusion
- ❑   Tight-Skins
- ❑   Data Madness

Since the original definition of an antipattern is a *literary* form of communication, we will discuss each antipattern in general. In addition, symptoms of the antipattern are identified along with suggested solutions. However, the solutions described in this chapter are only described in very general terms. Specific solutions for the antipatterns will be demonstrated, throughout this book, by the application of JOS development frameworks.

This book is written considering the following key points:

- ❑   Most developers are not architects. They do not have the time and energy to write the application architecture from the ground up and provide constant maintenance to it. Therefore, practical solutions using existing applications frameworks are more valuable than the code snippets demonstrating one part of the application architecture. So try to leverage other people's code. Every feature you use in application architecture is one less feature you have to write and maintain yourself.

- ❑   There are already several open source development frameworks ready for immediate use. Writing an architecture code might be an intellectual challenge for some developers. It is often a waste of time, resources, and energy for the organization employing them.

- ❑   Focus on the business logic. Most developers' job is to solve business problems. Every time you are confronted with writing a piece of code that is not directly related to solving a business problem, make sure whether or not you actually need to write it.

- ❑   Keep it simple. The most extensible and maintainable systems are ones that always focus on simplicity.

> **Architecture is done right when it has been implemented in the most straightforward fashion. Simplicity, above everything else, will guarantee the long-term maintainability and extensibility of an application.**

Now let's discuss the different web antipatterns in more detail.

Concern Slush

The Concern Slush antipattern is found in applications when the development team has not adequately separated the concerns of the application into distinct tiers (that is, the presentation, business, and data logics). Instead, the code for the applications is mixed together in a muddy slush of presentation, business, and data-tier logic. While development platforms like J2EE help the developer separate their application logic into distinct tiers, it is ultimately how the application is designed that determines how well defined the application tiers are. Technology can never replace good design and a strong sense of code discipline.

This makes the code extremely brittle. Changing even a small piece of functionality can cause a ripple effect across the entire application. In addition, every time a business rule needs to be modified or the structure of a data store changes, the developers have to search the application source code looking for all the areas affected by the change. This leads to a significant amount of waste of time.

This antipattern also tends to lead to insidious bugs creeping into the application, because invariably the developer will miss some code that needs to be modified. The bugs resulting from these missed changes might not manifest themselves for several months after the change to the original code was made. Hence, the development team has to spend even more time tracking down the missed code and fixing, testing, and redeploying it.

Most of the time the Concern Slush antipattern will emerge for one of the following reasons:

- **Lack of an application architect**
  The development team does not have a senior developer playing the role of an application architect. The application architect's primary role is to provide high-level design constructions for the application. The architect establishes the boundaries for each of the application tiers. They enforce development discipline within the team and ensure that the overall architectural integrity of the application stays in place.

- **Inexperience of the development team**
  The development team is new to enterpise development and writes its web applications without a thorough understanding of the technology it is working with.

  Often the developers are used to writing code in a procedural language (such as C or Visual Basic) and are suddenly appointed to write web-based applications with an object-oriented language like Java. The development team members continue to rely on their original training and continue to write code in a procedural fashion, never fully embracing object-oriented design techniques.

- **Extreme time pressures**
  The team realizes its mistakes during the development, but has been given an agressive deadline to be met. The developers toss caution to the wind and begin coding. They often do not realize how poorly designed the application is, until they begin the maintenance phase of the project.

- **Using an application prototype as the base for development**
  Often, the development team will work together on a quick prototype for an application, as a proof of concept. The code for the prototype is poorly designed. However, upon demonstrating the prototype, it becomes a huge success. The developers now fall victim to this success as they are put under a heavy pressure to deliver the prototyped application quickly. Therefore, they decide to use the prototype code as the basis for the application.

Symptoms

For web applications based on the Java platform, the symptoms for this antipattern will usually manifest in one of two ways:

❑   Overloading of responsibilities

❑   Indiscrete mixing of presentation, business, and data logic

The first symptom, overloading of responsibilities, occurs when a single or small group of servlets or JSP pages are responsible for all actions carried out by the application. A basic tenet of object-oriented design is that each class within the system should have small, well-defined, and discrete set of responsibilities.

A class, in this case a servlet or JSP page, is overloaded when the exact responsibilities of the class are not clear. Servlets and JSP pages that do not have well-defined responsibilities are often said to be "fat" or "heavy". The call to such a page always includes a number of control parameters that are used by the servlet or JSP page. These control parameters are used by conditional logic embedded by the servlet or JSP page to determine the code to be executed within the page.

In the second symptom, a servlet or JSP page mixes together presentation, business, and data logic into one massive procedure call. An example of this particular symptom is out.write() statements mixed with business logic and data logic. JSP pages are even more prone to this abuse because JSP scriptlets make it extremely easy, for even a novice web developer, to quickly build an application.

In the second symptom, we are assuming that no session Enterprise JavaBeans (EJBs) are being used in the application. When EJBs are used in an application most developers will gravitate towards putting the business logic in the EJBs. The Concern Slush antipattern manifests itself in EJBs, when the developer indiscriminately mixes data-access logic with the application's business logic in the EJB.

Solution

The solution is to provide software constructs that adequately separate the application's code into readily recognizable presentation, business, and data logic. For Java-based applications, the JSP Model-2 architecture is the recommended architectural model for building web applications. The JSP Model-2 is based on the concept of a Model-View-Controller (MVC) framework.

In an MVC framework, all requests made by the end user are routed through a controller class (usually a servlet) that determines the business object used to carry out the request. The data that the users request and the corresponding business object are considered as a model piece of the framework. After the business object has processed the user's request, the results are forwarded by the controller to the view portion of the framework. The view portion of the framework is responsible for the presentation logic that renders the results of the user's request to the end user. The diagram overleaf presents a conceptual view of an MVC framework:

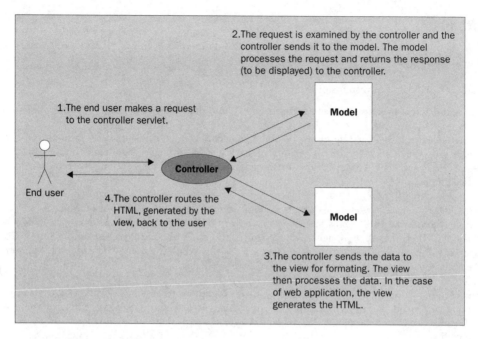

The two key features of the MVC framework are:

❑ The clean separation of the presentation, business, and data logic into self-contained software constructs. The MVC framework acts a natural roadmap, which helps the software developer ensure that they keep their application's logic broken into distinct pieces.

❑ The emphasis on building an application through declarative programming. Since all the access to presentation, business, and data logic is controlled through a single entity (that is, the controller), the developer can easily change the behavior of the application by changing the configuration data being fed to the controller. The application developer can completely "rewire" the code to display a different presentation interface or apply different business logic without having to touch the source code for the application.

Tier Leakage

The Tier Leakage antipattern occurs in applications that have been separated into three distinct layers of application logic. Tier leakage occurs when code and functionality from one tier are exposed to the other tiers.

This antipattern occurs when the application architect does not enforce the principle of "closed" tier architecture. A closed tier architecture allows each tier to communicate only with the tiers immediately above and below it. In other words, the presentation tier can only communicate with the business tier. It should never bypass the business tier and access data directly. The communication between the tiers happens via well-defined interfaces that do not expose the underlying implementation details of that tier to the one above.

In the case of Tier Leakage, the application architect breaks the application into three tiers, but they also allow communication between the tiers to be open. This means the presentation tier can still call and invoke services on the data-access tier. In addition, even if there is encapsulation of services, the underlying tier details still remain exposed. This allows the developers to bypass the application partitions put in place and use functionality they should not have access to.

The diagram below illustrates the differences between a closed and open tier architecture:

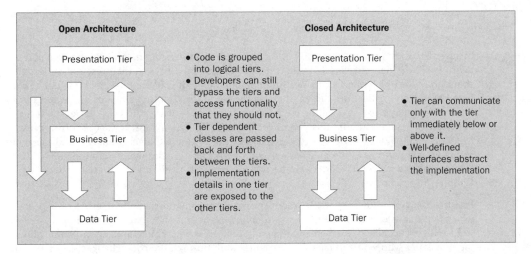

The end result of not enforcing a closed tier architecture is that, while various classes within the web application can be identified and grouped together in distinct tiers, there still exist dependencies between the tiers. This means that the changes to one tier can have side effects that ripple through the code in the other tiers.

This antipattern occurs when the development team has not defined discrete interfaces that hide the implementation details of one application tier from another. The causes for the Tier Leakage antipattern are very similar to those of the Concern Slush antipattern; developer inexperience, compressed delivery dates, and inappropriate reuse of an application prototype.

Symptoms

Some of the symptoms of Tier Leakage include:

❑ Changes to one tier break the code in other tiers

❑ You find that you cannot easily reuse a piece of code in one tier because of dependencies on a class in another tier

The first symptom is a common mistake. Instead of wrapping data retrieved from the data tier, the business tier exposes the details about the data tier, by allowing the data-tier objects to be passed back to the presentation tier. This results in the presentation class being unnecessarily exposed to the data-access technology being used to retrieve data (that is, JDBC, JDO, entity beans). It also tightly couples the presentation code to the physical column names, data types, and data relationships from the database. If physical details of the database change, developers need to walk through all of the code in the application to reflect the database changes.

The second symptom occurs when the developer allows tier specific classes to be passed back and forth between the different tiers. For example, you may have several classes, responsible for the business logic within your web application, which you'd want to reuse in a Swing based application. However, you cannot easily reuse the business logic, as it accesses an `HttpSession` object passed to it. The developer, rather than pulling the data out of the session object and then passing it to the business class, passes the `HttpSession` directly to the class.

Solution

There are three steps that can be taken to avoid tier leakage:

- ❏ Ensure that all the communication between the different tiers of an application takes place behind well-defined interfaces. Again, this means that one tier (say, the presentation tier) should only be able to access the tier immediately below it (say the business logic tier). In a Java-based web application, this can be accomplished through the judicious application of J2EE Design patterns. (We will be covering certain details of specific J2EE design patterns. For more information about this you may refer to *J2EE Design Patterns Applied*, Wrox Press, ISBN: 1-86100-528-8.) J2EE design patterns like the Business Object, Data Access Object, and Value Object patterns all do an excellent job of wrapping the implementation details of the classes within a particular tier. These design patterns will be described in greater detail in Chapter 5.

- ❏ Preform frequent code reviews. If you are using a version-control system, establish a process where nothing is checked into the version control system without another developer reviewing it. Provide a checklist of elements in the code that must be architecturally compliant. Make the developer who wants to check in the code, walk through the code changes they have made and have the reviewer compare this against the compliancy checklist.

  This review is designed to be very short (no more than five minutes long). It forces the developers to verbalize exactly what they have written and give the reviewer a chance to catch tier-leakage mistakes before they creep into the overall code base.

- ❏ Leverage JOS development frameworks, such as Struts, to abstract away the implementation details of one tier from the other. These frameworks provide services that allow you to minimize dependencies between the application tiers.

While any one of the steps shown above can help minimize the risk of Tier Leakage, you will probably find that using all three steps combined is the most effective. As you will see in later chapters, even with application frameworks such as Struts, you will still need to apply the J2EE design patterns within your application.

Using a development framework can still create dependencies in your code if you are not careful. You can still end up having your application being too tightly bound to the application development framework. Chapter 5 will look at how we can leverage various J2EE design patterns to cleanly separate your application code from the development framework.

Hardwired

While the Tier Leakage antipattern dealt with dependencies being created at the architectural level of the application, the Hardwired antipattern occurs when developers create dependencies at the application level. Hardwiring arises when the developer does not provide configurable plug-in points for screen navigation and application business rules. These items are hard coded into the application source code; thus, any changes to functionality require the source code to be altered, recompiled, and redeployed.

The Hardwired antipattern makes maintenance of web applications difficult because:

❑   Web applications can have thousands of pages of functionality. Hardwiring the pages that a user can navigate to directly in the application source code creates tight dependencies between the pages. This makes it difficult to rearrange the order in which screens are accessed. It also makes it nearly impossible to break screens into independent entities that can be reused across multiple applications.

❑   The business rules for a web application are in a constant state of flux. There is an unrelenting demand by organizations to provide a personalized web experience to their customers. Therfore, hardwiring the creation and invocation of business rules directly to a particular page demands the constant modification of the application source code by the web development team of the organization.

The Hardwired antipattern develops because the web development team does not use a declarative approach to build its applications. A declarative design approach separates the application's "what happens" functionality from the application's "how it happens" functionality.

In a declarative architecture, the application is broken into small pieces of functionality that can be configured together using metadata. Metadata is essentially data about data. In most application frameworks, metadata is used to define how a user's request is to be carried out and processed by the framework.

Metadata is usually stored in configuration files, independent of the application source code. When the application development team needs to change the behavior of the application, they do it by changing the metadata configuration. Using metadata to control application behavior is often termed declarative architecture. In a declarative architecture, you define certain behavior and the architecture code carries out the behavior. By using this type of architecture, new functionality can be added or existing behavior modified by changing the metadata. Thus the behavior of the application is not hardcoded and does not require a recompilation and redeployment for the changes to take place.

The advantage of a declarative architecture is that it allows the development team to introduce new functionality into the application, while minimizing the risk of ripple effects that the change will have throughout the system. The disadvantage is that it can be overdone to the point where the application becomes over abstracted, hard to maintain because of the complex configuration rules, and suffers from poor performance.

Symptoms

The symptoms for the Hardwired antipattern begin to manifest themselves, when changes to the application require functionality that was not in its original scope. The symptoms of hardwiring include:

❑ The hardcoding of navigation logic directly within the applications source code. If your development team has to search through all of the application's source code for changing a link, your application is showing signs of the Hardwired antipattern.

❑ An inability to change the workflow of the application without a significant amount of refactoring of the application's source code. If the application you are writing always assumes that data captured from the end user is always entered in a certain screen order, then the application is hardwired.

❑ There is no consistency in how or when a particular screen invokes the business rules. This inconsistency makes it difficult to maintain the application's code and also means that new logic or functionality cannot be "swapped" into the application. This is symptom particularly common in projects with large development teams.

One of the true indications that your application is suffering from the Hardwired antipattern is that a small navigation or business rule change causes major headaches for you or your development team.

Solution

The Hardwired antipattern can be refactored, by taking the responsibility of writing the code for screen navigation and business rule invocation out of the hands of the application developer. Instead, this logic should reside as a service within the application architecture. Since this service is no longer a responsibility for the developer, consistency can be enforced among the entire development team and much of the application's navigation, workflow, and business rule invocation functionality can be described as metadata.

The MVC pattern is again an excellent tool for refactoring this antipattern. The controller of the MVC is responsible for application navigation. The business logic for the application is cleanly separated from the presentation logic. Metadata is used to tie all of these different pieces together.

Even if an MVC development framework is used, the only true way to guarantee that a Hardwired antipattern does not develop is through strong software development practices. These practices include:

❑ Judicious use of design patterns to ensure that hardwiring does not occur between your application code and the development framework you are using to build the application. We will explore these design patterns in greater detail in Chapter 5.

❑ Write an application framework development guide that explains to your development team, how the application framework is partitioned into different pieces. Clearly identify the architectural best practices and identify those practices that violate the integrity of the framework. The framework developer's guide must be constantly updated, to ensure that material contained within it matches the current implementation of the framework. Depending on the complexity of the project, your development guide might be something as simple as a set of UML diagrams explaining the major framework components along with some notes about any design patterns used. Do not always rely on the JOS framework documentation. JOS projects can have haphazard documentation.

❑ Use the application framework development guide as a tool during code and design reviews. Hold these review sessions frequently and hold the developers accountable for adhering to standards defined in the guide.

Do not become overzealous while avoiding Hardwiring in you applications. It is easy to want to make everything in the application configurable.

> **Good application architecture lies in its simplicity. You always have to negotiate between the need to generalize and abstract framework functionality and the need to avoid tight dependencies. In the end, over abstraction or tight dependencies both lead to the same problem: code that is too complex to understand and maintain easily.**

The Stuts development framework takes a declarative approach for writing applications. This framework allows you change the behavior of the application by modifying configuration files. In both of these frameworks, application configuration is very easy and is designed to avoid the over-abstraction problems mentioned above.

Validation Confusion

The Validation Confusion antipattern revolves around the inconsistent application of validation and business logic in an application. Many web application developers do not clearly separate the application's validation logic from its business logic in an organized fashion.

The end result is the application consisting of a mess of JavaScript and server-side code for handling data validations. The data validation code is split between the front-end screens and also embedded within the business rules that carry out end-user requests. Logic for handling end user errors is often inconsistently applied and mixed with the business logic.

For the purpose of this book, validation logic is defined as any type of user interface code that involves:

❑ Formatting of data being presented or collected from the end user.

❑ Checking to ensure the user entered the required data.

❑ Type-checking to ensure that the data entered is the appropriate type. For instance, you want to make sure that when the user is asked to enter numerical data in a field, they do not enter character or strings (such as "abcd") as a numerical value.

❑ Simple bound checking logic to ensure that the data collected falls within a certain range (whether it is numeric or date data being collected)

Validation logic is considered extremely "lightweight". Validation rules are considered light, because changing them should not have a significant amount of impact on the overall business processes supported by the application. Business logic is the "heavyweight" cousin of validation logic. Business logic supports business processes. Changing this logic can have a significant impact on how a business is operated.

Why worry about the separation of validation logic from business logic? Failure to separate these two types of logic from one another makes it difficult to support the code. Since the validation logic is not centralized, developers have multiple spots to check when modifying a business rule.

More importantly, not cleanly partitioning the application's validation logic from its business logic can make it more difficult to reuse that business logic in another application. Validation rules are often very specific to an application. Business logic can be abstracted, generalized, and reused across multiple applications. However, with validation rules specific to the application embedded inside the business logic, a tight dependency is created that makes code reuse problematic.

A clean validation logic approach can help avoid previous antipatterns mentioned, namely Concern Slush and Tier leakage. The validation layer can be responsible for adapting the input provided by the user interface to the input required by the business logic. This can help prevent the user interface details from leaking down into the business logic.

This antipattern occurs when the web development team has not clearly defined how it is going to handle the validation of the data collected from the end user. The developers pass all of the data directly to the business rules in the application, without first putting the data through some kind of filter that ensures the data validity.

Symptoms

Validation Confusion can be spotted in one of the following cases:

❑ When asked where a particular validation rule for a screen resides, a developer has to search through presentation (as a language like JavaScript or JSP scriptlets) and business tier code to find the exact spot for the rule.

❑ The development team needs to constantly refactor code, because application specific validation rules are embedded inside the business logic it wants to reuse.

❑ There is no consistent mechanism for "how" validation errors are handled. End-users encounter different formats for errors being displayed. For example, in an application with Validation Confusion some of the errors might be displayed directly in the web browser while other errors will pop up in JavaScript alert windows. In short there is not consistency in the error handling that the end user experiences.

Solution

Refactoring the Validation Confusion antipattern can be accomplished by defining a consistent set of services used for form validation in the web application. These validation services are invoked before any of the business logic for the application is invoked. Any validation errors that occur are immediately processed and the end user is notified in a consistent and repeatable fashion.

This means that the validation for the application only resides in one tier of the application, using a consistent mechanism, for invoking the validation rules. This might mean having all of the application validation logic reside in a standard set of JavaScript class libraries, or, as is the case with Struts, moving all validation logic for a form to a set of Java classes that are invoked whenever the user submits data.

In Chapter 3 we will discuss the mechanism provided by Struts for handling form validation and errors.

Tight-Skins

Web-based applications have the ability to deliver unprecedented amounts of personalized content to the end user. Traditionally, companies pushed information out to their customers in a mass marketing approach. In this approach, customers were categorized into broad groups who shared similar interests and backgrounds. The company would then direct different advertising messages about their products to these groups. Mass marketing approach was considered successful if the organization running marketing campaign received a response rate of one percent.

The web development platform, with its thin-client, easy-to-use, and personalizable interface, has turned the mass marketing concept on its head. Web-based applications can deliver tightly-focused information and functionality to individual users, with very specific preferences and interests. Many of the sophisticated web applications that are currently online:

- ❑ Allow the end user to choose the information and content that they want to see

- ❑ Personalize the color, font, and layout of the web application user interface to reflect the user's personal choices

- ❑ Reach a global audience by having the web application presented in their language, using a look and feel appropriate for the end user's culture

However, the ability to deliver a customizable user interface to the end user requires some careful planning, in the design phase of a project. The Tight-Skins antipattern is a presentation-tier antipattern. It forms when the development team has not built its presentation tier to be flexible enough to handle personalized content for individual end users.

This antipattern can occur for a number of reasons:

- ❑ The original requirements of the application did not include an extensible user interface. However, requirements for the application changed. Since the development team had not planned interface flexibility upfront, it now has to face the challenge of refactoring the presentation tier of the application to support it.

- ❑ The development team was too focused on reuse at the business and data tier. It wrote the presentation tier in a monolithic fashion that did not have a component structure. Most developers are very comfortable thinking in terms of generalization, abstraction, and extensibility for server-side logic. However, the presentation code is often written with no real attempt to "templatize" it into components that can be easily swapped in and out of the application.

- ❑ The development team used the presentation code from the application prototype (if there was one) for the production application. This is usually done to save time and is again a reflection of the lack of design consideration for the user interface.

Unfortunately, the only way to combat the Tight-Skins antipattern, after it is formed, is to rewrite the user interface from scratch. This is why it is critical to identify personalization requirements for the application before any serious development work begins.

23

Symptoms

This antipattern has a number of symptoms including:

❑ The application's content is not separate from the application code. If you need to modify your application's source code to change the content delivered to the end user, this is a definite sign of a Tight-Skins antipattern. A common example would be when a JSP page has a significant amount Java scriptlets code and HTML mixed together. There are chances of tight coupling between some of the contents of the page and the JSP scriptlets.

❑ The application screens are not based on templates. Designing your application's screen so that it is divided into discrete components (that is, the header, the footer, navigation bars, etc.), without which you will find yourself propagating the same change across multiple screens.

❑ The presentation tier is hardcoded in one language. Many web applications start to support only one group of people. All content for the application is written in only that language. If the development team has to support multiple languages, it usually has to scour all code for any content that will be displayed to the end user then convert them over to the new language. This is especially painful, if more than two languages have to be supported.

Solution

The solution for the Tight-Skins antipattern involves cleanly separating application content from your Java source code. This way the content can be presented in multiple formats without having to wade through code. This also makes it easier to change how the content is to be displayed to the end user. Some ways of separating the application's content from its source include:

❑ Using JSP tag libraries to completely abstract any Java code from a JSP page. This way presentation content can easily be changed without having to wade through Java application code.

The Struts framework makes heavy use of custom JSP tag libraries. Some of the Struts tag libraries will be covered in greater detail in Chapter 3.

❑ Separating the application's content by making it external to the application's source code. Struts allows you to separate screen content and messages in a file independent of the application. This way, content can be changed without having to change the actual JSP page. This material will be covered in Chapters 3 and 4.

❑ Building your application's screens using the concept of a template. Templates divide the application screen into small components that can be easily plugged in and out. They also allow common elements in the presentation to be shared across all of the screens in the application. Velocity uses a templating language to accomplish this. Using Velocity makes it impossible to embed Java code inside the application. Chapter 6 of this book will introduce the reader to the Velocity templating language and its various uses.

Data Madness

Most web developers know that embedding data access logic inside of presentation code is poor design. Applications written in this fashion are difficult to maintain, and are tightly coupled with the underlying data structure of the database that they are manipulating. A change to the database can cause many elements of the user interface to be visited and often modified.

Many Java-based web development teams never allow the presentation layer of an application to directly obtain a database connection and use it to access a data store. Instead, they always wrap these calls inside the business tier. The development team never breaks out the **Create, Replace, Update, and Delete (CRUD)** logic associated with manipulating the data into a distinct set of classes. Instead, they intermix business and data access logic together inside the business tier.

The Data Madness antipattern forms when the application's architect does not decide how data-access logic is to be abstracted away from the other tiers in the application. When building a data-access tier, the following items have to be considered:

- ❑ How data is going to be accessed and manipulated

- ❑ Mapping relational data to Java-based objects

- ❑ Abstracting away physical details and relationships of the underlying data store

- ❑ Wrapping non-portable, vendor-specific functionality

- ❑ How transactions are going to be managed, particularly, transactions that cross multiple objects manipulating data from a data source

As most developers do not think of a data-access tier while designing, the formation of a Data Madness antipattern can significantly increase the amount of time and effort needed to complete a project. Consider the following:

- ❑ Most database access in Java is accomplished via the JDBC standard.

- ❑ The JDBC standard uses standard SQL code to retrieve and manipulate data from a relational database. It is very easy to write poorly behaving SQL. Most Java developers find it tedious to write and maintain a small task, like retrieving some data from a table that requires a lot of code.

- ❑ The JDBC API, while using Java objects in the actual API, does not take an object-orientated approach to data access. JDBC uses a relational model that retrieves data in a very row-oriented relational manner. This method of access is very clumsy and time consuming for a Java developer to work with.

- ❑ In a medium to large application, a significant amount of a developer's time can be spent doing nothing more than writing JDBC code to access data.

A significant amount of a development team's time is taken up writing data-access code (usually SQL code). Code that does not fit an object-oriented development model is prone to be coded improperly, and is scattered haphazardly through an application's business tier. This is the crux of the Data Madness antipattern.

Symptoms

Most development teams do not see the symptoms of the Data Madness antipattern until they are well along in their development efforts. The first symptoms of the Data Madness antipattern include the following:

- ❑ The repetition of the same data access logic within several business logic classes. This symptom is particularly prevalent in large development projects where very little development work is being done in the database (there are no stored procedures, triggers, or queries being executed inside the database). Developers are left to write their own data-access code, and often two developers will go after the same data for use in two different areas in the application and end up with almost identical data-access code.

❑ The dawning realization by the members of the development team that they are seriously behind schedule on the project. Upon examination they find that most of their efforts are spent writing database code.

❑ The sudden appearance of data-access helper classes and "homegrown" persistence frameworks within the application source code. These helper classes might help reduce the amount of code the developer is writing, but they do not solve the overall architectural issues of not having a well-defined data-access tier.

Later symptoms of the Data Madness antipattern usually appear in the maintenance and enhancement phase of the project:

❑ A database has to be reorganized for performance reasons. Several table relationships change and the development team faces a daunting refactoring project, as it has to pour through all of the source code and make modifications to reflect the underlying database change.

❑ The developers try to port the application to a new database platform, and have found that several key pieces of logic are relying on vendor-specific functionality. For example, one of the most common problems areas is the generation of primary keys for a database. Without a well-designed data-access tier, moving an application from SQL Server to Oracle can be a coding nightmare. SQL Server has the concept of auto-incrementing columns, while Oracle does not; it has sequence objects. This means that to port the code you need to find every SQL statement that uses sequences and change it. This is not a small task in a large project.

With a well-defined data access strategy in place, the development team could have abstracted how primary keys are generated, and centralized all of this logic in one class responsible for primary key generation.

❑ The development team wants to refactor the application to use the latest and greatest technology. (Java Data Objects, web services; you choose the buzzword.) Since the technology used to retrieve and manipulate data is not abstracted away from the classes using the data, the development team must again perform search and replace missions to find all code that uses the existing technology, and replace it.

Solution

Two steps can be taken to refactor the Data Madness antipattern:

❑ Provide a clearly defined data-access tier, which provides services that the business tier can use to access data. These services should abstract away the physical details of the database being accessed, any vendor-specific APIs being used, and how the data is actually being retrieved.

❑ Avoid writing data-access code, whenever possible. Use technologies that will let the developer map the underlying database tables to **Plain Old Java (POJ)** objects. These significantly reduce the amount of code that the development team must write and let it more clearly focus on the functionality of the application.

The first step above is a design-based approach involving the use of common J2EE data-tier patterns, like the Data Access Object and Value Object patterns, to abstract away database and data access details. These patterns are extremely easy to implement and when used help the development team maintain data-tier code without affecting the rest of the application.

The second step is a technology-based approach. Java is an object-oriented language that is not well suited to deal with the table-centric structure of relational databases. Instead of having the development team write its own SQL code, use an Object Relational (O/R) mapping tool to perform Create, Retrieve, Update, and Delete (CRUD) actions on behalf of the developers.

O/R mapping tools allow the development team to declare how data retrieved from the database maps to Java objects. O/R mapping is not a new concept. The J2EE API supports the concept of **Container-Managed Persistence (CMP)**-based entity beans. CMP-based entity beans allow the developer to provide O/R mappings to the J2EE application server and in turn, the application server generates all of the SQL code needed to access the database.

An alternative to entity beans is to use commercial O/R mapping tools. These tools have been available for years to C++ developers and have started gaining a significant amount of acceptance from the Java development community.

Commercial O/R mappings tools, while being very powerful, often carry long and expensive licensing agreements. They are often complicated to use and being a commercial product require a heavy investment in training, before the development team becomes proficient in their use.

However, over the last two years, JOS O/R mapping tools have started gaining more and more acceptance as an alternative means of building data access tiers. In Chapter 5 of this book, we are going to examine how one such JOS O/R mapping tool, ObjectRelationalBridge can be used to solve many of the problems created by the Data Madness antipattern.

Antipatterns, JOS Frameworks, and Economics

When web antipatterns form in an application, the cost of building and maintaining that application grows substantially. The development team's time is eaten up with the complexity that has crawled its way into the application. Less time is available to write real code and the code that is written is usually of mediocre quality.

Why are these antipatterns allowed to form? Developers do not purposely write poorly designed applications. We believe that web development frameworks can significantly reduce the occurrences of web antipatterns forming within an application. Antipatterns sometimes appear because applications are extremely complex to build and implement. Developers do not purposely go out and introduce these antipatterns. These antipatterns often occur because the developers try to manage the complexity of just implementing the application's business logic. At times, they do not realize that the decisions they make now will come at a high price later when an antipattern manifests itself.

A well-designed web development framework will promote consistency and structure for the development team. A framework will provide core application services for screen navigation, data validation, error handling, business rule management, and data persistence. With all of these benefits why haven't more Java web developers adopted the use of web development frameworks in their application development efforts? The reasons vary:

❑   Writing a web development framework is expensive

❑   Writing a development framework usually requires senior developers and architects with a significant amount of design expertise

- ❑ Development teams have not been able to build a business case for spending the money necessary to build an application framework

- ❑ The development team had to spend the time necessary to maintain the development framework

Until recently, open source development frameworks have not been readily available to developers. This meant that if a development team wanted to use a framework, the developers needed to build it themselves. Writing a homegrown development framework can be an expensive undertaking. It usually requires a group of senior developers with several months of uninterrupted time to design, implement, and thoroughly test the development framework.

Most IT organizations do not have senior developers and architects sitting around with nothing to do. Usually these individuals are extremely over allocated and giving them the time to focus on one problem requires commitment from the highest level of management. Even after the framework is completed, additional ramp-up time is needed as the framework developers begin training the development teams in how to use the framework.

For example, the Struts framework has a significant number of services embedded in it. To write an in-house version that offers even a fraction of the services offered by Struts, you have to take into consideration the resources contributed to the Struts framework:

- ❑ Struts was built by some of the finest developers currently in the industry. Many of these individuals were senior Java developers who command extremely high salaries.

- ❑ The Struts framework has had literally hundreds of individuals testing and debugging the framework. Most organizations could not even begin to provide a Quality Assurance (QA) team that could thoroughly debug a framework like Struts.

- ❑ Struts is now a mature framework that has literally hundreds of client implementations all running on a wide variety of hardware and Java platforms.

For an organization to build a framework like Struts for internal use with the same level of sophistication and quality assurance could literally cost between a half a million and a million dollars.

Let's not forget that even after a custom framework has been built, the costs of the framework continue to accumulate, as you begin to factor in the development resources needed to maintain and support the framework code base.

For organizations building their own application frameworks, it can take up to year or a year and a half before the organization starts seeing firm return on investment from its framework development efforts. (This includes the time needed to develop the framework and actually build two or three applications using the framework.) This is simply too large of a leap of faith for most companies to make.

Java open source development frameworks offer a viable alternative to building your own application architecture. These frameworks provide the following advantages:

- ❑ They are free to use. Most JOS frameworks have a liberal licensing agreement that lets you use the framework free of charge for building your applications. The only real restrictions that come into play with open source development tools is that the group sponsoring the tools places restrictions on repackaging the tools and selling them as your own.

❑ They are well supported. All of the open source development frameworks covered in this book enjoy a significant amount of support. High priority bugs that are discovered within the framework are usually fixed and the fixes made available for general use within hours. In addition, mailing lists and Internet news groups offer a wealth of information on how to solve common development problems encountered with JOS development frameworks.

This information is free of charge and unlike most commercial software products does not require an annual support contract. Some open source projects have groups willing to sell support for the product. (Such as, the JBoss Group at http://jboss.org, which not only builds the JBoss application server, but also offers different levels of paid support for the project.)

❑ They are extensible. If you find there are features lacking in the framework you have chosen, there is nothing stopping you or your development team from extending it. The source code is readily available for modification. Many of the features found in open source frameworks started out as the result of challenges encountered by developers using the framework. The developers extended the framework to handle their problem and then donated their solution back to the framework's code base.

There are a few downsides with open source development frameworks that should be noted:

❑ Documentation for an open source framework can be extremely vague. People writing the frameworks are donating most of their time and energy to do something that they love: write code. But the same level of attention is not paid to the mundane, but equally important task of writing documentation. Occasionally, a JOS development framework does require the developer to crack open a debugger to figure out what the framework is doing.

❑ Open source frameworks tend to be very Darwinistic when it comes to features in the framework. High priority bugs in the JOS frameworks are often found and fixed immediately. However, bugs that are of a low a priority for the JOS framework developers might never be fixed. This can be problematic for a development team using the framework that needs that particular bug fixed.

❑ JOS development frameworks are relatively new technology. Things can still go wrong with them and then cause unexpected behavior in your application. It is imperative that if your development team is going to write mission-critical software with a JOS framework, it needs to perform a significant amount of testing. In addition, the developers need to ensure that the framework that they have chosen to use is supported by a vibrant development group that actively supports their code.

Open source frameworks free a development team from having to invest its time in writing infrastructure code. Infrastructure code is the entry price you must pay before you can seriously begin writing an application. From the authors' anecdotal experiences, in many projects, up to 40-60% of development effort involve the implementation of infrastructure code. For the "we don't have time for architecture" development teams, that 40-60% of infrastructure development effort is usually spent in increased maintenance of the application over the course of its lifetime.

> **Trying to cut costs by implementing complex architectures shifts the upfront architect and infrastructure costs to the maintenance phase of the application.**

Ultimately, leveraging the functionality in open source frameworks translates into three direct benefits:

❑ Less complexity for the application developer in writing their applications

❑ More focus on writing code that has a direct benefit to the organization

❑ A significant cost-savings, by allowing the development team to access a significant amount of functionality without having to pay a dime for it

Both the benefits listed above allow the developers to produce higher quality code and deliver their applications more quickly to their end users.

From a management perspective, there are still some items to consider before you use a JOS development framework on your projects:

❑ Using a Java Open Source framework does not eliminate the need to have an application architect or architecture team. You still need individuals who can support JOS framework questions and issues.

❑ The initial adoption of a JOS framework does require extra time to be built into a project plan. The development team is going to need time to learn how to effectively use the JOS framework. This means that the first one or two applications built on the framework might take more time than they would have taken without using the framework.

❑ For the first application built on the framework, you should have someone who is experienced with the framework to mentor your team. This might require bringing in outside consulting resources. Consulting costs will be market rate if the JOS framework chosen is widely known and used (that is, Struts). For more obscure JOS frameworks, consulting costs could be significantly higher.

The JavaEdge Application

As stated earlier in this chapter, the purpose of this book is to provide a simple and straightforward roadmap that demonstrates how to successfully use the Jakarta web development frameworks. To do this, we are going to build a simple WebLog application (also known as a Blog). A WebLog, in its simplest form, is an electronic bulletin board where one user can post a story and other users can comment it. Often, a WebLog ends up to be a combination of reports on real-world events with a heavy dose of editorial bias from the storywriters and their commentators. Our WebLog is called the JavaEdge.

The requirements for the JavaEdge application are:

❑ **Visitor Registration**
Individuals who visit the JavaEdge Blog can register themselves to be the members of the JavaEdge community. By registering, the users can receive the weekly JavaEdge newsletter.

❑ **Browse Stories**
Visitors to the JavaEdge web site will be able to see the latest top ten stories posted by the JavaEdge community. When browsing the stories, the JavaEdge user will be able to see a short summary of the story. Clicking on a link next to each story will bring up the complete story listing.

❏ **Browse Comments**
When a user clicks on a link next to each story, they will be presented with not only a complete listing of the story they have chosen but also all of the comments associated with that particular story. Each posted comment will display the comment text, when the comment was posted, and who posted it.

❏ **Post Stories and Comments**
Individuals can post a story or comments for an already existing story. If the individuals choose to register themselves as JavaEdge members, any stories or comments posted by them will show the name they provided during the registration process. If they do not register as the JavaEdge members, they can still post stories and comments, but their name will not appear next to the story. Instead, the story will be posted as from a anonymous user.

❏ **User Registration**
Users can register to become the members of the JavaEdge community by providing some simple information (such as name, e-mail address, user-ID, password, etc.)

❏ **Search capabilities**
A user can search all the stories, posted on the JavaEdge web site, using a simple key word search engine. Any hits found by the search engine will be displayed as a list of URLs

The application code for JavaEdge is relatively sparse because the authors wanted to focus more on the underlying open source frameworks than building a full-blown application. In addition to demonstrating the capabilities of the Jakarta Java development frameworks, the application will illustrate some basic design principles that will ensure the long-term maintainability and extensibility of the JavaEdge code base.

Summary

Not every application developer needs to be an architect. However, all application developers need to have some basic understanding of software architecture. Otherwise, it is easy to make common design mistakes, which form into antipatterns that can make code difficult to support and extend.

This chapter has identified six common antipatterns that often spring up in web-based application development. These antipatterns are:

❏ Concern Slush

❏ Tier Leakage

❏ Hardwired

❏ Validation Confusion

❏ Tight-Skins

❏ Data Madness

Along with descriptions of these antipatterns, general solutions to these antipatterns were discussed. A common theme that has formed throughout our discussions of solutions is that JOS development frameworks offer a structured mechanism to develop applications and minimize the amount of infrastructure code being written. Developing an application framework is an expensive proposition. Open source frameworks have the advantage of being:

- ❑ Free of charge

- ❑ Supported by a large and enthusiastic development community

- ❑ Easily extended to support new features and functionality

We also discussed the requirements of the JavaEdge Application that we are going to develop in this book.

The rest of this book will demonstrate the technique to use the following open source frameworks to refactor the antipatterns discussed earlier:

- ❑ Struts web development framework

- ❑ Turbine/Velocity framework

- ❑ ObjectRelationalBridge (OJB)

- ❑ Lucene

- ❑ Ant

After reading this book you should have:

- ❑ A working definition of what an application framework is, the knowledge of the costs and efforts of building an application development framework, and the attractiveness of the open source framework.

- ❑ The ability to identify web antipatterns within your own projects. You should be able to understand the root causes of these antipatterns and the long-term architectural implications of the antipatterns.

- ❑ An understanding of what steps need to be taken to refactor the antipatterns.

- ❑ The ablity to use common JOS development frameworks, like Struts, to refactor these antipatterns out of your applications.

- ❑ A comprehensive set of best practices for each of the frameworks discussed in this book. These best practices will cover a range of topics including what are common development mistakes when using the framework and what design patterns can be used to supplement the services offered by the framework.

Creating a Struts-based MVC Application

Building a web-based application can be one of the most challenging tasks for a development team. Web-based applications often encompass functionality and data pulled from multiple IT systems. Usually, these systems are built on a wide variety of heterogeneous software and hardware platforms. Hence, the question that the team always faces is how to build web applications that are extensible and maintainable, even as they get more complex.

Most development teams attack the complexity by breaking the application into small manageable parts, which can be communicated via a well-defined interface. Generally, this is done by breaking the application logic into three basic tiers: the presentation tier, business logic tier, and data access tier. By layering the code into these three tiers, the developers isolate any changes made in one tier from the other application tiers. However, simply grouping the application logic into three categories is not enough for medium to large projects. When coordinating a web-based project of any significant size, the application architect for the project must ensure that all the developers write their individual pieces to a standard framework that their code will "plug" into. If they do not, the code base for the application will be in absolute chaos, because multiple developers will implement their own pieces using their own development style and design.

The solution is to use a generalized development framework, which has specific plug-in points for each of the major pieces of the application. However, building an application development framework from the ground up entails a significant amount of work. It also commits the development team to build and support the framework. Framework support forces the development team to exhaust those resources that could otherwise be used for building applications.

The next three chapters of this book will introduce the reader to a readily available alternative for building their own web application development framework, the **Apache Jakarta Group's Struts development framework**. These chapters do not cover every minute detail associated with the Struts development framework; instead, they guide readers on how to use Struts to build the JavaEdge appication, described in Chapter 1.

This chapter is going to focus on installing the Struts framework, configuring it, and building the first screen in the JavaEdge application. We cover the following topics in this chapter:

❑ A brief history of the Struts development framework

❑ A Struts-based application walkthrough

❑ Setting up your first Struts project, including the physical layout of the project, and an explanation of all the important Struts configuration files

❑ Configuring a Struts application. Some of the specific configuration issues that will be dealt with here are:

   ❑ Configuring the Struts ActionServlet

   ❑ Configuring Struts "actions" in the `struts-config.xml` file

❑ Best practices for Struts configuration.

In addition to our brief Struts configuration tutorial, we are going to discuss how Struts can be used to build a flexible and dynamic user interface. We will touch briefly some, but not all, of the customer JSP tag libraries available to the Struts developer. Some of the tag libraries that will be covered in this chapter include:

❑ Manipulating JavaBeans, by using the Struts bean tag library

❑ Making JSP pages dynamic by leveraging the conditional and iterating power of the Struts logic tag library

Let's begin our discussion with some of the common problems faced while building an application.

The JavaEdge Application Architecture

The JavaEdge application that we are going to develop, is a very simple WebLog (that is, a Blog) that allows the end users to post their stories and comment on the other stories. We have already discussed the requirements of the JavaEdge application in Chapter 1 in the section called *The JavaEdge Application*. The application is going to be written completely in Java. In addition, all the technologies used to build this application will be based on technology made available by the Apache Group's Jakarta project.

In this section, we'll focus on some of the architectural requirements needed to make this application extensible and maintainable. This application is built by multiple developers. To enforce consistency and promote code reuse, we will use an application development framework that provides plug-in points for the developers to add their individual screens and elements.

The framework used should alleviate the need for the individual JavaEdge developer to implement the infrastructure code that is normally associated with building an application. Specifically, the development framework should provide:

❏   A set of standard interfaces for plugging the business logic into the application. A developer should be able to add and modify new pieces of functionalities using the framework, while keeping the overall application intact (that is, a small change in the business logic should not require major updates in any part of the application).

❏   A consistent mechanism for performing tasks, such as end-user data validation, screen navigation, and invocation of the business logic. None of these tasks should be hardcoded into the application source code. Instead, they should be implemented in a declarative fashion that allows easy reconfiguration of the application.

❏   A set of utility classes or custom JSP tag libraries, which will simplify the process in which the developer builds new applications and screens. Commonly repeated development tasks, such as manipulating the data in a JavaBean, should be the responsibility of the framework and not the individual developer.

The chosen development framework must provide the scaffolding in which the application is to be built. Without this scaffolding, AntiPatterns like the Tier Leakage and Hardwired AntiPatterns will manifest themselves. (These two AntiPatterns were introduced in Chapter 1.) We will demonstrate how Struts can be used to refactor these AntiPatterns in this chapter. Now, let's start the discussion on the architectural design of the JavaEdge application.

The Design

The development team decided to use a Model-View-Controller (MVC) pattern, as the basis for the application architecture. The three core components of the MVC pattern, also know as a Model-2 JSP pattern by Sun Microsystems, are shown below:

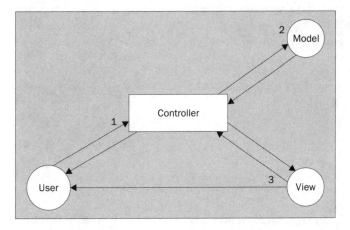

The numbers shown in the diagram represent the flow in which a user's request is processed. When a user makes a request to an MVC-based application, it is always intercepted by the controller (Step 1). The controller acts as a traffic cop, examining the user's request and then invoking the business logic necessary to carry out the requested action.

The business logic for a user request is encapsulated in the model (Step 2). The model executes the business logic and returns the execution control back to the controller. Any data to be displayed to the end user will be returned by the model via a standard interface.

The controller will then look up, via some metadata repository, how the data returned from the model is to be displayed to the end user. The code responsible for formatting the data to be displayed to the end user, is called the view (Step 3). View contains only the presentation logic and no business logic. When the view completes formatting the output data returned from the model, it will return execution control to the controller. The controller, in turn, will return control to the end user who made the call.

The MVC pattern is a powerful model for building applications. The code for each screen in the application consists of a model and a view. Neither of these components has explicit knowledge of the other's existence. These two pieces are decoupled via the controller, which acts as intermediary between these two components. The controller assembles, at run time, the required business logic and the view associated with a particular user request. This clean decoupling of the business and presentation logic allows the development team to build a pluggable architecture. As a result, new functionality and methods to format end-user data can easily be written, while minimizing the chance of any changes disrupting the rest of the application.

New functionality can be introduced into the application by writing a model and view and then registering these items to the controller of the application. Let's assume that you have a web application whose view components are JSP pages generating HTML. If you want to rewrite this application to generate PDF files rather than the HTML for the user's requests, you would only need to modify the view of the application. The changes you make to the view implementation will not have an impact on the other pieces of the application.

In a Java-based web application, the technology used to implement an MVC framework might look as shown below:

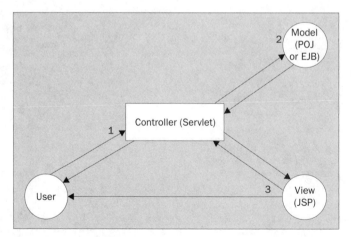

An MVC-based framework offers a very flexible mechanism for building web-based applications. However, building a robust MVC framework infrastructure requires a significant amount of time and energy from your development team. It would be better if you could leverage an already existing implementation of an MVC framework. Fortunately, the Struts development framework is a full-blown implementation of the MVC pattern.

In the next section, we are going to walk through the major components of the Struts architecture. While Struts has a wide variety of functionalities available in it, it is still in its most basic form an implementation of a Model-View-Controller pattern.

Using Struts to Implement the MVC Pattern

The Struts development framework (and many of the other open source tools used in this book) is developed and managed by the Apache Software Foundation's (ASF) Jakarta group. The ASF has its roots in the Apache Group. The Apache Group was a loose confederation of open source developers, who in 1995, came together and wrote the Apache Web Server. (The Apache Web Server is the most popular web server in use and runs over half of the web applications throughout the world.) Realizing that the group needed a more formalized and legal status, for protecting their open source intellectual property rights, the Apache Group reorganized as a non-profit corporation – the Apache Software Foundation – in 1999. The Jakarta group is a subgroup within the ASF, which is responsible for managing Java open source projects that the ASF is currently sponsoring.

The Struts development framework was initially designed by Craig R. McClanahan. Craig is a prolific open source developer, who is also one of the lead developers for another well-known Jakarta project, the Tomcat servlet container. He wrote the Struts framework to provide a solid underpinning for quickly developing JSP-based web applications. He donated the initial release of the Struts framework to the ASF, in May 2002.

All of the examples in this book are based on Struts release 1.0.2, which is the latest stable release. It is available for download from http://jakarta.apache.org/struts. There is currently a new release of Struts in beta testing, Release 1.1b. By the time this book is published, Release 1.1 will have been released, which supports all of the Struts features discussed in this book. When relevant, new features and functionality from Release 1.1b will be highlighted and discussed.

With this brief history of Struts, let's walk through how a Struts-based application works.

Walking Through Struts

Earlier in this chapter, we discussed the basics of the MVC pattern, on which the Struts development framework is based. Now, let's explore the workflow that occurs when an end user makes a request to a Struts-based application. The diagram overleaf illustrates this workflow:

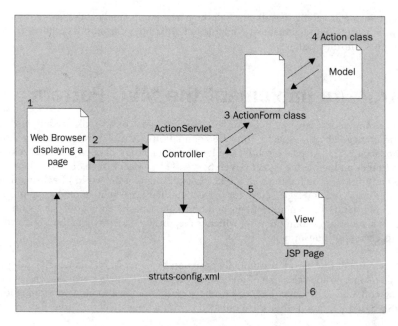

We are going to start our discussion with the end user looking at a web page (Step 1). This web page, be it a static HTML page or a JavaServer Page, contains a variety of actions that the user may ask the application to undertake. These actions may include clicking on a hyperlink or image that takes them to another page or submitting an online form that is to be processed by the application. All actions that are to be processed by the Struts framework will have a unique URL mapping (that is, /execute/*) or file extension (that is, *.do). This URL mapping or file extension is used by the servlet container to map all the requests over to the Struts **ActionServlet**.

The Struts `ActionServlet` acts as the controller for the Struts MVC implementation. The `ActionServlet` will take the incoming user request (Step 2) and map it to an action mapping defined in the `struts-config.xml` file. The `struts-config.xml` file contains all of the configuration information needed by the Struts framework to process an end-user's request. An <action> is an XML tag defined in the `struts-config.xml` file that tells the `ActionServlet` the following information:

❑ The **Action class** that is going to carry out the end user's request. An `Action` class is a Struts class that is extended by the application developer. Its primary responsibility is to contain all of the logic necessary to process an end user's request.

❑ An **ActionForm class** that will validate any form data that is submitted by the end user. It is extended by the developer. It is important to note that not every action in a Struts application requires an `ActionForm` class. An `ActionForm` class is necessary only when the data posted by an end user needs to be validated. An `ActionForm` class is also used by the `Action` class to retrieve the form data submitted by the end-user. An `ActionForm` class will have `get()` and `set()` methods to retrieve each of the pieces of the form data. It will be discussed in greater detail in Chapter 3.

❑ Where the users are to be forwarded after their request has been processed by the Action class. There can be multiple outcomes from an end user's request. Thus, an action mapping can contain multiple forward paths. A forward path, which is denoted by the <forward> tag, is used by the Struts ActionServlet to direct the user to another JSP page or to another action mapping in the struts-config.xml file.

Once the controller has collected all of the above information from the <action> element for the request, it will process the end user's request. If the <action> element indicates that the end user is posting the form data that needs to be validated, the ActionServlet will direct the request to the defined ActionForm class (Step 3).

An ActionForm class contains a method called validate(). (The configuration code examples, given later in this chapter, may help you to understand this discussion better.) The validate() method is overridden by the application developer and holds all of the validation logic that will be applied against the data submitted by the end user. If the validation logic is successfully applied, the user's request will be forwarded by the ActionServlet to the Action class for processing. If the user's data is not valid, an error collection called ActionErrors is populated by the developer and returned to the page where the data was submitted.

If the data has been successfully validated by the ActionForm class or the <action-mapping> does not define an ActionForm class, the ActionServlet will forward the user's data to the Action class defined by the action mapping (Step 4). The Action class has three public methods and several protected ones. For the purpose of our discussion, we will consider only the perform() method of the Action class. This method, which is overridden by the application developer, contains the entire business logic necessary for carrying out the end-user request.

Once the Action has completed processing the request, it will indicate to the ActionServlet where the user is to be forwarded. It does this by providing a key value that is used by the ActionServlet to look up from the action mapping. The actual code used to carry out a forward will be shown in the section called *Configuring the homePageSetup Action Element*. Most of the times, the user will be forwarded to a JSP page that will display the results of their request (Step 5). The JSP page will render the data returned from the model as an HTML page that is displayed to the end user. (Step 6)

In summary, a typical web screen, based on the Struts development framework, will consist of:

❑ One or more actions. Each action in the web page will map to exactly one <action> element defined in the struts-config.xml file. An action that is invoked by an end user will be embedded in an HTML or JSP page, as a hyperlink or as an action attribute inside a <form> tag. We will see some examples of this in the section called *Template Tags*.

❑ An <action> element that will define the ActionForm class, if any, that will be used to validate the form data submitted by the end user. It will also define which Action class will be used to process the end user's request.

❑ An ActionForm class that can use one or more forwards, defined in the <action> element, to tell the ActionServlet which JSP page should be used to render a response to the end user's request. Remember, multiple forwards can be defined within a single <action-mapping> element.

Now that we have completed a conceptual overview of how a single web page in a Struts application is processed, let's look at how a single page from the JavaEdge Blog is written and plugged into the Struts framework.

Getting Started: The JavaEdge Source Tree

Before diving into the basics of Struts configuration, we need to enumerate the different pieces of the JavaEdge application's source tree. The JavaEdge Blog is laid out in the following directory structure:

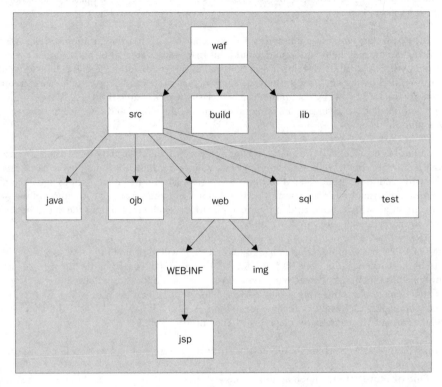

The root directory for the project called waf. There are several key directories underneath it, as discussed below:

- ❑ src: Contains the entire JavaEdge source code of the application. This directory has several subdirectories including:

  - ❑ java: All Java source files for the application.

  - ❑ ojb: All ObjectRelationalBridge configuration files. These files are discussed in greater detail in Chapter 5.

  - ❑ web: Contains the entire source code of the application that is going to be put in the WEB-INF directory. Files in this directory include any image file used in the application along with any JSP files.

- ❑ `sql`: Contains all of the MySQL-compliant SQL scripts for creating and pre-populating the WAF database used by the JavaEdge application.

- ❑ `build`: Contains the Ant build scripts used to compile, test, and deploy the application. The Ant tool is discussed in detail, in Chapter 8.

- ❑ `lib`: Contains the JAR files for the various open source projects used to build the JavaEdge application.

The JavaEdge application is built, tested, and deployed with the following software:

- ❑ **Tomcat-4.1.12**
  Tomcat is an implementation of the Sun Microsystems' Servlet and JSP specification. It is considered by Sun Microsystems to be the reference implementation for its specifications. The JavaEdge application is built and deployed around Tomcat. In Chapter 5, the open source application server bundle, JBoss 3.0.4/Tomcat 4.1.12, is used to run the application. Tomcat is available for download at http://jakarta.apache.org/tomcat. JBoss is an open source J2EE application server produced by the JBoss Group. It can be downloaded at http://jboss.org.

- ❑ **MySQL**
  MySQL is chosen, because it is one of the most popular open source databases available today. It is highly scalable and extremely easy to install and configure. It is available for download at http://mysql.com.

- ❑ **Ant**
  Versions 1.5 of the Apache Software Foundation's Ant build utility. It can be downloaded at http://jakarta.apache.org.

  - ❑ **Lucene**
    A Java-based Open Source search engine. It can be downloaded at http://jakarta.apache.org. It is discussed in detail in Chapter 7.

  - ❑ **Velocity**
    An alternative JOS development framework from the Jakarta Apache Group. Both Lucene and Velocity are discussed in greater detail in Chapter 6.

All of the source code used in this book can be downloaded from Wrox web site (**http://wrox.com/books/1861007817.htm**). We will not be discussing how to configure any of the development tools listed above in this chapter. For the information on how to configure these tools, to run the code examples in this book, please refer to the `readme.txt` file packaged with the source code.

We will start the JavaEdge Struts configuration, by configuring our application to recognize the Struts `ActionServlet`.

Configuring the ActionServlet

Any application that is going to use Struts must be configured to recognize and use the Struts `ActionServlet`. Configuring the `ActionServlet` in the `web.xml` file involves setting up two XML tag elements:

❑ A `<servlet>` tag, which defines the name of the corresponding servlet Java class and any initial configuration parameters that are passed to the servlet when it is loaded

❑ A `<servlet-mapping>` tag, which defines how the end user requests are going to be mapped to the Struts `ActionServlet`

The `<servlet>` tag that is used to configure the `ActionServlet` for the JavaEdge application is shown below:

```xml
<?xml version="1.0" encoding="ISO-8859-1"?>

<!DOCTYPE web-app
  PUBLIC "-//Sun Microsystems, Inc.//DTD Web Application 2.3//EN"
  "http://java.sun.com/j2ee/dtds/web-app_2_3.dtd">

<web-app>

  <!--Setting up the MemberFilter-->
  <filter>
    <filter-name>MemberFilter</filter-name>
    <filter-class>com.wrox.javaedge.common.MemberFilter</filter-class>
  </filter>

  <filter-mapping>
    <filter-name>MemberFilter</filter-name>
    <url-pattern>/execute/*</url-pattern>
  </filter-mapping>

  <!-- Standard Action Servlet Configuration (with debugging) -->
  <servlet>
    <servlet-name>action</servlet-name>
    <servlet-class>org.apache.struts.action.ActionServlet</servlet-class>
    <init-param>
      <param-name>application</param-name>
      <param-value>ApplicationResources</param-value>
    </init-param>
    <init-param>
      <param-name>config</param-name>
      <param-value>/WEB-INF/struts-config.xml</param-value>
    </init-param>
    <init-param>
      <param-name>debug</param-name>
      <param-value>2</param-value>
    </init-param>
    <init-param>
      <param-name>detail</param-name>
      <param-value>0</param-value>
    </init-param>
    <init-param>
      <param-name>validate</param-name>
      <param-value>true</param-value>
    </init-param>
    <init-param>
      <param-name>validating</param-name>
      <param-value>true</param-value>
    </init-param>
    <load-on-startup>2</load-on-startup>
```

```
    </servlet>

    <!-- Standard Action Servlet Mapping -->
    <servlet-mapping>
       <servlet-name>action</servlet-name>
       <url-pattern>/execute/*</url-pattern>
    </servlet-mapping>

    <!-- The Usual Welcome File List -->
    <welcome-file-list>
       <welcome-file>default.jsp</welcome-file>
    </welcome-file-list>

    <!-- Struts Tag Library Descriptors -->
    <taglib>
       <taglib-uri>/WEB-INF/struts-bean.tld</taglib-uri>
       <taglib-location>/WEB-INF/struts-bean.tld</taglib-location>
    </taglib>

    <taglib>
       <taglib-uri>/WEB-INF/struts-html.tld</taglib-uri>
       <taglib-location>/WEB-INF/struts-html.tld</taglib-location>
    </taglib>

    <taglib>
       <taglib-uri>/WEB-INF/struts-logic.tld</taglib-uri>
       <taglib-location>/WEB-INF/struts-logic.tld</taglib-location>
    </taglib>

    <taglib>
       <taglib-uri>/WEB-INF/struts-template.tld</taglib-uri>
       <taglib-location>/WEB-INF/struts-template.tld</taglib-location>
    </taglib>
 </web-app>
```

Anyone who is familiar with Java Servlet configuration will realize that there is nothing particularly sophisticated going on here. The `<filter>` and `<filter-mapping>` tags define a filter, written by the JavaEdge team, that checks if the user has logged into the application. If the user has not logged in yet, they will automatically be logged in as an anonymous user. This filter is called every time the Struts `ActionServlet` is invoked. The `<servlet>` tag defines all the information needed to use the Struts `ActionServlet` in the JavaEdge application. The `<servlet-name>` provides a name for the servlet. The `<servlet-class>` tag indicates the fully qualified Java class name of the Struts `ActionServlet`.

The Struts `ActionServlet` is highly configurable. The parameters shown in the above configuration are just some of the initialization parameters that can be used to control the behavior of the `ActionServlet`. More details about the parameters are provided in the table overleaf:

45

Parameter Name	Parameter Value
application	Name of the application resource bundle. Setting this attribute to `ApplicationResources` will tell the Struts `ActionServlet` to use the `ApplicationResources.properties` file.
config	Name and location of the Struts XML configuration file (called `struts-config.xml`). The `struts-config.xml` file is a general configuration file for the Struts framework and is used by several classes within Struts. The directory path stored here is the relative path based on the base URL of the application.
debug	The debugging level provided by the `ActionServlet`. Setting this parameter to 0 turns off all debugging in the `ActionServlet`. Setting this initialization parameter to 1 or 2 will give out different levels of debugging information, 2 being the highest level of debugging offered by the `ActionServlet`.
tempDir	Directory where any temporary files are stored, when files are uploaded to the `ActionServlet` class.
MaxFileSize	Maximum file size of an uploaded file. The file size specified is a number followed by a K for kilobytes, M for megabytes, or G for gigabytes.
validating	Determines whether the `struts-config.xml` file is validated against the `struts-config.dtd`. By default, this value is assumed to be `true`. It is highly recommended that you do not change this value.

Note: This is only a partial listing of the parameters for the Struts `ActionServlet`. For a full listing, please refer to the Struts Users Guide: http://jakarta.apache.org/struts/doc-1.0.2/userGuide.

Once the `<servlet>` element has been configured in the web.xml file, we need to define how the user requests are going to be mapped to the `ActionServlet`. This is done by defining a `<servlet-mapping>` tag in the web.xml file. The mapping can be done in one of two ways:

❑ URL prefix mapping

❑ Extension mapping

In URL prefix mapping, the servlet container examines the URL coming in and maps it to a servlet. The `<servlet-mapping>` for the JavaEdge application is shown below:

```
<web-app>
...
  <servlet-mapping>
    <servlet-name>action</servlet-name>
    <url-pattern>/execute/*</url-pattern>
  </servlet-mapping>
</web-app>
```

This servlet mapping indicates to the servlet container that any request coming into the JavaEdge application that has a URL pattern of /execute/* should be directed to the ActionServlet (defined by the <servlet-name> shown above) running under the JavaEdge application. For example, if we wanted to bring up the home page for the JavaEdge application we would point our browser to http://localhost:8080/JavaEdge/execute/homePageSetup, where JavaEdge is the application name, execute is the URL prefix, and homePageSetup is the Struts action.

> It is important to note that all URLs shown in our code examples are case-sensitive and must be entered exactly as they appear.

The servlet container, upon getting this request, would go through the following steps:

1. Determine the name of the application. The user's request indicates that they are making a request for the JavaEdge application. The servlet container will then look in the web.xml file associated with the JavaEdge application.

2. The servlet container will find the servlet that it should invoke. For this, it looks up for a <servlet-mapping> tag that matches a URL pattern called execute. In the JavaEdge web.xml file, this <servlet-mapping> tag maps to the ActionServlet (that is, the Struts ActionServlet).

3. The user's request is then forwarded to the ActionServlet running under the JavaEdge application. The homePageSetup, in the above URL, is the action the user would like the Struts framework to carry out. Remember, an action in Struts maps to an <action> element in the struts-config.xml file. (Note that we will be going through how to setup an <action> element in the section called *Configuring the homePageSetup Action Element*). This <action> element defines the Java classes and JSP pages that will process the user's request.

The second way to map the user's request to the ActionServlet is to use extension mapping. In this method, the servlet container will take all URLs that map to a specified extension and send them to the ActionServlet for processing. In the example below, all of the URLs that end with a *.st extension will map to the Struts ActionServlet:

```
<web-app>
  <servlet-mapping>
    <servlet-name>action</servlet-name>
    <url-pattern>*.st</url-pattern>
  </servlet-mapping>
</web-app>
```

If we used extension mapping to map the user's requests to the ActionServlet, the URL to get the JavaEdge home page would be http://localhost:8080/JavaEdge/homePageSetup.st, where JavaEdge is the application name, homePageSetup is the Struts action, and .st is the extension.

For the JavaEdge application, being built in the next four chapters, we will be using the URL prefix method (this is the best practice for setting up and pre-populating the screens).

Configuring the homePageSetup Action Element

As the servlet configuration is completed for the JavaEdge application, let's focus on setting up and implementing our first Struts action, the homePageSetup action. This action sends the user to the JavaEdge home page. However, before the user actually sees the page, the action will retrieve the latest postings from the JavaEdge database. These postings will then be made available to the JSP page, called homepage.jsp. This page displays the latest ten stories in a summarized format and allows the user to log in to JavaEdge and view their personal account information. In addition, the JavaEdge reader is given a link to see the full story and any comments made by the other JavaEdge readers.

To set up the homePageSetup action, the following steps must be undertaken:

1. A Struts <action> element must be added in the struts-config.xml file.

2. An Action class must be written to process the user's request.

3. A JSP page, in this case the homePage.jsp, must be written to render the end user's request.

It is important to note that Struts follows all of Sun Microsystems' guidelines for building and deploying a web-based applications. The installation instructions, shown here, can be used to configure and deploy Struts-based application in any J2EE-compliant application server or servlet container.

Setting up your first struts-config.xml file is a straightforward process. This file can be located in the WEB-INF directory of the JavaEdge project, downloaded from Wrox web site (http://wrox.com/books/1861007817.htm). The location of the struts-config.xml file is also specified in the config attribute, in the web.xml entry of the ActionServlet.

The struts-config.xml file has a root element, called <struts-config>:

```
<?xml version="1.0" encoding="ISO-8859-1"?>
<!DOCTYPE struts-config
  PUBLIC "-//Apache Software Foundation//DTD Struts Configuration 1.0//EN"
          "http://jakarta.apache.org/struts/dtds/struts-config_1_0.dtd">
<struts-config>
...
</struts-config>
```

All actions, for the JavaEdge application, are contained in a tag called <action-mappings>. Each action has its own <action> tag. To set up the homeSetupAction, we would add the following information to the struts-config.xml file:

```
<?xml version="1.0" encoding="ISO-8859-1"?>
<!DOCTYPE struts-config
  PUBLIC "-//Apache Software Foundation//DTD Struts Configuration 1.0//EN"
          "http://jakarta.apache.org/struts/dtds/struts-config_1_0.dtd">
<struts-config>
  <action-mappings>
    <action
      path="/homePageSetup"
      type="com.wrox.javaedge.struts.homepage.HomePageSetupAction"
      unknown="true">
      <forward name="homepage.success" path="/WEB-INF/jsp/homePage.jsp"/>
    </action>
  </action-mappings>
</struts-config>
```

An action has a number of different attributes that can be set. In this chapter, we will only be concerned with the path, type, and unknown attributes of the <action> element. The other <action> element attributes are discussed in the *Chapter 3*. Let's now discuss the above-mentioned attributes briefly.

❑   path
    Holds the action name. When an end user request is made to the ActionServlet, it will search all of the actions defined in the struts-config.xml and try to make a match, based on the value of the path attribute.

> Note that all values in the **path** attribute for an action must start with a forward slash ("**/**"), to map to the attribute. If you fail to put this in your **path** attribute, Struts will not find your action.

❑   If the ActionServlet finds a match, it will use the information in the rest of the <action> element, to determine how to fulfill the user's request. In the above example, if the users point their web browsers to http://localhost:8080/JavaEdge/homePageSetup, the ActionServlet will locate the action by finding the <action> element's path attribute that matches /homePageSetup. It is important to note that all path names are case-sensitive.

❑   type
    Holds the fully qualified name of the Action class. If the user invokes the URL shown in the above bullet, the ActionServlet will instantiate an Action class of type com.wrox.javaedge.struts.homepage.HomePageSetupAction. This class will contain all of the logic to look up the latest ten stories, which are going to be displayed to the end user.

❑   unknown
    Can be used by only one <action> element in the entire struts-config.xml file. When set to true, this tag tells the ActionServlet to use this <action> element as the default behavior, whenever it cannot find a path attribute that matches the end user's requested action. This prevents the user from entering a wrong URL and, as a result, getting an error screen. Since the JavaEdge home page is the starting point for the entire application, we set the homePageSetup action as the default action for all unmatched requests. If more than one <action> tag has its unknown attribute set to true, the first one encountered in the struts-config.xml will be used and all others will be ignored. If the unknown attribute is not specified in the <action> tag, the Struts ActionServlet will take it as false. The false value simply means that Struts will not treat the action as the default action.

An <action> tag can contain one or more <forward> tags. A <forward> tag is used to indicate where the users are to be directed after their request has been processed. It consists of two attributes, name and path. The name attribute is the name of the forward. The path attribute holds a relative URL, to which the user is directed by the ActionServlet after the action has is completed. The value of the name attribute of the <forward> tag is a completely arbitrary name. However, this attribute is going to be used heavily by the Action class defined in the <action> tag. Later in this chapter, when we demonstrate the HomePageSetupAction class, we will find out how an Action class uses the <forward> tags for handling the screen navigation. When multiple <forward> tags exist in a single action, the Action class carrying out the processing can indicate to the ActionServlet that the user can be sent to multiple locations.

Sometimes, you might have to reuse the same `<forward>` across multiple `<action>` tags. For example, in the JavaEdge application, if an exception is raised in the data-access tier, it is caught and rewrapped as a `DataAccessException`. The `DataAccessException` allows all exceptions raised in the data access tier, to be handled uniformly by all of the `Action` classes in the JavaEdge application. (Refer to Chapter 4 for the exception handling). When a `DataAccessException` is caught in an `Action` class, the JavaEdge application will forward the end user to a properly formatted error page. Rather than repeating the same `<forward>` tag in each Struts action defined in the application, you can define it to be global. This is done by adding a `<global-forwards>` tag, at the beginning of the `struts-config.xml` file:

```xml
<?xml version="1.0" encoding="ISO-8859-1"?>
<!DOCTYPE struts-config
  PUBLIC "-//Apache Software Foundation//DTD Struts Configuration 1.0//EN"
          "http://jakarta.apache.org/struts/dtds/struts-config_1_0.dtd">
<struts-config>
  <global-forwards type="org.apache.struts.action.ActionForward">
    <forward name="system.error" path="/WEB-INF/jsp/systemError.jsp"/>
  </global-forwards>
  <action-mappings>
       …..
  </action-mappings>
</struts-config>
```

The `<global-forwards>` tag has one attribute called `type`, which defines the `ActionForward` class that forwards the user to another location. Struts is an extremely pluggable framework, and it is possible for a development team to override the base functionality of the Struts `ActionForward` class, with their own implementation. If your development team is not going to override the base `ActionForward` functionality, the `type` attribute should always be set to `org.apache.struts.action.ActionForward`. After the `<global-forwards>` tag is added to the `struts-config.xml` file, any `Action` class in the JavaEdge application can redirect a user to `systemError.jsp`, by indicating to the `ActionServlet` that the user's destination is the `system.error` forward.

Now let's discuss the corresponding `Action` class of the homePageSetup, that is, `HomePageSetupAction.java`.

Building HomePageSetupAction.java

The `HomePageSetupAction` class, which is located in `src/java/com/wrox/javaedge/struts/homepage/HomePageSetupAction.java` file, is used to retrieve the top postings made by JavaEdge users. The code for this `Action` class is shown below:

```java
package com.wrox.javaedge.struts.homepage;

import org.apache.struts.action.Action;
import org.apache.struts.action.ActionMapping;
import org.apache.struts.action.ActionForm;
import org.apache.struts.action.ActionForward;
import javax.servlet.http.HttpServletRequest;
import javax.servlet.http.HttpServletResponse;
import javax.servlet.http.HttpSession;
import org.apache.struts.action.ActionErrors;
import org.apache.struts.action.ActionError;
```

```
import com.wrox.javaedge.story.*;
import com.wrox.javaedge.story.dao.*;
import com.wrox.javaedge.common.*;
import java.util.*;


/**
 *  Retrieves the ten latest posting on JavaEdge.
 */

public class HomePageSetupAction extends Action {

/**
 *  The perform() method comes from the base Struts Action class. We
 *  override this method and put the logic to carry out the user's
 *  request in the overriding method.
 *  @param mapping An ActionMapping class that will be used by the Action
 *  class to tell the ActionServlet where to send the end user.
 *
 *
 *  @param form The ActionForm class that will contain any data submitted
 *  by the end user via a form.
 *  @param request A standard Servlet HttpServletRequest class.
 *  @param response A standard Servlet HttpServletResponse class.
 *  @return An ActionForward class that will be returned to the
 *  ActionServlet indicating where the user is to go next.
 */

    public ActionForward perform(ActionMapping mapping,
                                 ActionForm form,
                                 HttpServletRequest request,
                                 HttpServletResponse response) {

      try {
/**
 *  Create a Story Data Access Object and use it to retrieve
 *  all of the top stories.
 */

        StoryDAO storyDAO = new StoryDAO();
        Collection topStories = storyDAO.findTopStory();


        //Put the collection containing the top stories into the request

        request.setAttribute("topStories", topStories);
      } catch(DataAccessException e) {
        System.out.println("Data access exception raised in
                           HomePageSetupAction.perform()");
        e.printStackTrace();
        return (mapping.findForward("system.error"));
      }

      return (mapping.findForward("homepage.success"));
    }
}
```

Before we begin the discussion the HomePageSetupAction class, let's have a look at the Command design pattern.

The Power of the Command Pattern

The `Action` class is an extremely powerful development metaphor, because it is implemented using a Command design pattern. According to the Gang of Four (Erich Gamma, Richard Helm, Ralph Johnson, and John Vlissides) a Command pattern:

> *"Encapsulates a request as an object, thereby letting you parameterize clients with different requests..."*
> *–Design Patterns, Elements of Reusable Object-Oriented Software, page.233*

A Command pattern lets the developer encapsulate a set of behaviors in an object, and provides a standard interface for executing that behavior. Other objects can also invoke the behavior, but they have no exposure to how the behavior is implemented. This pattern is implemented with a concrete class, abstract class, or interface. This parent class contains a single method (usually named `perform()` or `execute()`) that carries out some kind of action. The actual behavior for the requested action is implemented in a child class (which, in our example, is `HomePageSetupAction`), extending the Command class. The Struts `Action` class is the parent class in the Command pattern implementation. The diagram below illustrates the relationship between the `Action` and `HomePageSetupAction` classes:

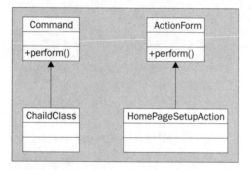

The use of the Command design pattern is one of reasons why Struts is so flexible. The `ActionServlet` does not care how a user request is to be executed. It only knows that it has a class that descends from the `ActionForm` and will have a `perform()` method. When the end user makes a request, the `ActionServlet` just executes the `perform()` method in the class that has been defined in the `struts-config.xml`. If the development team wants to change the way in which an end user request is processed, it can do it in two ways: either directly modify the logic in the `Action` class or write a new `Action` class and modify the `struts-config.xml` file to point to the new `Action` class. The `ActionServlet` never knows that this changed has occurred. Later in this section, we will discuss how Struts' flexible architecture can be used to solve the Hardwired AntiPattern. With this discussion on the Command pattern, let's go back to the `HomePageSetupAction` class.

The first step, in writing the `HomeSetupAction` class, is to extend the Struts `Action` class.

```
public class HomePageSetupAction extends Action
```

Next, the `perform()` method for the class needs to be overridden. (In the `Action` class source code, there are several `perform()` methods that can be overridden. Some of these are deprecated. Other methods allow you to make request to Struts from a non-HTTP based call. For the purpose of this book, we will only by dealing with HTTP-based `perform()` methods.)

> Note that if you are using Struts 1.1 then the **preform()** method has been deprecated, so you should use **execute()** instead.

```
public ActionForward perform(ActionMapping mapping,
                             ActionForm form,
                             HttpServletRequest request,
                             HttpServletResponse response){
...
}
```

The perform()/execute() method signature takes four parameters:

❏   ActionMapping
    Finds an ActionForward from the struts-config.xml and returns it to the
    ActionServlet. This ActionForward class contains all the information needed by the
    ActionServlet to forward the end users to the next page in the application.

❏   ActionForm
    A helper class that is used to hold any form data submitted by the end user. The ActionForm
    class is not being used in our HomePageSetupAction class shown earlier. This class will be
    discussed in greater detail in Chapter 3 and Chapter 4.

❏   HttpServletRequest
    A standard HttpServletRequest object passed around within the servlet.

❏   HttpServletResponse
    A standard HttpServletResponse object passed around within the servlet.

Now let's look at the actual implementation of the perform() method.

```
StoryDAO storyDAO = new StoryDAO();
Collection topStories = storyDAO.findTopStories();
```

The first step, carried out by the perform() method, is to instantiate a StoryDAO object and use it to
retrieve a Collection object of StoryVO. Each StoryVO object contained within the collection
topStories represents a single row of the data retrieved from the story table in the JavaEdge database.
The StoryDAO is an implementation of a J2EE **Data Access Object (DAO) pattern**. This pattern hides all
the implementation details of how the data is retrieved and manipulated from the database.

> *The term "J2EE patterns" is a bit of a misnomer. The Data Access Object pattern and Value Object*
> *pattern – also known as a Communication Object pattern –were used in other languages before Java.*
> *However, they were called J2EE patterns when the patterns were explained in the book* Core J2EE
> Design Patterns: Best Practices and Design Strategies, Prentice Hall (ISBN: 0-13-064884-1).

The StoryVO object is an implementation of a J2EE **Value Object (VO) pattern**. A Value Object pattern
wraps the data being passed between the different tiers in a simple Java class containing get() or set()
methods to access the data. The physical details of the data are abstracted away from the application
consuming the data. The DAO and VO design patterns, along with the JavaEdge database tables, will be
discussed in greater detail in Chapter 5.

After the `storyDAO.findTopStories()` method is executed, the `topStories` object will be placed as an attribute of the `request` object:

```
request.setAttribute("topStories", topStories);
```

The `Collection` is being placed in the `request`. As a result, when the `ActionServlet` forwards this to the `homepage.jsp` page (as defined in the `struts-config.xml` file), the `homePage.jsp` will be able to walk through each item in the `topStories Collection` and display the data in it to the end-user.

Once the story data has been retrieved, an `ActionForward` will be generated by calling the `findForward()` method, in the `mapping` object passed into the `perform()` method:

```
return (mapping.findForward("homepage.success"));
```

If a `DataAccessException` is raised, while executing the call to the `storyDAO.findTopStories()` method, the exception will be caught and processed:

```
try {
    ...
} catch(DataAccessException e) {
  System.out.println("Data access exception raised in  " +
                     "HomePageSetupAction.perform()");
  e.printStackTrace();
  return (mapping.findForward("system.error"));
}
```

You will notice that, when the `DataAccessException` is caught, the user is redirected to the global forward `system.error`.

We have finished configuring the `struts-config.xml` file and built an `Action` class to pre-populate the JavaEdge's home screen with story data. Before we look at the JSP file, `homePage.jsp`, let's discuss how to refactor the Hardwired AntiPattern.

Refactoring the Hardwired AntiPattern

The declarative architecture of the Struts development framework provides a powerful tool for avoiding or refactoring a Hardwired antipattern. (Refer to Chapter 1, for the discussion of Hardwired and other antipatterns.)

All activities performed by the user, in a Struts-based application should be captured within an `<action>` tag defined in the `struts-config.xml` file. Using an `<action>` tag gives the developer flexibility in the way in which the screen navigation and application of business rules are carried.

According to the author's experience, while building a Struts application, `<action>` elements defined within the application fall into three general categories:

❑ **Setup Actions**
   Used to perform any activities that take place before the user sees a screen. In the JavaEdge Home Page example, we used the `/HomePageSetup` action to retrieve the top stories from the JavaEdge database and place them in an attribute in the `HttpServletRequest` object.

❑ **Form Actions**
   Actions that will process the data collected from the end user.

❑ **Tear-Down Actions**
   Can be invoked after a user's request has been processed. Usually, it carries out any cleanup action, needed after the user's request has been processed.

These three types of actions, are purely conceptual. There is no way in the Struts <action> tag, to indicate that the action being defined is a Setup, Form, or Tear-Down action. However, this classification is very useful for your own Struts applications. A Setup action allows you to easily enforce "pre-condition" logic before sending a user to a form. This logic ensures that, before the user even sees the page, certain conditions are met. Setup actions are particularly useful when you have to pre-populate a page with data. In Chapters 3 and Chapter 4, when we discuss how to collect the user data in Struts, we will find several examples of a Setup action used to pre-populate a form. In addition putting a Setup action before a page gives you more flexibility in maneuvering the user around. This Setup action can examine the current application state of the end users, based on which it can navigate them to any number of other Struts actions or JSP pages.

A Form action is invoked when the user submits the data entered in an HTML form. It might insert a record into a database or just perform some simple data formatting on the data entered by the user.

A Tear-Down action is used to enforce "post-condition" logic. This logic ensures that after the user's request has been processed, the data needed by the application is still in a valid state. Tear-Down actions might also be used to release any resources, previously acquired by the end-user.

As you become more comfortable with Struts, you will prefer chaining together the different actions. You will use the Setup action enforce pre-conditions that must exist when the user makes the initial request. The Setup action usually retrieves some data from a database and puts it in one of the different JSP page contexts (that is, page, request, session, or application context). It then forwards the user to a JSP page that will display the retrieved data. If the JSP page contains a form, the user will be forwarded to a Form action that will process the user's request. The Form action will then forward the user to a Tear Down action that will enforce any post-condition rules. If all post-conditions rules are met, the Tear Down action will forward to the next JSP page the user is going to visit.

It's important to note that by using the strategies defined above, you can change application behavior by reconfiguring the struts-config.xml file. This is a better approach than to go constantly into the application source code and modify the existing business logic.

With this discussion on the Hardwired antipattern, let's have a look at homepage.jsp, which renders the HTML page that the user will see after the request has been processed.

Constructing the Presentation Tier

Now we are going to look at how many of the Struts custom JSP tag libraries can be used to simplify the development of the presentation tier. With careful design and use of these tag libraries, you can literally write JSP pages without ever writing a single Java scriptlet. The Struts development framework has four sets of custom tag libraries:

- ❑ Template tags
- ❑ Bean tags
- ❑ Logic tags
- ❑ HTML tags

We will not be discussing the Struts HTML tag libraries in this chapter. Instead, we will discuss these tags in Chapter 3.

Before we begin our discussion of the individual tag libraries, the web.xml file for the JavaEdge application has to be modified, to include the following Tag Library Definitions (TLDs):

```xml
<web-app>
...
  <taglib>
    <taglib-uri>/WEB-INF/struts-bean.tld</taglib-uri>
    <taglib-location>/WEB-INF/struts-bean.tld</taglib-location>
  </taglib>

  <taglib>
    <taglib-uri>/WEB-INF/struts-html.tld</taglib-uri>
    <taglib-location>/WEB-INF/struts-html.tld</taglib-location>
  </taglib>

  <taglib>
    <taglib-uri>/WEB-INF/struts-logic.tld</taglib-uri>
    <taglib-location>/WEB-INF/struts-logic.tld</taglib-location>
  </taglib>

  <taglib>
    <taglib-uri>/WEB-INF/struts-template.tld</taglib-uri>
    <taglib-location>/WEB-INF/struts-template.tld</taglib-location>
  </taglib>
</web-app>
```

With these TLDs added to the web.xml file, we now begin our discussion by looking at the Struts <template> tags.

Template Tags

The template tag libraries are used to break a JSP screen into small manageable pieces, which can easily be customized and plugged into the application. All of the screens in the JavaEdge application are going to be broken into four distinct parts:

❑ A title that will appear at the top of the web browser window.

❑ A header section containing various links for navigating around the JavaEdge application. This section will be displayed at the top of every screen.

❑ A content section, where screen-specific content will be placed.

❑ A footer section, which will contain a blue bar going across the bottom of the page.

The first step, in setting up the JavaEdge application to use the templates, is to actually define a template that will be used for the pages. The JavaEdge template is defined in a file named template.jsp. The code for this file is shown below:

```jsp
<%@ taglib uri='/WEB-INF/struts-template.tld' prefix='template' %>

<head>
  <title><template:get name='title'/></title>
</head>
<html>
  <body>
```

```
      <p>
        <template:get name='header'/>
        <template:get name='content'/>
        <template:get name='footer'/>
      </p>
    </body>
  </html>
```

The template above sets up an HTML page with four different template plug-in points. Each plug-in is going to allow the individual screen implementing the template to define its own content for that particular plug-in point. These plug-in points can be identified by the `<template:get>` tags, embedded throughout the `template.jsp` file. The `homePage.jsp` file implements the above template, by using the Struts template tags `<template:insert>` and `<template:put>`:

```
<%@ page language="java" %>
<%@ taglib uri="/WEB-INF/struts-bean.tld" prefix="bean" %>
<%@ taglib uri="/WEB-INF/struts-html.tld" prefix="html" %>
<%@ taglib uri="/WEB-INF/struts-logic.tld" prefix="logic" %>
<%@ taglib uri="/WEB-INF/struts-template.tld" prefix="template" %>

<template:insert template='template.jsp'>
  <template:put name='title' content='Todays Top Stories' direct='true'/>
  <template:put name='header' content='header.jsp'/>
  <template:put name='content' content='homePageContent.jsp'/>
  <template:put name='footer' content='footer.jsp'/>
</template:insert>
```

The `<template:insert>` tag is used to indicate the template that will be used to build the page. In the `homePage.jsp` file, we are telling the `<template:insert>` tag to use the `template.jsp` file. The JSP files that are plugged into the template can be set as the absolute paths based on the application's root (that is, `/WEB-INF/jsp`) or the paths relative to the where the `template.jsp` file is located. Since all of the JSP files for the JavaEdge application, are located in one directory, we have chosen not to fully define a relative URL in the individual JSP files. Once we have indicated where the template is located, we can begin plugging in the content we want to display to the end user.

The content is going to be plugged into the template through the use of the `<template:put>` tag. This tag allows the developer to plug either a literal string value or the contents of a file into the template. To use a literal string value, the `direct` attribute of the `<template:put>` tag must be set to `true`. For example, in the `homePage.jsp` file above:

```
<template:put name='title' content='Today&#39;s Top Stories' direct='true'/>
```

The above call will cause the following HTML code to be generated, when the user is directed to the `homePage.jsp` by the `ActionServlet`.

```
<title>Today&#39;s Top Stories</title>
```

To use the contents of a file in the template, we use the `<template:put>` tag without the `direct` attribute or with the `direct` attribute set to `false`. In `homePage.jsp`, the following code will load the contents of the file `homePageContent.jsp` and process any JSP code or custom tags from that file appropriately:

```
<template:put name='content' content='/WEB-INF/jsp/homePageContent.jsp'/>
```

To summarize, the template tag library has three tags:

Tag Name	Tag Description
`<template:insert>`	Defines the template that will be used in the JSP page.
`<template:put>`	Allows the developer to load the contents of a file or define a literal string, which will be plugged into the template. If the developers want to use a literal string in the template, they must have the `direct` attribute for this tag set to `true`.
`<template:get>`	Defines plug-in point within the template where content can be loaded.

Now, if you have configured the JavaEdge application based on the download instructions on the Wrox web site (http://wrox.com/books/1861007817.htm), you should be able to bring up the JavaEdge home page (Remember the URL to bring up this page is http://localhost:8080/JavaEdge/execute/homePageSetup. Later on, in the chapter, we will discuss ways to redirect the user to /homePageSetup action, when they first come to the JavaEdge application.). The JavaEdge home page should look like:

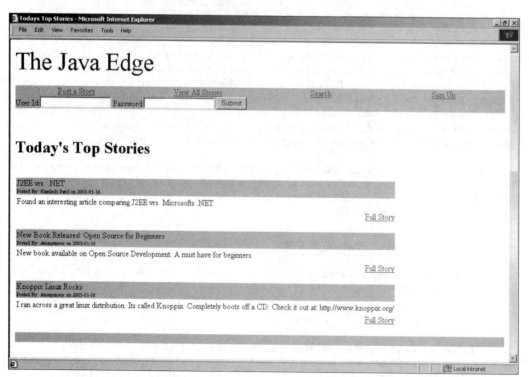

We are now going to show all the header, content, and footer code that is used throughout the JavaEdge application. We are not going to immediately explain what the code does, because this explanation will be explained as we discuss the other Struts tag libraries.

The Screen Header: header.jsp

The header.jsp file generates the menu bar above each of the JavaEdge application pages:

```jsp
<%@ page language="java" %>
<%@ taglib uri="/WEB-INF/struts-bean.tld" prefix="bean" %>
<%@ taglib uri="/WEB-INF/struts-html.tld" prefix="html" %>
<%@ taglib uri="/WEB-INF/struts-logic.tld" prefix="logic" %>
<%@ taglib uri="/WEB-INF/struts-template.tld" prefix="template" %>


<p>
  <font size="7">
    <bean:message key="javaedge.header.title"/>
  </font>
</p>

<div align="center">
  <center>
    <html:form action="login">
      <table border="0" cellpadding="0" cellspacing="0" style="border-
        collapse: collapse" bordercolor="#111111" width="100%"
        id="AutoNumber1" bgcolor="#FF66FF">
        <tr>
          <logic:notEqual scope="session" name="memberVO"
           property="memberId" value="1">
            <td width="16%" bgcolor="#99CCFF" align="center">
              <bean:message key="javaedge.header.logout"/>
            </td>
          </logic:notEqual>

          <logic:notEqual scope="session" name="memberVO"
           property="memberId" value="1">
            <td width="17%" bgcolor="#99CCFF" align="center">
              <bean:message key="javaedge.header.myaccount"/>
            </td>
          </logic:notEqual>

          <td width="17%" bgcolor="#99CCFF" align="center">
            <bean:message key="javaedge.header.postastory"/>
          </td>

          <td width="17%" bgcolor="#99CCFF" align="center">
            <bean:message key="javaedge.header.viewallstories"/>
          </td>

          <logic:notPresent scope="session" name="memberVO">
            <td width="17%" bgcolor="#99CCFF" align="center">
              <bean:message key="javaedge.header.signup"/>
            </td>
          </logic:notPresent>
        </tr>
```

```
      <tr>
        <logic:equal scope="session" name="memberVO" property="memberId"
         value="1">
          <td width="16%" bgcolor="#99CCFF" align="left" colspan="4">
            <bean:message key="javaedge.header.userid"/>
            <input type="text" name="userId"/>
            <bean:message key="javaedge.header.password"/>
            <input type="password" name="password"/>
            <html:submit property="submitButton" value="Submit"/>
            <html:errors property="invalid.login"/>
          </td>
        </logic:equal>
      </tr>

    </table>
  </html:form>
  </center>
</div>
```

The Home Page Content: homePageContent.jsp

The homePageContent.jsp will generate the output that will be displayed in the middle of the application screen. The HTML generated in this middle section is going to be the majority of the JavaEdge application; the end user will interact with:

```
<%@ page language="java" %>
<%@ taglib uri="/WEB-INF/struts-bean.tld" prefix="bean" %>
<%@ taglib uri="/WEB-INF/struts-html.tld" prefix="html" %>
<%@ taglib uri="/WEB-INF/struts-logic.tld" prefix="logic" %>
<%@ taglib uri="/WEB-INF/struts-template.tld" prefix="template" %>

<p>
  <font size="7">
    <bean:message key="javaedge.header.title"/>
  </font>
</p>

<div align="center">
  <center>
    <html:form action="login">
      <table border="0" cellpadding="0" cellspacing="0" style="border-
        collapse: collapse" bordercolor="#111111" width="100%"
        id="AutoNumber1" bgcolor="#FF66FF">
        <tr>
          <logic:notEqual scope="session" name="memberVO"
           property="memberId" value="1">
            <td width="16%" bgcolor="#99CCFF" align="center">
              <bean:message key="javaedge.header.logout"/>
            </td>
          </logic:notEqual>

          <logic:notEqual scope="session" name="memberVO"
           property="memberId" value="1">
            <td width="17%" bgcolor="#99CCFF" align="center">
              <bean:message key="javaedge.header.myaccount"/>
            </td>
          </logic:notEqual>
```

```
                <td width="17%" bgcolor="#99CCFF" align="center">
                  <bean:message key="javaedge.header.postastory"/>
                </td>

                <td width="17%" bgcolor="#99CCFF" align="center">
                  <bean:message key="javaedge.header.viewallstories"/>
                </td>

                <logic:notPresent scope="session" name="memberVO">
                  <td width="17%" bgcolor="#99CCFF" align="center">
                    <bean:message key="javaedge.header.signup"/>
                  </td>
                </logic:notPresent>
              </tr>

              <tr>
                <logic:equal scope="session" name="memberVO" property="memberId"
                 value="1">
                  <td width="16%" bgcolor="#99CCFF" align="left" colspan="4">
                    <bean:message key="javaedge.header.userid"/>
                    <input type="text" name="userId"/>
                    <bean:message key="javaedge.header.password"/>
                    <input type="password" name="password"/>
                    <html:submit property="submitButton" value="Submit"/>
                    <html:errors property="invalid.login"/>
                  </td>
                </logic:equal>
              </tr>

          </table>
        </html:form>
      </center>
    </div>
```

The Screen Footer: footer.jsp

The footer.jsp file generates the blue footer bar at the end of each JavaEdge screen:

```
<%@ page language="java" %>
<%@ taglib uri="/WEB-INF/struts-bean.tld" prefix="bean" %>
<%@ taglib uri="/WEB-INF/struts-html.tld" prefix="html" %>
<%@ taglib uri="/WEB-INF/struts-logic.tld" prefix="logic" %>
<%@ taglib uri="/WEB-INF/struts-template.tld" prefix="template" %>

<table border="0" cellpadding="0" cellspacing="0" style="border-collapse:
 collapse" bordercolor="#111111" width="100%" id="AutoNumber1"
 bgcolor="#FF66FF">
  <tr bgcolor="#99CCFF">
    <td>
       
    </td>
  </tr>
</table>
```

Bean Tags

Well-designed JSP pages use JavaBeans to separate the presentation logic, in the application, from the data that is going to be displayed on the screen. A JavaBean is a regular class that can contain the data and logic. In our home page example, the `HomePageSetupAction` class retrieves a set of `StoryVO` classes into a collection and puts them into the session. The `StoryVO` class is a JavaBean that encapsulates all of the data, for a single story, posted in the Java Edge database. Each data element, stored within a `StoryVO` object, has a `get()` and `set()` method for each property. The code for the `StoryVO` class is shown below:

```java
package com.wrox.javaedge.story;

import java.util.Vector;

import com.wrox.javaedge.common.ValueObject;
import com.wrox.javaedge.member.MemberVO;

/**
 *  Holds Story data retrieved from the JavaEdge database.
 *  @todo Need to finish documenting this class
 */

public class StoryVO extends ValueObject {

  private Long storyId;
  private String storyTitle;
  private String storyIntro;
  private byte[] storyBody;
  private java.sql.Date submissionDate;
  private Long memberId;
  private MemberVO storyAuthor;
  public Vector comments = new Vector(); // of type StoryCommentVO

  public Long getStoryId() {
    return storyId;
  }

  public void setStoryId(Long storyId) {
    this.storyId = storyId;
  }
  public String getStoryTitle() {
    return storyTitle;
  }

  public void setStoryTitle(String storyTitle) {
    this.storyTitle = storyTitle;
  }

  public String getStoryIntro() {
    return storyIntro;
  }

  public void setStoryIntro(String storyIntro) {
    this.storyIntro = storyIntro;
  }
  public String getStoryBody() {
    return new String(storyBody);
  }
```

```
public void setStoryBody(String storyBody) {
  this.storyBody = storyBody.getBytes();
}

public java.sql.Date getSubmissionDate() {
  return submissionDate;
}

public void setSubmissionDate(java.sql.Date submissionDate) {
  this.submissionDate = submissionDate;
}

public Vector getComments() {
  return comments;
}

public void setComments(Vector comments) {
  this.comments=comments;
}

public MemberVO getStoryAuthor() {
  return storyAuthor;
}

public void setStoryAuthor(MemberVO storyAuthor) {
  this.storyAuthor = storyAuthor;
}

} // end StoryVO
```

The JSP specification defines a number of `<jsp>` tags that give the developer the ability to manipulate the contents of a JavaBean.

The Struts bean tag library offers a significant amount of functionality beyond that offered by the standard `<jsp>` tag libraries. The functionality provided by the bean tag library can be broken into two broad categories of functionality:

❑ Generating output from existing screen data.

❑ Creating new JavaBeans. These new JavaBeans can hold the data specified by the developer or retrieved from web artifacts, such as the cookie or a value stored in an HTTP header.

We are going to begin with the most common use of the Struts bean tag, the retrieval and display of data from a JavaBean.

Bean Output

There are two bean tags available for generating output in the Struts bean library. They are:

❑ `<bean:write>`

❑ `<bean:message>`

The `<bean:write>` tag retrieves a value from a JavaBean and writes it to the web page being generated. Examples of this tag can be found throughout the homePageContent.jsp file. For example, the following code will retrieve the value of the property (storyTitle) from a bean, called story, stored in the page context:

```
<bean:write name="story" scope="page" property="storyTitle"/><BR/>
```

To achieve the same result via a Java scriptlet would require the following code:

```
<%
  StoryVO story = (StoryVO) pageContext.getAttribute("story");

  if (story!=null){
    out.write(story.getStoryTitle());
  }
%>
```

The <bean:write> tag supports the concept of the nested property values. For instance, the StoryVO class has a property called storyAuthor. This property holds an instance of a MemberVO object. The MemberVO class contains the data about the user who posted the original story. The homePageContent.jsp page retrieves the values from a MemberVO object, by using a nested notation in the <bean:write> tag. For instance, to retrieve the first name of the user who posted one of the stories to be displayed, the following syntax is used:

```
<bean:write name="story" property="storyAuthor.firstName"/>
```

In the above example, the <bean:write> write tag is retrieving the storyAuthor by calling story.getStoryAuthor() and then the firstName property by calling storyAuthor.getFirstName()

The <bean:write> tag has the following attributes that can be configured:

Attribute Name	Attribute Description
name	The name of the JavaBean to be retrieved.
scope	The scope, in which to look for the JavaBean. Valid values include page, request, and session. If this attribute is not set, the <bean:write> tag will start searching for the bean at the page level and continue until it finds the bean.
property	The name of the property to be retrieved from the JavaBean. The <bean:write> tag uses the reflection to call the appropriate get() method of the JavaBean, from which you are retrieving the data. Therefore, your JavaBean has to follow the standard JavaBean naming conventions (that is, a get prefix followed by the first letter of the method name capitalized).
filter	Determines whether or not characters that are significant in HTML, should be replaced with their & counterparts. For example, if the data retrieved from a call to StoryVO.getTitle() contained an & symbol, setting the filter attribute to true would cause the <bean:write> tag to write the character as &amp. The default value for this attribute is true.
ignore	When set to true, this attribute tells the <bean:write> not to throw a runtime exception, if the bean name cannot be located in the scope specified. The <bean:write> will simply generate an empty string to be displayed in the page. (If scope is not specified, the same rules apply here, as specified above.)
	If this attribute is not set or set to false, a runtime exception will be thrown by the <bean:write> tag, if the requested bean cannot be found.

The second type of tag for generating output is the Struts `<bean:message>` tag. The `<bean:message>` tag is used to separate the static content from the JSP page in which it resides. All the contents are stored in a properties file, independent of the application. The properties file consists of a name-value pair, where each piece of the text that is to be externalized is associated with a key. The `<bean:message>` tag will use this key to look up a particular piece of text from the properties file.

To tell the name of the properties file to the `ActionServlet`, you need to make sure that the `application` parameter is set in the `web.xml` file. The properties file, called `ApplicationResources.properties`, is placed in the `classes` directory underneath the `WEB-INF` directory of the deployed application. In the JavaEdge source tree, the `ApplicationResources.properties` file is located in *working directory*/waf/src/web/WEB-INF/classes (where the `working directory` is the one in which you are editing and compiling the application source).

For the purpose of the JavaEdge application, an `<init-param>` tag must be configured as shown below:

```
<servlet>
  ...
  <init-param>
    <param-name>application</param-name>
    <param-value>ApplicationResources</param-value>
  </init-param>
</servlet>
```

The static content for the JavaEdge application has not been completely externalized using the `<bean:message>` functionality. Only the `header.jsp` file has been externalized. The following `<bean:message>` example, taken directly from `header.jsp`, will return the complete URL for the JavaEdge login page:

```
<bean:message key="javaedge.header.logout"/>
```

When this tag call is processed, it will retrieve the value for the `javaedge.header.logout` key from the `ApplicationResources.properties` file. All of the name-value pairs from the `ApplicationResources.properties` file used in the `header.jsp` are shown below:

```
javaedge.header.title=The Java Edge
javaedge.header.logout=<a href="/JavaEdge/execute/LogoutSetup">Logout</a>
javaedge.header.myaccount=<a href="/JavaEdge/execute/MyAccountSetup">My
Account</a>
javaedge.header.postastory=<a href="/JavaEdge/execute/postStorySetup">Post a
Story</a>
javaedge.header.viewallstories=<a href="/JavaEdge/execute/ViewAllSetup">View All
Stories</a>
javaedge.header.signup=<a href="/JavaEdge/execute/signUpSetup">Sign Up</a>
javaedge.header.search=<a href="/JavaEdge/execute/SearchSetup">Search</a>
```

If the `<bean:message>` tag cannot find this key in the `ApplicationResources.properties` file, the `<bean:message>` tag will throw a runtime exception.

The <bean:message> tag has the following attributes:

Attribute Name	Attribute Description
key	Key, in the properties file, for which the <bean:message> tag is going to look.
arg0	Parameter value that can be passed into the text string retrieved from the properties file. For instance, if a property had the value: `hello.world=Hi {0}!` using <bean:message key="hello.world" arg="John"/> would return the following text to the output stream: Hi John!. The <bean:message> tag can support at most five parameters being passed to a message.
arg1	Second parameter value that can be passed to the text string retrieved from the properties file.
arg2	Third parameter value that can be passed to the text string retrieved from the properties file.
arg3	Fourth parameter value that can be passed to the text string retrieved from the properties file.
arg4	Fifth parameter value that can be passed to the text string retrieved from the properties file.
bundle	The name of the bean in which the MessageResources object containing the application messages is stored.
locale	The name of the bean in which our Locale object is stored.

Let's have an interesting discussion on the Tight Skins antipattern, before moving on to bean creation.

The Tight Skins Antipattern

Recollecting our discussion in Chapter 1, the Tight Skins antipattern occurs when the development team does not have a presentation tier whose look and feel can be easily customized. The Tight Skins antipattern is formed, when the development team embeds the static content in the JSP pages. Any changes to the static content result in having to hunt through all of the pages in the application and making the required changes.

As we saw above, the <bean:message> tag can be used to centralize all the static content, in an application, to a single file called ApplicationResources.properties. However, the real strength of this tag is that it makes it very easy to write internationalized applications that can support multiple languages. The JavaEdge header toolbar is written to support only English. However, if you want the JavaEdge's header toolbar to support French, you need to follow the following steps:

1. Create a new file, called ApplicationResources_fr.properties.

The _fr extension to the ApplicationResources.properties file is not just a naming convention followed here. These extensions are part of the ISO-3166 standard. For a complete list of all of the country codes supported by this standard, please visit http://www.ics.uci.edu/pub/ietf/http/related/iso639.txt.

2. Copy all of the name-value pairs from the JavaEdge's application into the new `ApplicationResources_fr.properties` file. Translate all of the static contents in these name-value pairs to French. Also, if the JavaEdge application is going to support only French, you may rename the file from `ApplicationResources_fr.properties` to `ApplicationResources.properties` and replace the existing `ApplicationResources.properties` file. However, if you want to support English and French at the same time, you to need to tell the Struts which `java.util.Locale` is to be used for the user. A `Locale` object is part of the standard Java SDK and is used to hold the information about a region. For more details on the `Locale` object, please refer the Sun JDK documentation (available at http://java.sun.com).

3. To support both English and French concurrently, you could ask the users the language in which they want to see the site, when they are registering for a JavaEdge account. Their language preference could be stored in the JavaEdge database. If the user chooses French as their language preference, then anytime that user logs into the JavaEdge application, the following code could be executed in any `Action` class to switch the language preference from English over to French:

```
HttpSession session = request.getSession();
session.setAttribute(org.apache.struts.action.Action.LOCALE_KEY,
                     new java.util.Locale(LOCALE.FRENCH, LOCALE.FRENCH) );
```

Struts stores a `Locale` object, in the session, as the attribute key `org.apache.struts.action.Action.LOCALE_KEY`. Putting a new `Locale` object (which is instantiated with the values for French) will cause Struts to reference the `ApplicationResources_fr.properties` file, for the time for which the user's session is valid. (Or at least, until a new `Locale` object, containing another region's information is placed in the user's session.)

Bean Creation

Struts offers a number of helper tags (bean creation tags), for creating the JavaBeans to be used within a JSP page. With these tags, a number of tasks can be carried out within the JSP page, without the need to write Java scriptlet code. These tasks include:

❑ Retrieve a value from a cookie and create a new JavaBean to hold the cookie's contents

❑ Retrieve an HTTP parameter and store its value in a new JavaBean

❑ Retrieve a configuration element of Struts (such as a forward, mapping, or form Bean) and store its information in a JavaBean

❑ Retrieve an object from the JSP page context (that is, the application, request, response, or session objects)

❑ Define a new JavaBean from scratch and place a value in it

❑ Copy the contents of a single property from an existing JavaBean into a new JavaBean

The table below gives a brief summary of the different <bean> creation tags available:

Bean Name	Bean Description
`<bean:cookie>`	Creates a new JavaBean to hold the contents of the specified cookie. To retrieve a cookie named `shoppingCart` into a bean, we use the following syntax: `<bean:cookie id="cart" name="shoppingCart" value="None"/>` This call creates a new JavaBean called `cart`, which will hold the value stored in the cookie `shoppingCart`. The `value` attribute tells the bean to store the string `None`, if the cookie cannot be found. If the `value` attribute is not specified and the cookie cannot be found, a runtime exception will be raised.
`<bean:parameter>`	Creates a new JavaBean to hold the contents of a parameter retrieved from the `HttpServletRequest` object. To retrieve a request parameter, called `sendEmail`, from the `HttpServletRequest` we use the following code: `<bean:parameter id="sendEmailFlag" name="sendEmail" value="None"/>` Like the `<bean:cookie>` tag, if the `value` attribute is not specified and the requested parameter is not located, a runtime exception will be raised.
`<bean:struts>`	Creates a new JavaBean to hold the contents of a Struts configuration object. `<bean:struts id="homePageSetupMap" forward="/homePageSetup"/>` The above `<bean:struts>` tag will retrieve the `homePageSetup` action and place the corresponding object into JavaBean called `homePageSetupMap`.
`<bean:page>`	Creates a new JavaBean to hold an object retrieved from the JSP page context. The following example will retrieve the session object from the `HttpServletRequest` object and place it as a JavaBean called `hSession`. `<bean:page id="hSession" property="session"/>`
`<bean:include>`	Creates a JavaBean to hold the content returned from a call to another URL. The following example will take the content retrieved from a call to `/test.jsp` page and place it in a JavaBean called `testInclude`: `<bean:include id="testInclude" name="/test.jsp"/>`
`<bean:resource>`	Retrieves the data from a file located in a Web Application Resource (WAR) file. This data can be retrieved as a string or `InputStream` object by the tag. The following code will create a new JavaBean, called `webXmlBean`, which will hold the contents of the `web.xml` file as a string: `<bean:resource id="webXmlBean" name="/web.xml"/>`

Bean Name	Bean Description
`<bean:header>`	Creates a new JavaBean and populates it with an item retrieved from the HTTP header. `<bean:header id="httpReferer" name="referer"/>` In the above example, the `referer` property is being pulled out of the HTTP header and placed in a bean called `httpReferer`. However, since no `value` attribute is being defined, a runtime exception will be thrown, if the `referer` value cannot be found in the HTTP header.
`<bean:define>`	Creates a new JavaBean and populates it with a string value defined by the developer. The `<bean:define>` tag given below creates a JavaBean called `hello`, that will hold the ever popular phrase, `Hello World`. This bean will be placed in a session of the application. `<bean:define id="hello" value="Hello World" scope="session"/>`

We have not used any of the bean creation tags in the JavaEdge application. There is simply no need to use them for any of the pages in the application. Also, in the author's opinion, most of the bean creation tags can be used in an `Action` class using Java code. According to the author's experience, the overuse of the bean creation tags can clutter up the presentation code and make it difficult to follow.

For full details on the bean creation tags you can visit the following URLs: http://jakarta.apache.org/struts/doc-1.0.2/struts-bean.html#define (which lists all of the bean tags and provides an explanation of all their attributes) and http://jakarta.apache.org/struts/doc-1.0.2/api/org/apache/struts/taglib/bean/package-summary.html (which shows several working examples for each of the `<bean>` tags).

Logic Tags

The logic tag library gives the developer the ability to add conditional and iterative control to the JSP page, without having to write Java scriptlets. These tags can be broken into three basic categories:

❑ Tags for controlling iteration.

❑ Tags for determining, whether a property in an existing JavaBean is equal to, not equal to, greater than, or less than another value. In addition, there are logic tags that can determine whether or not a JavaBean is present within a particular JSP page context (that is, page, request, session, or application scope).

❑ Tags for moving (that is, redirecting or forwarding) a user to another page in the application.

Iteration Tags

The logic tag library has a single tag, called `<logic:iterate>`, which can be used to cycle through a `Collection` object in the JSP page context. Recollect that in the `HomePageSetupAction` class, a collection of `StoryVO` objects is placed into the `request`. This collection holds the latest ten stories posted to the JavaEdge site. In the `homePageContent.jsp` page, we cycle through each of the `StoryVO` objects in the `request`, by using the `<logic:iterate>` tag:

```
<logic:iterate id="story" name="topStories" scope="request"
              type="com.wrox.javaedge.valueobject.StoryVO">
  <TR bgcolor="#99CCFF">
    <TD>
      <bean:write name="story" scope="page" property="storyTitle"/><BR/>
      ...
</logic:iterate>
```

In the above code snippet, the `<logic:iterate>` tag looks up the `topStories` collection in the `request` object of the JSP page. The `name` attribute defines the name of the collection. The `scope` attribute defines the scope, in which the `<logic:iterate>` tag is going to search for the JavaBean. The `type` attribute defines the Java class that is going to be pulled out of the collection. In this case, it is `StoryVO`. The `id` attribute holds the name of the JavaBean, which holds a reference to the `StoryVO` pulled out of the collection. When referencing an individual bean in the `<logic:iterate>` tag, we will use the `<bean:write>` tag. The `name` attribute of the `<bean:write>` tag must match the `id` attribute defined in the `<logic:iterate>`.

```
<bean:write name="story" scope="page" property="storyTitle"/>
```

Keep in mind the following points, while using the `<logic:iterate>` tag:

- Multiple types of collections can be supported by the `<logic:iterate>` tag. These types include:

  - Vector

  - ArrayList

  - Arrays of objects

  - Java Enumeration objects

  - Java Iterator objects

- The `<logic:iterate>` tag supports the use of only the arrays of objects. It does not support arrays containing primitive data values.

- If your collection can contain `null` values, the `<logic:iterate>` tag will still go through the actions defined in the loop. It is the developer's responsibility to check if the a `null` value is present by using the `<logic:present>` or `<logic:notPresent>` tags. (These tags will be covered in the next section, *Conditional Tags*.)

Conditional Tags

The Struts development framework also provides a number of tags to perform basic conditional logic. Using these tags, a JSP developer can perform a number of conditional checks on the common servlet container properties. These conditional tags can check for the presence of the value of a piece of data stored as one of the following types:

- Cookie

- HTTP Header

- `HttpServletRequest` Parameter

- JavaBean

- A property on a JavaBean

For instance, in the `header.jsp`, the Struts conditional `<logic:present>` and `<logic:notPresent>` tags are used to determine which menu items are available for a JavaEdge end user. If the user has been successfully authenticated, there will be a JavaBean, called `memberVO`, present in the user's session. (The code that actually authenticates the user and places a `memberVO` class in session is located in the `LoginAction.java` class. If you are interested in seeing the code please review it in this class.) This JavaBean contains all of the user's personal information and preferences. Let's look at a code snippet from the `header.jsp`:

```
<logic:notPresent scope="session" name="memberVO" >
  <td width="16%" bgcolor="#99CCFF" align="center">
    <bean:message key="javaedge.header.login"/>
  </td>
</logic:notPresent>
<logic:present scope="session" name="memberVO">
  <td width="16%" bgcolor="#99CCFF" align="center">
    <bean:message key="javaedge.header.logout"/>
  </td>
</logic:present>
```

In the JSP above code, a column containing a link to the login URL will be rendered only if the JavaEdge user has not yet logged into the application. The `<logic:notPresent>` checks the user's session to see if there is a valid `memberVO` object present in the session. The `<logic:present>` tag in the above code checks if there is a `memberVO` object in the user's session. If there is one, a column will be rendered containing a link to the logout page.

The `<logic:present>` and `<logic:notPresent>` tags are extremely useful, but, in terms of applying the conditional logic, are extremely blunt instruments. Fortunately, Struts provides us with a number of other conditional logic tags.

Suppose that the user authentication scheme was changed and the JavaEdge application set a flag indicating that the user was authenticated, by placing a value of `true` or `false` in a cookie called `userloggedin`. You could rewrite the above code snippet, as follows, to use the `<logic:equals>` and `<logic:notEquals>` tags:

```
<logic:notEquals cookie="userloggedin" value="true">
  <td width="16%" bgcolor="#99CCFF" align="center">
    <bean:message key="javaedge.header.login"/>
  </td>
</logic:notEquals>
<logic:equals cookie="userloggedin" value="true">
  <td width="16%" bgcolor="#99CCFF" align="center">
    <bean:message key="javaedge.header.logout"/>
  </td>
</logic:equals>
```

We can even use the `<logic:equals>` and `<logic:notEquals>` tag to check a property in a JavaBean. For instance, we could rewrite the authentication piece of the JavaEdge application to set an attribute (called `authenticated`) in the `memberVO` object to a hold a string value of `true` or `false`. We could then check the property in the `memberVO` JavaBean using the following code:

```
<logic:notEquals name="memberVO" property="authenticated" scope="session"
                 value="true">
  <td width="16%" bgcolor="#99CCFF" align="center">
    <bean:message key="javaedge.header.login"/>
  </td>
</logic:notEquals>

<logic:equals name="memberVO" property="authenticated" scope="session"
              value="true">
  <td width="16%" bgcolor="#99CCFF" align="center">
    <bean:message key="javaedge.header.logout"/>
  </td>
</logic:equals>
```

When applying the conditional logic tags against a property on a JavaBean, keep two things in mind:

❑   The scope that you are looking for the JavaBean. If you do not define a scope attribute, all of the contexts in the JSP will be searched. If you define this attribute and the value you are looking for is not there, a runtime exception will be thrown by the Java tag.

❑   Chaining the property values of a JavaBean using a "." notation. You can find examples of the "." notation in the section called *Bean Output*, in this chapter.

There are some other conditional logic tags available. These include:

❑   <logic:greaterThan>:
    Checks if the value retrieved from a JavaBean property, HttpServletRequest parameter, or HTTP header is greater than the value stored in the value attribute of the <logic:greaterThan> tag.

❑   <logic:lessThan>:
    Checks if the value retrieved from a JavaBean property, HttpServletRequest parameter, or HTTP header value is less than the value stored in the value attribute of the <logic:lessThan> tag.

❑   <logic:greaterEqual>:
    Checks if the value retrieved from a JavaBean property, HttpServletRequest parameter, or HTTP header value is greater than or equal to the value stored in value attribute of the <logic:greaterEqual> tag.

❑   <logic:lessEqual>:
    Checks if the value retrieved from a JavaBean property, HttpServletRequest parameter, or HTTP header value is less than or equal to the value stored in the value attribute of the <logic:lessEqual> tag.

The logic tags shown above will try to convert the value they are retrieving to a float or double and perform a numeric comparison. If the retrieved value cannot be converted to a float or double, these tags will perform the comparisons based on the string values of the items being retrieved.

Here's another interesting discussion about the Tight Skins antipattern.

The Tight Skins AntiPattern Revisited

A common requirement, for many web applications, is to provide a different look and feel for the same screen(s), depending on who the user is. Many development teams will embed the conditional checks in the JSP code of the application to determine which piece of the screen is to be rendered for the user. However, embedding the conditional logic into every page, for each different user role, is very shortsighted solution. In applications with more than two user roles, it becomes very cumbersome to implement role-based presentation. The JSP code has `<logic>` tags spread all over it and becomes a nightmare to maintain. This is a Tight Skin antipattern, because customizing the look and feel of the page to a particular class of the user becomes very difficult.

The JSP code for checking the user's role becomes tightly intertwined with the JSP code rendering the HTML page. However, using the Struts `<template>` and `<logic>` tags, we can simplify role-based presentation. Also, this makes it very easy to have an application that can support different looks and feels for the same screens.

Let's look at a simple example of using the `<template>` and `<logic>` tags for role-based presentation in the JavaEdge application. Suppose, in the JavaEdge website, we want to provide different headers, footers, and content based on whether the visitor of the JavaEdge site is a registered member or an anonymous user. For the register member, we might want to have a different presentation interface, which provides more functionalities and features than that available to a non-registered member. We could rewrite the `homePage.jsp` file to perform the following logic:

```jsp
<%@ page language="java" %>
<%@ taglib uri="/WEB-INF/struts-bean.tld" prefix="bean" %>
<%@ taglib uri="/WEB-INF/struts-html.tld" prefix="html" %>
<%@ taglib uri="/WEB-INF/struts-logic.tld" prefix="logic" %>
<%@ taglib uri="/WEB-INF/struts-template.tld" prefix="template" %>

<template:insert template='template.jsp'>
  <logic:present scope="session" name="memberVO">
    <template:put name='title' content='Todays Top Stories' direct='true'/>
    <template:put name='header' content='header_member.jsp'/>
    <template:put name='content' content='homePageContent_member.jsp'/>
    <template:put name='footer' content='footer_member.jsp'/>
  </logic>
  <logic:notPresent scope="session" name="memberVO">
    <template:put name='title' content='Todays Top Stories' direct='true'/>
    <template:put name='header' content='header.jsp'/>
    <template:put name='content'
                  content='homePageContent.jsp'/>
    <template:put name='footer' content='footer.jsp'/>
  </logic>
</template:insert>
```

The JavaEdge application has two user roles, anonymous and member. In more sophisticated applications, where we might have several different roles, we can customize the look and feel of each screen to a specific user using the above approach. Every time we need to add a role, we modify the base template for each screen to include new plug-in points for the header, screen content, and footer JSP files specific to that role.

By using Struts templates and performing the conditional checks in the template file for each page, we partition the presentation code for each role. Each role has its own JSP files for rendering the application screens. This makes maintaining the JSP code for the individual role easier and lessens the risk that modifications made for one role break the user interface for all the other roles.

Movement Tags

These logic tags, in the Struts tag library, offer the developer the ability to redirect the user to a new URL. The two movement logic tags are:

❑　<logic:forward>: Forwards the user to a specified global <forward> tag defined in the struts-config.xml file.

❑　<logic:redirect>: Performs a redirect to a URL specified by the developer.

Let's see how these two tags can be used. To bring up the JavaEdge application, the user needs to point the browser to http://localhost:8080/JavaEdge/homePageSetup. This forces the users to know they have to do the /homePageSetup action. An easier solution would be to allow them to go to http://localhost:8080/JavaEdge.

In a non-Struts based application, this could be accomplished by setting up a <welcome-file-list> tag in the application's web.xml file. This tag allows you to define the default JSP or HTML file, which is presented when the user comes to the application and does not define a specific page. However, this is a problem for Struts applications. The <welcome-file-list> allows the developer to specify only file names and not URLs or Struts actions.

However, using the movement logic tags provides you with the ability to work around this shortcoming. First, we will demonstrate a solution using a <logic:forward> tag. We still need to set up the <welcome-file-list> tag in web.xml file of the JavaEdge. We are going to set up a file, called default.jsp, for the default file to be executed.

```
<web-app>
  ...
  <welcome-file-list>
    <welcome-file>default.jsp</welcome-file>
  </welcome-file-list>
</web-app>
```

Next, we add a new <forward> tag, called default.action, to <global-forwards> tag in the struts-config.xml file of the JavaEdge.

```
<struts-config>
  <global-forwards type="org.apache.struts.action.ActionForward">
    <forward name="system.error" path="/WEB-INF/jsp/systemError.jsp"/>
    <forward name="default.action" path="/execute/homePageSetup"/>
  </global-forwards>
  ...
</struts-config>
```

The last step is to write the default.jsp file. This file contains two lines of code:

```
<%@ taglib uri="/WEB-INF/struts-logic.tld" prefix="logic" %>
<logic:forward name="default.action"/>
```

We can perform the same functionality with the <logic:redirect> tag. If we implement the default.jsp using a <logic:redirect> tag, we still need to setup default.jsp in the web.xml file. However, we do not need to add another <forward> tag to the <global-forwards> located in struts-config.xml. Instead, we just need to write the default.jsp in the following manner:

```
<%@ taglib uri="/WEB-INF/struts-logic.tld" prefix="logic" %>
<logic:redirect page="/execute/homePageSetup"/>
```

The above code will generate a URL relative to the JavaEdge application
(http://localhost:8080/Javaedge/execute/HomePageSetup). We are not restricted, while using the
`<logic:redirect>`, to redirect to a relative URL. We can also use a fully qualified URL and even
redirect the user to another application. For instance, we could rewrite the `default.jsp` as follows:

```
<%@ taglib uri="/WEB-INF/struts-logic.tld" prefix="logic" %>
<logic:redirect href="http://localhost:8080/JavaEdge/execute/homePageSetup"/>
```

Using both the `<logic:redirect>` and the `<logic:forward>` is equivalent to calling the
`redirect()` method in the `HttpSessionServletResponse` class in the Java Servlet API. The
difference between the two tags is the that the `<logic:forward>` tag will let you forward only to a
`<global-forward>` defined in the `struts-config.xml` file. The `<logic:redirect>` tag will let
you redirect to any URL.

The `<logic:redirect>` tag has a significant amount of functionality. However, we have had a brief
introduction to what the `<logic:redirect>` tag can do. A full listing of all the attributes and
functionalities of this tag can be found at http://jakarta.apache.org/struts/doc-1.0.2/struts-
logic.html#redirect.

Summary

In this chapter, we explored the basic elements of a Struts application and how to begin using Struts to
build the applications. To build a Struts application we need to know:

- ❑ The basic components of a Struts application:
  - ❑ `ActionServlet`: Is the controller in the Struts MVC implementation. It takes all user
    requests and tries to map them to an `<action>` entry in the `struts-config.xml` file.
  - ❑ `action`: Defines a single task that can be carried by the end user. Also, it defines the class that
    will process the user's request and the JSP page that will render the HTML the user sees.
  - ❑ `Action` class: Contains the entire logic to process a specific user request.
  - ❑ `ActionForm`: Is associated with an `<action>` tag in the `struts-config.xml` file. It
    wraps all the form data submitted by the end user and also can perform validation on the
    data entered by the user.
  - ❑ JSP pages: Are used to render the HTML pages that the users will see, as a result of their
    request to the ActionServlet.
- ❑ The configuration files necessary to build a Struts application:
  - ❑ `web.xml`: This file contains the entire ActionServlet configuration, the mapping of user
    requests to the ActionServlet, and all the Struts Tag Library Definitions (TLDs).
  - ❑ `struts-config.xml`: This file contains all the configuration information for a
    Struts-based application.

❏ `ApplicationResources.properties`: This file is a central location for static content for a Struts application. It allows the developer to easily change the text or internationalize an application.

❏ The different Struts tag libraries for building the presentation piece of the application. These tags libraries include:

  ❏ `<template>`: Gives the developer a set of JSP tags to break down an application screen into pluggable components that can be easily swapped in and out.

  ❏ `<bean>`: Provides the developer with JSP tags for generating output from a JavaBean and creating a JavaBean from common JSP web artifacts.

  ❏ `<logic>`: Can be used to apply the conditional logic in the JSP page, through `Collections` stored in the user's JSP page context, and redirect the user to another page.

  ❏ `<html>`: These tags are not discussed in this chapter. However, they offer a significant amount of functionality and are discussed in Chapters 3 and Chapter 4.

We also identified some different areas where Struts can be used to refactor the web antipatterns, that might form during the design and implementation of the web-based applications. Refactoring of the following antipatterns was discussed:

❏ **Hardwired Antipattern**
  We looked at how to chain together Struts actions, to perform the pre-condition, form processing, and post-condition logic. This segregation of the business logic into the multiple applications provides a finer control over the application of the business logic and makes it easier to redirect the user to different Struts actions and JSP pages.

❏ **Tight Skins Antipattern**
  While examining this antipattern, we looked at how to use the `<template>` and `<logic>` tags to implement role-based presentation logic.

This chapter lays the foundation for the material covered in Chapters 3 and Chapter 4. In the next chapter, we are going to cover how to implement web-based forms using the Struts form tags. We will also look at the Struts HTML tag library and how it simplifies form development. Finally, the next chapter will focus on how to use the Struts `ActionForm` class, to provide a common mechanism for validating user data and reporting validation errors back to the user.

Form Presentation and Validation with Struts

In the previous chapter, all of our Struts examples were built around very simple screens, which were populated with data retrieved from the JavaEdge application. However, most web applications require a high degree of interaction, with end users often submitting the data via HTML forms.

This chapter is going to look at how to simplify the construction of HTML forms and form handling code, using the Struts development framework. We are going to discuss, from both a conceptual and implementation point of view, how the Struts framework can provide a configurable and consistent mechanism for building web forms. This chapter is going to cover the following topics:

❑ Validating HTML form data using the `ActionForm` class:

   ❑ How the `validate()` method of the `ActionForm` class is used to validate data against the user

   ❑ Error handling when a validation rule is violated

❑ Pre-populating an HTML form with data

❑ Configuring Struts for processing HTML form data

❑ Simplifying the development of HTML form pages using the Struts HTML tag libraries

Problems with Form Validation

Most web development teams do not have a consistent strategy for collecting the data from the end user, validating it, and returning any error messages that need to be displayed. They use a hodge-podge of different means of collecting and processing the user's data. Two commonly used mechanisms include embedding JavaScript in the HTML or JSP page rendering the form, and mixing the validation logic for the screen with the business logic in the business tier of the application. This inconsistency in the form processing often results in:

❑ Customers, whether they are internal (such as employees) or external (such as purchasers), have a disjointed experience while using the web-based applications of the organization. Each application requires the customer to have a different set of skills and an understanding of how the application works and how to respond to errors. In larger applications, this inconsistency can exist even between different pages in the same application.

❑ Validation logic is strewn through the different layers of the application. This increases the amount of time required to perform application maintenance. The maintenance developer, who is rarely the same as the code developer, often has to hunt for the location of the validation logic and know multiple development languages (JavaScript for validation rules enforced in the browser, Java for validation logic in the middle tier, and a stored procedure language for validation logic in the database).

❑ Validation logic is used differently across different browsers. JavaScript, though "standardized", is implemented differently across browsers. Developers of a web browser take great liberties in the way in which they implement the JavaScript European Computer Manufacturers Association (ECMA) standard. Often, they provide their own browser-specific extensions, which make cross-browser viewing (and portability) of the application difficult.

❑ The application code is difficult to reuse. With validation logic strewn throughout the tiers of an application, it is difficult to pick up that validation code and reuse it in another application. The developer has to take care of the dependencies that are present before reusing the validation code, because there is no clean separation between the validation and business logic.

All the problems identified above are the symptoms of the Validation Confusion antipattern. Recollecting the discussion in Chapter 1, the Validation Confusion antipattern occurs due to one of the following reasons:

❑ No clear distinction between the validation logic of the form data and the business logic that processes the user's request

❑ Lack of a pluggable interface, which allows the developer to easily modify the validation logic for a particular screen

❑ No standardized mechanism for identifying validation violations and notifying them to the end user

Fortunately, the Struts framework provides a rich set of software services for building and managing the form data. These services allow a developer to handle the form validation in a consistent fashion. Much of the logic normally associated with capturing and presenting the errors becomes the responsibility of the Struts framework and not the application developer.

Using Struts for Form Validation

To build an HTML form in Struts we need to have the following pieces in place:

❑ A Struts `ActionForm` class, which is used to hold the data collected from the end user and perform any validations on that data. This class provides a simple-to-use "wrapper", which eliminates the need for developers to pull the submitted data out of the `HttpServletRequest` object associated with the end user's request.

❑ A Struts `Action` class to carry out the user's request. In the process of carrying out the user's request, any business rules that should be enforced will be executed and any database insert, updates, or deletes will be performed.

❑ A JSP page, which uses the Struts HTML tag libraries to render the form elements that are going to appear on the page.

Tying all of these pieces together is the `struts-config.xml` file. This file will have entries in it for defining the Struts `ActionForm` classes used in the application, which `ActionForm` classes are going to be used with which action, and whether an `ActionForm` class is going enforce the validation against the submitted data. Each Struts action processing the form data must have its corresponding `<action>` tag modified, to indicate which `ActionForm` class will be used by the action.

Let's discuss what happens when the user submits the data in an HTML form. The diagram below shows what happens when the user submits the form data to a Struts-based application.

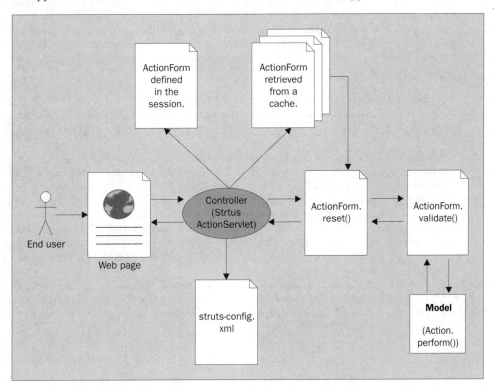

1. The `ActionServlet` examines the `struts-config.xml` file, to determine if an `ActionForm` class has been defined to validate the user's request. An `ActionForm` simplifies the form processing, but it is not required to access the form data submitted by the end user. An `Action` class can still access the submitted form data, by calling the `getParameter()` method in the request object passed into its `perform()` method. However, this bypasses all of the validation and error handling support in Struts.

2. If the action does not have an `ActionForm` class defined for it, the `ActionServlet` will check an internal cache to see if the `ActionForm` exists in the user's session or request. (Whether or not the `ActionForm` for the action class is supposed to live in the session or the request is controlled by an entry in the `struts-config.xml` file. Configuration of the `struts-config.xml` file is discussed in the section called *The struts-config.xml File*.)

3. If the `ActionForm` class has been defined to exist in the user's session, the `ActionServlet` will check if an `ActionForm` instance already exists in the session. If it exists, the `ActionServlet` will pull the `ActionForm` out of the session and populate its properties with values from the request. If it does not exist in the session, the `ActionServlet` will create a new instance of the `ActionForm` class, populate it with the data from the request, and put it in the session.

4. If the `ActionForm` class has been defined to exist in the user's request, the `ActionServlet` will check its internal cache to see if an appropriate `ActionForm` class already exists. If an instance is available in the cache, the `ActionServlet` will take it out of the cache and call its `reset()` method. The `reset()` method puts the `ActionForm` class instance in a default state before populating it with the form data submitted by the end user. The `reset()` method is called only if the `ActionForm` is to be put in the user's request. If the `ActionForm` instance is stored in the user's session, the `reset()` method will not be invoked.

Whether or not the `ActionServlet` places the `ActionForm` class in the user's request or session is determined by the `scope` attribute in the `<action>` tag. We will be exploring the `<action>` tag in greater detail in the section called *The struts-config.xml File*.

5. Once the `reset()` method has been called, the `validate()` method of `ActionForm` is invoked. The `validate()` method will enforce the validation rules on the form data submitted by the end user. If the data successfully passes all validations, the `ActionServlet` will invoke the `perform()` method, in the `Action` class, responsible for processing the user's request. If a validation error occurs, the `ActionServlet` will redirect the user back to the screen where the data was submitted. The user will then have to correct the validation violations before they can continue. We will be covering how Struts is notified of a validation error in the section called *Validating the Form Data*.

Once the user's data has successfully passed all the form validation, the `perform()` method will be invoked in the `Action` class associated with the action. Remember that the Java class that carries out the end user's request, is defined via the `type` attribute in the `<action>` element. We suggest you to refer to Chapter 2, to understand how to configure a Struts action, before continuing.

Implementing Form Validation with Struts

Let's begin the discussion of form handling by Struts, by looking at how an HTML form is processed by Struts when a user submits it. We are going to use the Post a Story page from the JavaEdge application (discussed in Chapter 3) as our example.

This page can be accessed by either clicking the Post a Story link in the menu bar at the top of every JavaEdge page or pointing our browser to http://localhost:8080/javaedge/execute/postStorySetup. The Post a Story page is used by a JavaEdge user to submit a story that the other users visiting this page can read.

If you have successfully reached this page, you will see the following screen:

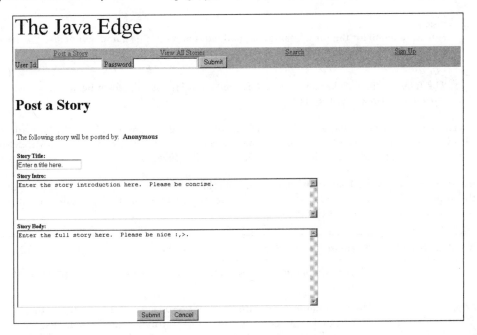

Let's begin by looking at how to setup our `struts-config.xml` class to use `ActionForm` objects.

The struts-config.xml File

To use an `ActionForm` class to validate the data collected from a user form, the `struts-config.xml` file for the application must be modified. These modifications include:

❑ Adding a `<form-beans>` tag, which will define each of the `ActionForm` classes used in the application

❑ Modifying the `<action>` tag processing the user's request, to indicate that before the user's request is processed, it must be validated by an `ActionForm` class

The `<form-beans>` tag holds one or more `<form-bean>` tags within it. This tag appears at the top of the `struts-config.xml` file. Each `<form-bean>` tag corresponds to only one `ActionForm` class in the application. For the JavaEdge application, the `<form-beans>` tag looks as shown below:

```
<form-beans>
  <form-bean name="postStoryForm"
             type="com.wrox.javaedge.struts.poststory.PostStoryForm"/>
  ...
  <form-bean> //more form-bean definitions.
</form-beans>
```

The `<form-bean>` element has two attributes. They are:

❑ name
  A unique name for the form bean being defined. Later on, this name will be used to associate this form bean with an `<action>` element. This attribute is a required field.

❑ type
  The fully-qualified class name of the `ActionForm` class that the form bean represents. This attribute is also a required field.

The `<form-bean>` actually has a third optional attribute called `className`. This attribute allows you to plug in a new base `ActionForm` class. For most purposes, the default `ActionFormBean` defined in the `<init-parameters>` tag of the `ActionServlet` will suffice.

Once a `<form-bean>` has been defined, we can use it in an `<action>` element to perform validation of the form data. To add the validation to a `<form-bean>`, we must supply four additional attributes in an `<action>` element. These attributes are:

Attribute Name	Attribute Description
name	Maps to the name of the `<form-bean>` that will be used to process the user's data.
scope	Defines whether or not the `ActionForm` class will be created in the user's request or session context. The `scope` attribute can be used only when the name attribute is defined in the `<action>` tag. If the name attribute is present, the `scope` attribute is an optional tag. The default value for the `scope` attribute is `request`.
validate	A Boolean attribute that indicates whether or not the submitted form data will be validated. If it's `true`, the `validate()` method in the `ActionForm` class and the `perform()` method in the `Action` class will be invoked. If it's `false`, then the `validate()` method will not be invoked, but the `perform()` method in the `Action` class defined in the tag will be executed. The `validate` attribute is used only when the name attribute has been defined in the tag. The default value for the `validate` attribute is `true`.
input	Used to define where the user should be redirected, if a validation error occurs. Usually, the user is redirected back to the JSP page where the data was submitted. It is not required if the name attribute is not present.

The /postStory action, processing the data entered by the user in the postAStory.jsp page, is shown below:

```
<action path="/postStory"
        input="/WEB-INF/jsp/postStory.jsp"
        name="postStoryForm"
        scope="request"
        validate="true"
        type="com.wrox.javaedge.struts.poststory.PostStory">
  <forward name="poststory.success" path="/javaedge/execute/homePageSetup"/>
</action>
```

Struts ActionForm Class

The Struts ActionForm class is used to hold the entire form data submitted by the end user. It is a helper class that is used by the ActionServlet to hold the form data, which it has pulled from the end user's request object. The application developer can then use the ActionForm to access the form through get() and set() method calls.

The ActionForm class not only provides a convenient wrapper for the request data but also validates the data submitted by the user. However, an Action class is not required to have an ActionForm class. An Action class can still access the form data, submitted by the end user, by calling the getParameter() method in the request object passed into its perform() method.

To build an ActionForm class, the developer needs to extend the base Struts ActionForm class and override two methods in it, reset() and validate(). Just to review, the reset() method is overridden by the developer when an ActionForm class for an action is to be stored in the user's request context. The reset() method clears the individual attributes, in the ActionForm class, to ensure that the ActionForm class is properly initialized before it is populated with the user's form data. The validate() method is overridden by the developer. This method will contain all of the validation logic used in validating the data entered by the end user.

In addition, the application developer needs to define all the form elements that are going to be collected by the ActionForm class as private attributes in the class. For each defined attribute, there must be corresponding get() and set() methods that follow the standard JavaBean naming conventions.

> You must implement a get() and set() method for each form element captured off the screen. These get() and set() method should follow the standard JavaBean naming conventions. The first letter of the word after the get()/set() should be capitalized along with the first letter of each word in the method, thereafter. All other letters in the method name should be in a lower case. The Struts framework uses Java reflection to read the data from and write data to the ActionForm class. An exception will be raised if the get() or set() method is not present for a piece of data submitted.

For the Post a Story page, we are going to write a Struts ActionForm class called PostStoryForm.java. This class will hold the story title, the story introduction, and the body of the story. In addition, it will contain the validation code for the data being submitted by the user. The class diagram shown below illustrates the class relationships, methods, and attributes for the Struts ActionForm class and the PostStoryForm class:

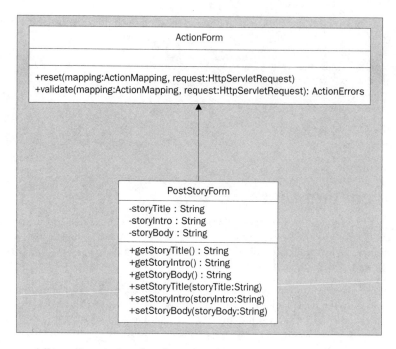

It is very easy to fall into the mindset that there must be one `ActionForm` class for each HTML form from which the data is collected. In small-to-medium size applications, there is nothing wrong in using a single `ActionForm` placed in the user's session. All the forms in the application will use this `ActionForm` to hold the data collected from the user.

This simplifies the collection of the data because your application has only one `ActionForm` instance that you have to work with. By using a single `ActionForm` class and placing it in the user's session, you can very easily implement a wizard-based application that will remember each piece of user information entered. As the user steps back and forth through the wizard, the data can easily be retrieved from the single `ActionForm` class.

The problem with using a single `ActionForm` class in the user's session is that the application will not scale as well. Remember, the objects placed in the user's session have a reference held until the session times out and the objects are garbage-collected. Do not place `ActionForm` objects in the session merely as a convenience. The other problem with this method occurs if the users are carrying out a long-lived transaction. If the users lose their connection or close their browser, any of the data entered till then will be lost. To ensure that as much of the user's data is captured and persisted as possible, break the application into smaller transactions. Use an `ActionForm` class for each application screen and persist the data in the `ActionForm` class as soon as the users submit their data. Place the `ActionForm` class into the request so that server resources are not unnecessarily used.

The code for the `PostStoryForm` class is shown below. However, the `reset()` and `validate()` methods for this class are not displayed. They will be discussed in the sections called *Using the reset() Method* and *Validating the Form Data*, respectively.

```
package com.wrox.javaedge.struts.poststory;

import org.apache.struts.action.Action;
import org.apache.struts.action.ActionMapping;
import org.apache.struts.action.ActionForm;
import org.apache.struts.action.ActionForward;
import org.apache.struts.action.ActionErrors;
import org.apache.struts.action.ActionError;
import org.apache.struts.action.ActionServlet;
import org.apache.struts.util.MessageResources;
import com.wrox.javaedge.common.VulgarityFilter;

import javax.servlet.http.HttpServletRequest;
import javax.servlet.http.HttpServletResponse;
import javax.servlet.http.HttpSession;

public class PostStoryForm extends ActionForm {

  String storyTitle = "";      //defined as empty string
  String storyIntro = "";
  String storyBody  = "";

  /**
   *  Validates all data posted from the Post Story page.
   */
  public ActionErrors validate(ActionMapping mapping,
                               HttpServletRequest request) {

    ...
  }

  /**
   *  Used to clear out the values stored in a PostStoryForm class's
   *      attributes.
   */
  public void reset(ActionMapping mapping, HttpServletRequest request) {
    ...
  }

  /** Getter for property storyTitle.
   * @return Value of property storyTitle.
   */
  public java.lang.String getStoryTitle() {
    return storyTitle;
  }

  /** Setter for property storyTitle.
   * @param storyTitle New value of property storyTitle.
   */
  public void setStoryTitle(java.lang.String storyTitle) {
    this.storyTitle = storyTitle;
  }

  /** Getter for property storyIntro.
   * @return Value of property storyIntro.
```

```
  */
  public java.lang.String getStoryIntro() {
    return storyIntro;
  }


/** Setter for property storyIntro.
 * @param storyIntro New value of property storyIntro.
 */
public void setStoryIntro(java.lang.String storyIntro) {
    this.storyIntro = storyIntro;
}


/** Getter for property storyBody.
 * @return Value of property storyBody.
 */
public java.lang.String getStoryBody() {
    return storyBody;
}


/** Setter for property storyBody.
 * @param storyBody New value of property storyBody.
 */
public void setStoryBody(java.lang.String storyBody) {
    this.storyBody = storyBody;
}
}
```

Using the reset() Method

The reset() method is used to ensure that an ActionForm class is always put in a "clean" state, before the ActionServlet populates it with the form data submitted in the user's request. In the struts-config.xml, the developer can choose to place an ActionForm for a specific Struts action either in the user's session or request.

If the developer declares that the ActionForm is to be placed in the session, the reset() method will not be invoked. The ActionServlet will bypass the reset() method, populate the properties in the ActionForm with the data from the user's request, and then call the validate() method of the ActionForm.

The reset() method is invoked only if the developer has declared that the ActionForm class should be stored in the request. This method is necessary because Struts maintains a cache for each of the declared ActionForm classes. A single instance of an ActionForm class can be shared by multiple users for different requests at different times. Hence, the developer must implement the reset() method to ensure that the end user never gets some other user's data.

> You do not have to override the **reset()** method while building an **ActionForm**. However, if you declare an **ActionForm** class to be stored in the request, and not the session, it is always a good idea to implement a **reset()** method to clear the contents of the **ActionForm** class properties.

Implementing the `reset()` method for the `PostStoryForm`, will set all its properties to an empty string. The `reset()` method for the `PostStoryForm` class is shown below:

```
public void reset(ActionMapping mapping,
                  HttpServletRequest request) {
    storyTitle = "";
    storyIntro = "";
    storyBody  = "";
}
```

Pre-populating an ActionForm with Data

So far, we have talked about using the `reset()` method to ensure that the contents of an `ActionForm` class are cleared, before the `ActionServlet` places data in it from the user request. However, an `ActionForm` class can also be used to pre-populate an HTML form with data. The data populating the form might be text information retrieved from a properties file or a database.

To pre-populate an HTML form with data, we need to have the following Struts elements in place:

❑   A Struts pre-setup action, which will be called before a user is redirected to a JSP page, displaying an HTML form pre-populated with the data. The concept of pre- and post-setup actions is discussed in Chapter 2.

❑   An `ActionForm` class whose `reset()` method will pre-populate the form fields with data retrieved from the `ApplicationResources.properties` file. The `ApplicationResources.properties` file is discussed in Chapter 2.

❑   A JSP page, which uses the Struts HTML tag libraries to retrieve the data from the `ActionForm` class.

For example, we can pre-populate the HTML form for the **Post a Story** page with some simple instructions on what data is supposed to go in each field. For this example, we are going to use the following files:

❑   `PostStoryForm.java`

❑   `PostStorySetupAction.java`

❑   `postStoryContent.jsp`

We are only going to look at the `PostStoryForm` and the `PostStorySetupAction` Java classes. The `postStoryContent.jsp` file will use the Struts HTML tag library to read the values out of the `PostStoryForm` object stored in the request and display them in each field. The `postStoryContent.jsp` and Struts HTML tag library is discussed in the section called *The Struts HTML Tag Library*.

PostStoryForm.java

Writing the `reset()` method for a `PostStoryForm` to pre-populate the `ActionForm` with the instructions for each field in the form is a straightforward task:

```
public void reset(ActionMapping mapping,
                  HttpServletRequest request) {
  ActionServlet servlet = this.getServlet();
  MessageResources messageResources = servlet.getResources();

  storyTitle =
    messageResources.getMessage("javaedge.poststory.title.instructions");
  storyIntro =
    messageResources.getMessage("javaedge.poststory.intro.instructions");
  storyBody =
    messageResources.getMessage("javaedge.poststory.body.instructions");
}
```

The `reset()` method above reads values from the `ApplicationResources.properties` file and uses them to populate the properties of the `PostStoryForm` object.

The Struts development framework provides an easy-to-use wrapper class, called `MessageResources`, for directly accessing the data in the `ApplicationResources.properties` file. To retrieve an instance of the `MessageResources` class, you first need to get a reference to the `ActionServlet` that is currently processing the `ActionForm` object. Fortunately, the `ActionForm` class provides a `getServlet()` method that will retrieve an instance of the `ActionServlet`:

```
ActionServlet servlet = this.getServlet();
```

Once an instance of the `ActionServlet` is retrieved, a call to its `getResources()` method will retrieve a `MessageResources` object that wraps all the values stored in the `ApplicationResources.properties` file:

```
MessageResources messageResources = servlet.getResources();
```

After getting an instance of a `MessageResources` object, you can pass the message key of the item that you want to retrieve to the `getMessage()`. The `getMessage()` method will retrieve the desired value:

```
messageResources.getMessage("javaedge.poststory.title.instructions");
```

If the key passed to the `getMessage()` method cannot be found, a value of `null` will be returned. The following are the name-value pairs from the `ApplicationResources.properties` file used to pre-populate the `PostStoryForm`:

```
javaedge.poststory.title.instructions=Enter a title here.
javaedge.poststory.intro.instructions=Enter the story introduction here.  Please
be concise.
javaedge.poststory.body.instructions=Enter the full story here. Please be nice.
```

The `PostStoryForm.reset()` method is a very simple example of how to pre-populate a form with the data contained in an `ActionForm` class. In reality, many applications retrieve their data from an underlying relational database rather than from a properties file. How the `reset()` method on the `PostStoryForm` is invoked, is yet to be explored. Let's take a look at the `PostStorySetupAction.java` and see how we can trigger the `reset()` method.

PostStorySetupAction.java

Triggering the `PostStoryForm.reset()` method does not require any coding in the `PostStorySetupAction.java` file. All that the `PostStorySetupAction` class is going to do is to forward the user's request to the `postStoryContent.jsp`. So what role does the `PostStorySetupAction.java` play, if its `perform()` method just forwards the user on to a JSP page? How is the `reset()` method in the `PostStoryForm` class called?

If we set a Struts `<action>` tag in the `struts-config.xml` file to use an `ActionForm` and tell the `ActionServlet` to put the `PostStoryForm` in the user's request, the `reset()` method in the `PostStoryForm` class will be invoked.

When a user clicks on the **Post a Story** link in the JavaEdge header, they are asking the `ActionServlet` to invoke the `/postStorySetup` action. This action is configured to use the `ActionForm` class of `PostStoryForm`. The `PostStoryForm` is going to be put in the user's request context by the `ActionServlet`.

Since the `ActionForm` class for the `/postStorySetup` action is the `PostStoryForm` class and the `PostStoryForm` class is going to be placed into the user's request context, the `reset()` method in the `PostStoryForm` class will be invoked. The `reset()` method is going to initialize each of the attributes in the `PostStoryForm` class to hold a set of simple instructions pulled from the `ApplicationResources.properties` file.

After the `reset()` method has been invoked the `ActionServlet` will place any submitted form data in the `PostStoryForm` instance. Since the user has not actually submitted any data, the `PostStoryForm` class will still hold all of the values read from the `ApplicationResources.properties` file. The `ActionServlet` will then invoke the `perform()` method in the `PostStorySetupAction` class, which will forward the user to the `postStoryContent.jsp` page. This page will display a form, pre-populated with instructions.

In summary, to pre-populate the form, we need to perform the following two steps:

1. Write a Struts `Action` class called `PostStorySetupAction.java`. The `perform()` method of this class will pass the user on to `postStoryContent.jsp`.

2. Set up an action called `/postStorySetup` in the `struts-config.xml` file. This action will use the `PostStoryForm` class.

The code for `PostStorySetupAction.java` is shown below:

```
package com.wrox.javaedge.struts.poststory;

import org.apache.struts.action.Action;
import org.apache.struts.action.ActionMapping;
import org.apache.struts.action.ActionForm;
import org.apache.struts.action.ActionForward;
import javax.servlet.http.HttpServletRequest;
import javax.servlet.http.HttpServletResponse;
import javax.servlet.http.HttpSession;
```

```
public class PostStorySetupAction extends Action {
  public ActionForward perform(ActionMapping mapping,
                               ActionForm form,
                               HttpServletRequest request,
                               HttpServletResponse response){

    return (mapping.findForward("poststory.success"));
  }
}
```

The `perform()` method just forwards the user to the `postStoryContent.jsp` page, by returning an `ActionForward` mapped to this page:

```
return (mapping.findForward("poststory.success"));
```

The `poststory.success` mapping corresponds to the `<forward>` element, defined for the following `<action>` tag of `/postStorySetup`:

```
<action path="/postStorySetup"
        type="com.wrox.javaedge.struts.poststory.PostStorySetupAction"
        name="postStoryForm"
        scope="request"
        validate="false">
  <forward name="poststory.success" path="/WEB-INF/jsp/postStory.jsp"/>
</action>
```

The `name` attribute shown above tells the `ActionServlet` to use an instance of `PostStoryForm`, whenever the user invokes the `/postStorySetup` action:

```
name="postStoryForm"
```

Remember, the value of the `name` attribute must refer to a `<form-bean>` tag defined at the beginning of the `struts-config.xml` file.

The `scope` attribute tells the `ActionServlet` to place the `PostStoryForm` as an attribute in the `HttpServletRequest` object:

```
scope="request"
```

Setting the `validate` attribute to `false`, in the above tag, will cause the `ActionServlet` not to invoke the `validate()` method of the `PostStoryForm`. This means the `reset()` method in the `PostStoryForm` object is going to be invoked and placed in the user's request, but no data validation will take place.

Since no data validation takes place, the `perform()` method of `PostStorySetupAction` will be invoked. Remember, the `Action` class that carries out the end user's request is defined via the `type` attribute:

```
type="com.wrox.javaedge.struts.poststory.PostStorySetupAction"
```

Another Technique for Pre-population

There is another technique for pre-populating an ActionForm with data. It is discussed here because implementing your Struts application using this technique can cause long-term maintenance headaches.

In the PostStorySetupAction.java, you could implement the perform() method so that it creates an instance of PostStoryForm and invokes its reset() method directly. After the reset() method is invoked, the PostStoryForm can then be set as an attribute in the request object passed in the perform() method. The following code demonstrates this technique:

```
public class PostStorySetupAction extends Action {
   public ActionForward perform(ActionMapping mapping,
                                ActionForm form,
                                HttpServletRequest request,
                                HttpServletResponse response){

      PostStoryForm postStoryForm = new PostStoryForm();
      postStoryForm.setServlet(this.getServlet());
      postStoryForm.reset(mapping, request);
      request.setAttribute("postStoryForm", postStoryForm);

      return (mapping.findForward("poststory.success"));
   }
}
```

This technique does not require you to provide any additional configuration information in the <action> tag. The above code carries out all the actions that the ActionServlet would carry out.

However, using this approach has two long-term architectural consequences. First, the above approach has tightly coupled the PostStoryForm class to the PostStorySetupAction class. In the future, if the development team wants the /postStorySetup to use something other than the PostStoryForm class for the pre-population or form validation, it must rewrite the perform() method. This becomes a tedious task, if the PostStoryForm class is present throughout multiple applications and a developer needs to switch it with another ActionForm class. If the developer had used the first technique and associated the PostStoryForm and PostStorySetup by declaring their usage in the struts-config.xml, a few small changes to the file could have easily switched the ActionForm class populating the postStoryContent.jsp page.

The second problem is that it takes control of the ActionForm away from the ActionServlet. The responsibility for managing the ActionForm shifts from the ActionServlet to the application developer. If the Struts development team changes how the ActionForm class is processed by the ActionServlet, the developers run the risk of having their application code break when they try to upgrade to the next release of Struts.

> **If you have to work on the application framework, consider redesigning the task you are trying to execute. Stepping outside the application framework, as in the example shown above, can lead to long-term maintenance and upgrade issues. The Struts architecture tries to remain very declarative and controlling the application flow programmatically breaks one of the fundamental tenants of Struts.**

Validating the Form Data

As discussed earlier, a common mistake in web application development is for there to be no clear distinction between business logic and validation logic. The ActionForm class helps the developers to solve this problem, by allowing them to enforce lightweight validation rules against the data entered by a user. By encapsulating these validation rules in the ActionForm class, the developer can clearly separate the validation rules from the business logic that actually carries out the request. The business logic is placed in the corresponding Action class for the end user's request.

A web developer can override the validate() method and provide their own validation rules for the submitted data, while writing their own ActionForm class. If the developer does not override the validate() method, none of the data submitted will have any validation logic run against it.

The validate() method for the PostStoryForm class is going to enforce three validation rules:

❑ The users must enter a story title, story introduction, and story body. If they leave any field blank, they will receive an error message indicating that they must enter the data.

❑ The users are not allowed to put vulgarity in their application. The validate() method will check the data entered by the user for any inappropriate words.

❑ Each field in the Post a Story page is not allowed to exceed a certain length, otherwise, the user will get an error message.

It is important to note that, in all cases, the users will not be allowed to continue until they correct the validation violation(s).

The validate() method for the PostStoryForm class is as shown below:

```
public ActionErrors validate(ActionMapping mapping,
                             HttpServletRequest request) {
   ActionErrors errors = new ActionErrors();

   checkForEmpty("Story Title", "error.storytitle.empty",
                 getStoryTitle(), errors);
   checkForEmpty("Story Intro", "error.storyintro.empty",
                 getStoryIntro(), errors);
   checkForEmpty("Story Body",  "error.storybody.empty",
                 getStoryBody(), errors);

   checkForVulgarities("Story Title", "error.storytitle.vulgarity",
                       getStoryTitle(), errors);
   checkForVulgarities("Story Intro", "error.storyintro.vulgarity",
                       getStoryIntro(), errors);
   checkForVulgarities("Story Body",  "error.storybody.vulgarity",
                       getStoryBody(), errors);

   checkForLength("Story Title", "error.storytitle.length", getStoryTitle(),
                  100, errors);
   checkForLength("Story Intro", "error.storyintro.length", getStoryIntro(),
                  2048, errors);
   checkForLength("Story Body", "error.storybody.length", getStoryBody(),
                  2048, errors);

   return errors;
}
```

The first step in the `validate()` method is to instantiate an instance, called `errors`, of the `ActionErrors` class:

```
ActionErrors errors = new ActionErrors();
```

The `ActionErrors` class is a Struts class that holds one or more instances of an `ActionError` class. An `ActionError` class represents a single violation of one of the validation rules being enforced in the `ActionForm` class. If a form element submitted by an end user violates a validation rule, an `ActionError` will be added to the to the `errors` object.

When the `validate()` method completes, the `errors` object will be returned to the `ActionServlet`:

```
return errors;
```

If the `errors` object is `null` or contains no `ActionErrors`, the `ActionServlet` will allow the business logic to be carried out, based on the end user's request. This is done by invoking the `perform()` method in the `Action` class associated with the request.

Let's look at the `checkForVulgarities()` method, to see how an `ActionError` class is actually created when a validation rule is violated. The `checkForEmpty()` and `checkForLength()` methods will not be discussed in detail, but the code for these methods is shown below:

```
/**
 *  Ensures that the field being checked is not null
 */
private void checkForEmpty(String fieldName, String fieldKey, String value,
                          ActionErrors errors) {
  if (value.trim().length() == 0) {
    ActionError error = new ActionError("error.poststory.field.null",
                                        fieldName);
    errors.add(fieldKey, error);
  }
}


/**
 * Ensures that the field in question does not exceed a maximum length
 */
private void checkForLength(String fieldName, String fieldKey, String value,
                            int maxLength, ActionErrors errors){
  if (value.length() > maxLength){
    ActionError error = new ActionError("error.poststory.field.length",
                                        fieldName);
    errors.add(fieldKey, error);
  }
}
```

Creating an ActionError

The `checkForVulgarities()` method is as shown below:

```
/**
 * Ensures that the field being checked does not violate our vulgarity list
 */
private void checkForVulgarities(String fieldName, String fieldKey,
                                 String value, ActionErrors errors) {

    VulgarityFilter filter = VulgarityFilter.getInstance();

    if (filter.isOffensive(value)){
        ActionError error = new ActionError("error.poststory.field.vulgar",
                                            fieldName);
        errors.add(fieldKey, error);
    }
}
```

The first line in this method retrieves an instance of the `VulgarityFilter` into a variable called `filter`:

```
VulgarityFilter filter = VulgarityFilter.getInstance();
```

The `VulgarityFilter` class is implemented using a singleton design pattern and wraps a collection of words that are considered to be offensive. The code for the class is shown below:

```
package com.wrox.javaedge.common;

public class VulgarityFilter {

    private static VulgarityFilter filter = null;

    private static String[] badWords = {"Stupid", "Idiot", "Moron", "Dummy",
                                        "Flippin", "Ninny"};

    static {
        filter = new VulgarityFilter();
    }

    public static VulgarityFilter getInstance(){
        return filter;
    }

    public boolean isOffensive(String valueToCheck){
        String currentWord = "";

        for (int x = 0; x <= badWords.length - 1; x++){
            if (valueToCheck.toLowerCase().indexOf(badWords[x].toLowerCase())
                != -1) {
                return true;
            }
        }

        return false;
    }
}
```

The `VulgarityFilter` class has a single method called `isOffensive()`, which checks if the text passed in is offensive. A value of `true` returned by this method indicates the user has entered data that contains offensive text:

```
if (filter.isOffensive(value))
```

When a vulgarity is found, a new `ActionError` is created and added to the `errors` object passed to the `checkForVulgarity()` method:

```
ActionError error = new ActionError("error.poststory.field.vulgar",
                                    fieldname);
errors.add(fieldKey, error);
```

There are five constructors that can be used to instantiate an `ActionError` class. The first parameter of each of these constructors is a lookup key, which Struts uses to find the text of the error message displayed to the end user. Struts will look for all error messages in the `ApplicationResources.properties` file associated with the application. The error messages for the **Post a Story** page are shown below:

```
error.poststory.field.null=The following field: {0} is a required field.  Please
provide a value for {0}.<br/>
error.poststory.field.vulgar=You have put a vulgarity in your {0} field.  Please
refer to our <a href="/javaedge/policy.html">terms of use policy.</a><br/>
error.poststory.field.length=Your {0} field is too long.<br/>
```

When the user violates the vulgarity validation rule and the `checkForVulgarity()` method creates an `ActionError`, the lookup key `error.poststory.field.vulgar` will be used to return the following error message:

```
The following field: {0} is a required field.  Please provide a value for
{0}.<br/>
```

The error message can contain at most four distinct parameter values. The parameter values are referenced by using the notation: {number}, where the `number` is between zero and three. In the above example, only one parameter is inserted into the error message. A summary of the five constructors in the `ActionError` class is given below:

ActionError Constructor	Description
`ActionError(String lookupKey)`	Retrieves the error message from the `ApplicationResources.properties` file.
`ActionError(String lookupKey, String param0)`	Retrieves the error message from the `ApplicationResources.properties` file and passes in one parameter.
`ActionError(String lookupKey, String param0, String param1)`	Retrieves the error message from the `ApplicationResources.properties` file and passes in two parameters.

Table continued on following page

ActionError Constructor	Description
`ActionError(String lookupKey, String param0, String param1, String param2)`	Retrieves the error message from the `ApplicationResources.properties` file and passes in three parameters.
`ActionError(String lookupKey, String param0, String param1, String param2, String param3)`	Retrieves the error message from the `ApplicationResources.properties` file and passes in four parameters.

After the `error` object has been created, it is later added to the `errors` object by calling the `add()` method in `errors`:

```
errors.add(fieldKey, error);
```

The `add()` method takes two parameters:

❑ A key that uniquely identifies the added error within the `ActionErrors` class. This key must be unique and can be used to look up a specific error in the `ActionErrors` class.

❑ An `ActionError` object containing the error message.

Viewing the Errors

The Struts `ActionServlet` checks if there are any errors in the returned `ActionErrors` object and determines if a validation error was returned by the `validate()` method. If there are any `ActionError` objects in the returned `ActionErrors` instance, it means that the validation errors were found. If the value returned from the `validate()` method is `null` or contains no `ActionError` objects, no validation errors were found.

If the Struts `ActionServlet` finds that there are errors present in the `ActionError` object, it will redirect the user to the path set in the `input` attribute for the action. Most of the time, the value in this `input` tag is the JSP page where the data was entered. The `ActionForm` object holding the user's data will still be in the request. Thus, any data entered by the user in the form will appear pre-populated in the form. How does Struts present the user with all the errors raised in the `validate()` method? It does this using the `<html:errors/>` tag. This tag is found in the Struts HTML custom JSP tag library. (There are several other form-related custom tags in the HTML tag library. We will be discussing the full HTML tag library in the section called *The Struts HTML Tag Library*). There are two ways of using this tag:

❑ To write each error message, stored within the `ActionErrors` class, to the JSP out `PrintWriter` class

❑ To retrieve a specific error message from the `ActionErrors` class and place it next to the specific fields

Writing All Error Messages to the JSP Page

To perform the first action, you must import the Struts HTML tag library and place the `<html:errors/>` tag where you want the errors to appear. For instance, in the `postStoryContent.jsp`, we use this tag in the following manner:

```
<%@ page language="java" %>
<%@ taglib uri="/WEB-INF/struts-html.tld" prefix="html" %>

<BR/><BR/>
<H1><bean:message key="javaedge.poststory.text.header"/></H1>

<html:errors/>
```

This code will write all the errors messages in the `ActionErrors` class returned by `validate()` method of the `PostStoryForm` immediately below the header of the page. The following example shows the type of error messages that can be presented to the end-user:

```
You have put a vulgarity in your Story Title field. Please refer to our <a
href="/javaedge/policy.html">terms of use policy.</a><br/>
The following field: Story Intro is a required field. Please provide a value for
Story Intro.<br/>
The following field: Story Body is a required field. Please provide a value for
Story Body.<br/>
```

It is extremely important to note that the `<html:errors/>` tag will write the error text exactly as it has been defined in the `ApplicationResources.properties` file. This means that the developer must provide HTML tags to format the appearance of the error message. This also includes putting any `<br/>` tags for the appropriate line breaks between the error messages. The `<html:errors/>` tag allows the application developer to define a header and footer for a collection of error messages. Headers and footers are defined by including an `errors.header` property and `errors.footer` property in the `ApplicationResources.properties` file. These two properties can contain text (and HTML code) that will appear immediately before and after the errors written by the `<html:errors/>` tag. The following snippet shows these properties for the JavaEdge application:

```
errors.header=<h3><font color="red">Important Message</font></h3><ul>
errors.footer=</ul><hr>
```

Even if you do not want to use the `errors.header` and `errors.footer` properties to generate an error header and footer, you must still define them in the `ApplicationResources.properties` with no values. For example:

```
errors.header=
errors.footer=
```

If you do not include these properties, you will get a null value appearing before and after your list of errors.

The `<html:errors/>` tag provides a very simple and consistent error handling mechanism. Front-end screen developers only need to know that they have to put an `<html:errors/>` tag in their JSP form pages to display any validation errors. The job of the server-side developers is simplified because they can easily validate the form data submitted by the end user and communicate any errors back to the user by populating an `ActionErrors` object.

Keeping in mind all the discussion that we had so far, when the end users violate a validation rule on the Post a Story page they will see the following output:

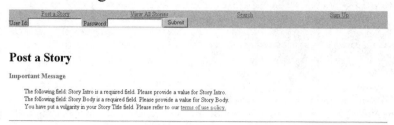

The following field: Story Intro is a required field. Please provide a value for Story Intro.
The following field: Story Body is a required field. Please provide a value for Story Body.
You have put a vulgarity in your Story Title field. Please refer to our terms of use policy.

Retrieving a Single Error Message

The <html:errors/> tag by itself is somewhat inflexible, because you have to present all the validation errors caused by the end user at a single spot on the screen. Many application developers like to break the validation errors apart and put them next to the field that contains the invalid data.

Fortunately, the <html:errors/> tag allows you to pull a single error message from an ActionErrors object. It has an attribute called `property`. This attribute will let you retrieve an error message, using the key value that was used while adding the error message to the ActionErrors object. For example, when a user enters a word that violates the vulgarity filter, we add that validation error to the errors object by calling:

```
errors.add(fieldKey, error);
```

The fieldKey variable passed to the errors.add() method is the name we have chosen to represent that particular error. For example, if the user typed the word dummy into the story title field, this would violate the vulgarity validation rule and a new ActionError class would be instantiated. The new ActionError would be added to the errors class and would have a fieldKey value of error.storytitle.vulgarity.

If you wanted to put that specific error message directly above the Story Title field label, you could rewrite the postStoryContent.jsp with the following code:

```
<TR>
  <TD>
    <font size="1" color="red">
      <html:errors property="error.storytitle.vulgarity"/>
    </font>
    <bean:message key="javaedge.poststory.form.titlelabel"/>
    <html:text name="postStoryForm" property="storyTitle"/>
  </TD>
</TR>
```

By using the <html:errors/> tag in the manner shown above, you can cause the postStoryContent.jsp to generate an error message that may look like the one shown below:

Important Message

You have put a vulgarity in your Story Title field. Please refer to our <u>terms of use policy.</u>

The following story will be posted by: **Anonymous**

Story Title:

Dummy

Story Intro:

> You must remember that if you are going to scatter the individual validation errors throughout the screen, you need to make sure you set the `errors.header` and `errors.footer` properties, in `ApplicationResources.properties`, to no value. Otherwise, every error message rendered in the page will include the contents of the `errors.headers` and `errors.footer` properties.

Error Handling and Pre-population

After discussing how HTML errors are handled in Struts, you might be a little bit confused. Why does the form show up with all of the fields pre-populated with the data that the user just entered? Why doesn't the `reset()` method in the `ActionForm` class reset all the values?

The reason is simple. When the `validate()` method is invoked and if there are validation errors, the `ActionServlet` is going to look at the value of the `input` attribute in the `<action>` tag. The `input` attribute almost invariably points back to the JSP where the user entered the data. Remember, the `reset()` method gets called only when an action is invoked. Redirecting the user back to a JSP page will not invoke the `reset()` method. If the JSP page to which the user is redirected uses the Struts HTML tag library and an `ActionForm` in the user's request or session, it will pull the data out of the `ActionForm` and pre-populate the form elements with that data. Thus, when a validation error occurs the user sees the validation errors and a pre-populated form.

If you want to force the reset of all the elements in a form, after the validation occurs, you need to point the `input` attribute in the `<action>` element to an action (usually a `SetupAction` of some kind).

The Struts HTML Tag Library

As we have seen earlier in this chapter, Struts provides the `ActionForm` and the `Action` classes as the means of validating and processing the data submitted by the end user. The Struts development framework also provides a JSP tag library, called the HTML tag library, which significantly simplifies the development of HTML-based forms. The HTML tag library allows the developer to write JSP pages that tightly integrate with an `ActionForm` class.

The Struts HTML tag library can be used to generate HTML form controls and read data out of an `ActionForm` class in the user's session or request. It also helps developers avoid writing significant amounts of scriptlet code to pull the user data out of JavaBeans (that is, the `ActionForm` objects) in the user's request and/or session. When combined with the other Struts tag libraries, as discussed in Chapter 2, a developer can write very dynamic and data-driven web pages without ever having to write a single line of JSP scriptlet code.

The Struts HTML tag library contains a wide variety of tags for generating HTML form controls. We are not going to cover every tag in the Struts HTML tag library. Instead, we are going to go through the most commonly used tags and explore their usage. For a full list of the different tags available in the Struts HTML tag library, you can visit http://jakarta.apache.org/struts. The tags discussed in this chapter include:

Tag Name	Tag Description
`<html:form>`	Renders an HTML `<form>` tag
`<html:submit>`	Renders a submit button
`<html:cancel>`	Renders a cancel button
`<html:text>`	Renders a text field
`<html:textarea>`	Renders a textarea field
`<html:select>`	Renders an HTML `<select>` tag for creating drop-down boxes
`<html:option>`	Renders an HTML `<option>` control that represents a single box in a dropdown
`<html:checkbox>`	Renders an HTML checkbox
`<html:radio>`	Renders an HTML radio control

Let's begin the discussion of the Struts HTML tag library by looking at the `postStoryContent.jsp` page:

```
<%@ page language="java" %>
<%@ taglib uri="/WEB-INF/struts-bean.tld" prefix="bean" %>
<%@ taglib uri="/WEB-INF/struts-html.tld" prefix="html" %>
<%@ taglib uri="/WEB-INF/struts-logic.tld" prefix="logic" %>
<%@ taglib uri="/WEB-INF/struts-template.tld" prefix="template" %>

<BR/>
<BR/>
<H1>
  <bean:message key="javaedge.poststory.text.header"/>
</H1>

<html:errors/>

<html:form action="postStory">
  <TABLE>
    <TR>
```

```
       <TD>
         <bean:message key="javaedge.poststory.text.intro"/>
         <logic:present scope="session" name="memberVO">
           <B>
             <bean:write name="memberVO" scope="session"
                        property="firstName"/> 
             <bean:write name="memberVO" scope="session"
                        property="lastName"/>
           </B><BR/>
         </logic:present>

         <logic:notPresent scope="sessiom" name="memberVO">
           <B>Anonymous</B>
         </logic:notPresent>

       </TD>
       <TD>
         <BR/><BR/> 
       </TD>
     </TR>

     <TR>
       <TD>
         <bean:message key="javaedge.poststory.form.titlelabel"/>
         <html:text property="storyTitle"/>
       </TD>
     </TR>

     <TR>
       <TD>
         <bean:message key="javaedge.poststory.form.introlabel"/>
         <html:textarea property="storyIntro" cols="80" rows="5"/>
       </TD>
     </TR>

     <TR>
       <TD>
         <bean:message key="javaedge.poststory.form.bodylabel"/>
         <html:textarea property="storyBody" cols="80"
                           rows="10"/>
       </TD>
     </TR>

     <TR>
       <TD align="center"><html:submit property="submitButton"
           value="Submit"/>
       </TD>
     </TR>
   </TABLE>
</html:form>
```

Setting Up a Struts HTML Form

Before using the individual Struts HTML tag within a JSP page, three steps must be undertaken:

1. Import the Struts HTML Tag Library Definitions (TLDs)

2. Define an <html:form> tag, within the page, that will map to an <action> tag defined in the struts-config.xml file

3. Define an <html:submit> button to allow the user to submit the entered data

The Struts HTML TLD is imported as shown below:

```
<%@ taglib uri="/WEB-INF/struts-html.tld" prefix="html" %>
```

Next, we use the Struts HTML tags. Just as in a static HTML page, we need to define a <form> tag that will encapsulate all the HTML form controls on the page. This is done by using the <html:form> tag.

```
<html:form action="postStory">
    ...
</html:form>
```

The <html:form> tag has a number of different attributes associated with it. However, we will not be discussing every <html:form> attribute in detail. Some of the <html:form> attributes are given below:

Attribute Name	Attribute Description
action	Maps to the <action> tag that will carry out the user's request when the form data is submitted. This is a required field.
method	Determines whether the form will be sent as a GET or POST. This is not a mandatory field and if it is not specified, Struts will generate the <form> tag to use a POST method.
Name	The name of the JavaBean that will be used to pre-populate the form controls. The <html:form> tag will check if this bean is present in the user's session or request. The scope attribute below defines whether to look into the user's session or request. If no JavaBean is found in the context defined in the scope attribute, the <html:form> tag will create a new instance of the bean and place it into the scope defined by the scope attribute. The class type of the created JavaBean is determined by the type attribute below.
scope	Determines whether the bean should look in the user's session or request for the JavaBean named in the name attribute above. The value for this attribute can be either "session" or "request".
type	Fully qualified Java class name for the JavaBean being used to populate the form.

Attribute Name	Attribute Description
onsubmit	Lets the developer define a JavaScript onSubmit() event handler for the generated form.
onreset	Lets the developer define a JavaScript onReset() event handler for the generated form.
Focus	Name of the field that will have focus when the form is rendered.

The most important of these attributes is the action attribute. It maps to an <action> element defined in the struts-config.xml file. If no name, scope, or type attribute is specified in the <html:form> tag, the ActionForm that will be used to populate the form its fully qualified Java name, and the scope in which it resides will be pulled from the <action> tag in struts-config.xml file.

In the <html:form> tag used in the postStoryContent.jsp, all the ActionForm information would be retrieved by the ActionServlet, by looking at the name attribute in the <action> tag of postStory action in the struts-config.xml file:

```
<action path="/postStory"
  input="/WEB-INF/jsp/postStory.jsp"
  name="postStoryForm"
  scope="request"
  validate="true"
  type="com.wrox.javaedge.struts.poststory.PostStory">
  <forward name="poststory.success" path="/javaedge/execute/homePageSetup"/>
</action>
```

Since the value of name (postStoryForm) is defined as a <form-bean> element in the struts-config.xml, the ActionServlet can figure out its fully qualified Java class name and instantiate an instance of that class.

> It is a good practice to use the **action** attribute rather than the **name, scope,** and **type** attributes, to define the JavaBean that will populate the form. Using this attribute gives you more flexibility, by allowing you to change the **ActionForm** class in one location (**struts-config.xml**) rather than searching multiple JSP pages.

Let's look at the HTML generated by the <html:form> tag shown earlier:

```
<form name="postStoryForm" method="POST"
      action="/javaedge/execute/postStory">
```

The name attribute generated tells the ActionServlet of Struts that the postStoryForm bean, defined in the <form-beans> tag of the struts-config.xml, is going to be used to hold all the data posted by the user. The default method of the form (since we did not define one in the <html:form> tag) is going to be a POST method. The action attribute contains the URL to which the form data is going to be submitted. Since the action of the <html:form> tag was postStory, the <html:form> generated the action attribute (for the corresponding <form> tag) is /javaedge/execute/postStory.

The last step in setting up an HTML form is using the Struts <html:submit> tag to generate an HTML submit button:

```
<html:submit property="submitButton" value="Submit"/>
```

In addition to the <html:submit> tag, the Struts tag library has HTML tags for creating cancel buttons. When an <html:cancel> tag is used an HTML button will be rendered that, when clicked, will cause the ActionServlet to bypass the validate() method in the ActionForm that is associated with the form.

Even though the validate() method is bypassed, the perform() method for the Action class (in this case PostStory.java) linked with the form will be invoked. This means that, if you want to use an <html:cancel> button in your page, the perform() method must to detect when the cancel button is invoked and act accordingly. For instance, let's say the following <html:cancel> tag was added to the postStoryContent.jsp file:

```
<html:cancel value="Cancel"/>
```

The validate() method in the PostStoryForm class would not be called. However, the perform() method on the PostStory class would be invoked. The perform() method taken from the PostStory class could be written in the following manner:

```
public ActionForward perform(ActionMapping mapping,
                             ActionForm form,
                             HttpServletRequest request,
                             HttpServletResponse response){

  if (this.isCancelled(request)){
    System.out.println("*****The user pressed cancel!!!");
    return (mapping.findForward("poststory.success"));
  }

  //Add the story data to the database.
  ...
  return (mapping.findForward("poststory.success"));
}
```

If you did not want the code in the perform() method to be executed, you will have to use a method called isCancelled() to detect if the user pressed a cancel button. The isCancelled() method is inherited from the base Struts Action class. This method looks for a parameter in the user's request, called org.apache.struts.taglib.html.CANCEL. If it finds this parameter, it will return true indicating to the developer (writing the perform() method code) that the user clicked the cancel button.

The parameter name, org.apache.struts.taglib.html.CANCEL, maps to the name attribute in the <input> tag generated by the <html:cancel> button. The HTML button generated by the <html:cancel> tag shown earlier looks like:

```
<input type="submit" name="org.apache.struts.taglib.html.CANCEL"
       value="Cancel">
```

Unlike the <html:submit> tag, the property attribute on the <html:cancel> tag is rarely set.

> If you set the **property** attribute in the **<html:cancel>** button, it will override the default value generated and you will not be able to use the **isCancelled()** method to determine if the user wants to cancel the action.

Using Text and TextArea Input Fields

The postStoryContent.jsp files use text <input> and textarea tags to collect the data from the end user. The <html:text> and <html:textarea> tags are used to generate the text <input> and textarea tags, respectively. For instance, the postContent.jsp page uses the <html:text> tag to generate an HTML text <input> tag by using:

```
<html:text property="storyTitle"/>
```

The <html:text> tag has a number of attributes, but the most important are name and property. The name attribute defines the name of the ActionForm bean that the input field is going to map to. The property attribute defines the property in the ActionForm bean that is going to map to this input field. There are two things that you should keep in mind while working with the property attribute:

❑ The property attribute will map to a get() and set() method in the ActionForm bean. This means that value must match the standard JavaBean naming conventions. For instance, the value storyTitle is going to be used by the ActionServlet to call the getStoryTitle() and setStoryTitle() methods in the ActionForm.

❑ The value in a property attribute can be nested by using a ".". notation. Let's assume that the ActionForm method had a property called member that mapped to a MemberVO object containing the user data. The developer could set the value of the property attribute to be "member.firstName". This would translate into a call to the getMember().getFirstName() and getMember().setFirstName() methods of PostStoryForm class.

> If you refer to the Struts documentation on the Jakarta web site, you will notice that almost every Struts HTML tag has a **name** attribute in it. This attribute is the name of the JavaBean to and from which the HTML tag will read and write data. You do not have to supply a **name** attribute for the HTML form attributes we are describing in the following sections. If you do not supply a **name** attribute and if the **<html:*>** control is inside an **<html:form>** tag, the **<html:*>** control will automatically use the **ActionForm** associated with the **<html:form>** tag.

The <html:textarea> input tag behaves in a similar fashion to the <html:text> tag. The <html:textarea> tag uses the column and row attributes to define the width and length of the textarea the user can type in:

```
<html:textarea name="postStoryForm" property="storyIntro" cols="80" rows="5"/>
```

The above tag will generate an <input> tag called storyInto that will be 80 columns wide and five rows long.

Drop-down Lists, Checkboxes, and Radio Buttons

Most HTML forms are more than just a collection of the simple text field controls. They use drop-down lists, checkboxes, and radio buttons to collect a wide variety of information. While the postStoryContent.jsp file did not contain any of these controls, it is important to understand how the Struts framework renders these controls using the HTML tag library. Let's begin the discussion by the looking at the drop-down list.

Drop-down List

A drop-down list HTML control provides a list of options that a user can select from. However, the user sees only the item that has been selected. All of the other items are hidden until the user clicks on the drop-down box. On clicking the box, the rest of the options will be displayed and the user will be able to make a new choice.

Since the Post a Story page does not have a drop-down box, we will have to step away from it briefly. Using the Struts HTML tag library, there are two ways of rending a drop-down box:

❑   Use an <html:select> tag and build a static list of options by hard-coding a static list of <html:option> tags in the code

❑   Use an <html:select> tag and dynamically build the list by reading the data from a Java collection object using the <html:options> tag

The <html:select> tag renders a <select> tag in HTML. The <html:option> tag renders a single option for placement in the drop-down list. If you want to display a drop-down list containing a list of name prefixes, you would write the following code in your JSP file:

```
<html:select property="someBeanProperty">
  <html:option value="NS">Please select a prefix</form:option>
  <html:option value="Mr.">Mr.</form:option>
  <html:option value="Ms.">Ms.</form:option>
  <html:option value="Mrs.">Mrs.</form:option>
  <html:option value="Dr.">Dr.</form:option>
</html:select>
```

The above code snippet would generate the following HTML:

```
<select name="someBeanProperty">
  <option value="NS">Please select a prefix</option>
  <option value="Mr.">Mr.</option>
  <option value="Ms.">Ms.</option>
  <option value="Mrs.">Mrs.</option>
  <option value="Dr.">Dr.</option>
</select>
```

The <html:select> tag has one important attribute, the property attribute. It is the name of the ActionForm method that will store the item selected from the drop-down list. The <html:option> tag must always be contained within an <html:select> tag. The value attribute in the <html:option> tag specifies the value that will be sent in the user's request for the selected item from the drop-down list, when they hit the "submit" button.

The `<html:select>` and `<html:option>` tag work well while generating a drop-down list that does not change. However, if you want to create a drop-down list based on the data that is dynamic, such as the data pulled from a database, you need to the use the `<html:options>` tag. The `<html:options>` allows you to generate an `<option>` list from a Java `Collection` object.

Let's assume that in a `SetupAction` class we created a `Vector` object and populated it with the prefix codes. We then put that code in the `request` object as shown below:

```
Vector prefixes = new Vector();
prefixes.add("NS");
prefixes.add("Mr.");
prefixes.add("Ms.");
prefixes.add("Mrs.");
prefixes.add("Dr.");
request.setAttribute("prefixes", prefixes);
```

We could then render this collection into a drop-down list using the following code:

```
<html:select property="someBeanProperty">
  <html:options name="prefixes">
</html:select>
```

CheckBoxes

Setting up a checkbox to appear on an HTML form is easy to do. It just requires the use of a checkbox flag. To create a checkbox on a form, the following syntax can be used:

```
<html:checkbox property="someBeanProperty" value="true"/>
```

The `property` attribute for the checkbox matches the name of the `property` in the `ActionForm` for which the checkbox is going to get and set data. The `value` attribute is the value that will be sent in the HTTP request if the user checks the checkbox. If no value is specified, then the default value will always be on.

One important thing to remember is that when a checkbox is not checked, no value will be passed in the HTTP request. This also means that the value that was already set in the `property` in the `ActionForm` associated with the checkbox will not change. You have to check the `request` to see if the checkbox is present in the request. If it is not, you have to set the `ActionForm` property to a `false` or `off` value:

```
if (request.getAttribute("someBeanProperty") == null) {
  this.setSomeBeanProperty(false);
}
```

This is important because otherwise if the submitted data has a validation error and the `ActionServlet` returns the user to the screen, where they entered data, any checkboxes that had been moved from a checked to an unchecked state would still show up on the screen as checked.

So in your `validate()` method in the `ActionForm` you must check the `request` object to see if the checkbox parameter was passed as a `request` attribute. If it was not, you must set the corresponding property in the `ActionForm` to be `false`. This has to be done before you start doing any validation of the form data, or else you will end up with your form data inconsistently handling the checkbox information passed to it. This also means that if you want to pre-populate a form with checkboxes set in an off status, the `reset()` method of the `ActionForm`, being used to populate the page must set the properties in the `ActionForm` that map to the checkboxes to a `false` value.

Radio Buttons

To render a radio button in a form, we use the `<html:radio>` tag. This tag has two core attributes: `property` and `value`. These two attributes are similar in behavior to the `<html:checkbox>` tag. The `property` attribute defines the name of the property in the `ActionForm` that the radio button maps to. The `value` attribute is the value that will be sent, if the radio button is selected when the user submits the form.

To group a set of radio button controls together, so that only one of a group of radio buttons can be set, can be accomplished by setting each radio button's `property` attribute to point the same `ActionForm` property.

If we wanted to use a radio button, instead of the drop-down list to show a selection of prefixes to the user, we could write the following code:

```
<LI>Mr. <html:radio property="someBeanProperty" value="Mr."/>
<LI>Ms. <html:radio property="someBeanProperty" value="Ms."/>
<LI>Mrs. <html:radio property="someBeanProperty" value="Mrs."/>
<LI>Dr. <html:radio property="someBeanProperty" value="Dr."/>
```

The HTML generated by the above code would look as shown below:

```
<LI>Mr. <input type="radio" name="someBeanProperty" value="Mr.">
<LI>Ms. <input type="radio" name="someBeanProperty" value="Ms.">
<LI>Mrs. <input type="radio" name="someBeanProperty" value="Mrs.">
<LI>Dr. <input type="radio" name="someBeanProperty" value="Dr.">
```

Dynamic Forms and Validation

The current stable release of Struts, v1.0.2, provides powerful development metaphors for capturing, processing, and validating the form data submitted by an end user. In medium-to-large projects, implementing an individual `ActionForm` class for each screen in the application can turn into a significant amount of work. The developers will find that they are writing a large number of `ActionForm` classes to capture the data, but are basically providing the same types of validation rules against the data.

The next release of the Strut framework, v1.1b (b standing for beta), offers two new features that promise significant reduction in the amount of work associated with building the form classes. These two new features are:

❑ Dynamic Forms

❑ The Validator Framework

Let's take a look at these new features and see how they can be used to build our previous example, the Post a Story page. Note that since this is a beta version of Struts, the features and their implementations described here might differ slightly when version 1.1 of the framework is released.

Dynamic Forms

As we discussed earlier in the chapter, to use Struts form processing capabilities, developers need to explicitly extend the Struts `ActionForm` class. They need to implement getter or setter methods for each of the form fields they wanted to capture in the class and override the `reset()` and `validate()` method inherited from the `ActionForm` class.

Struts v1.1b now gives the development team the ability to declaratively define an `ActionForm` class without writing a single line of code. To do this, we need to first define a `<form-bean>` class in the `struts-config.xml`. The following code shows the `<form-bean>` entry that is used to define the `ActionForm` (`postStoryForm`) class in the **Post a Story** page:

```xml
<struts-config>
  <form-beans>
  <!-- Old postStoryDefinition. Please note that it uses user defined type.
        <form-bean name="postStoryForm"
                   type="com.wrox.javaedge.struts.poststory.PostStoryForm"/>
  -->
    <form-bean name="postStoryForm"
               type="org.apache.struts.action.DynaActionForm">
      <form-property name="storyIntro" type="java.lang.String"
                     initial="Please enter a story intro!"/>
      <form-property name="storyBody"  type="java.lang.String"
                     initial="Please enter a story body!"/>
      <form-property name="storyTitle" type="java.lang.String"
                     initial="Please enter a story title!"/>
    </form-bean>

    <!-- Rest of the ActionForm definitions-->
    </form-beans>
  <!-- Rest of the struts-config.xml file -->
</struts-config>
```

Just like the standard non-dynamic Struts `ActionForm` class, we need to define the dynamic `ActionForm` class as a `<form-bean>` entry in the `struts-config.xml`. However, while defining a dynamic `ActionForm`, we do not provide our own `ActionForm` class in the `type` attribute of the `<form-bean>` tag. Instead, we use the `org.apache.struts.Action.DynaActionForm` in the `type` attribute:

```xml
<form-bean name="postStoryForm"
           type="org.apache.struts.action.DynaActionForm">
```

Using the `DynaActionForm` class tells Struts that we will be using a dynamic `ActionForm`. Once we have defined the `<form-bean>`, we need to define the individual properties in it. This is equivalent to writing a `get()`/`set()` method in a non-dynamic `ActionForm` class:

```xml
<form-property name="storyIntro" type="java.lang.String"
               initial="Please enter a story intro!"/>
<form-property name="storyBody"  type="java.lang.String"
               initial="Please enter a story body!"/>
<form-property name="storyTitle" type="java.lang.String"
               initial="Please enter a story title!"/>
```

Just like the non-dynamic example shown earlier in the chapter, our dynamic `ActionForm` (`postStoryForm`) definition has three properties: `storyIntro`, `storyBody`, and `storyTitle`. Each of these properties has a corresponding `<form-property>` tag.

A `<form-property>` tag has three attributes:

Attribute Name	Attribute Description
name	The name of the property and the value that will be referenced by the Struts HTML tag libraries, while accessing and setting the form data. This is a mandatory attribute.
type	Fully-qualified Java class name of the attribute being set. This is a mandatory attribute.
initial	The initial value that the attribute will be populated with when the `reset()` method for the `ActionForm` class is invoked. Since, this is a dynamic form, the developer does not have to override the `reset()` method on the form.

Defining the `<form-bean>` and its corresponding `<form-property>` tags is sufficient to tell Struts to use a dynamic `ActionForm` class. The `postStoryContent.jsp` page, which pulls the data from the `postStoryForm` form bean, does not have to be modified. It does not care whether we are using a non-dynamic or dynamic `ActionForm`.

Pulling the data from a dynamic form bean in the Struts `Action` class is done a little differently than in a non-dynamic form bean. The following code shows the rewritten `PostStoryForm` class (that is, the `Action` class), pulling the data from the dynamic `postStoryForm` form bean defined above:

```
package com.wrox.javaedge.struts.poststory;

import java.util.Vector;

import javax.servlet.http.HttpServletRequest;
import javax.servlet.http.HttpServletResponse;
import javax.servlet.http.HttpSession;

import org.apache.struts.action.Action;
import org.apache.struts.action.ActionForm;
import org.apache.struts.action.ActionForward;
import org.apache.struts.action.ActionMapping;
import org.apache.struts.action.DynaActionForm;

import com.wrox.javaedge.common.ApplicationException;
import com.wrox.javaedge.member.MemberVO;
import com.wrox.javaedge.story.StoryManagerBD;
import com.wrox.javaedge.story.StoryVO;
import com.wrox.javaedge.story.dao.StoryDAO;

public class PostStory extends Action {
```

```
public ActionForward perform(ActionMapping mapping,
                             ActionForm form,
                             HttpServletRequest request,
                             HttpServletResponse response){

  if (this.isCancelled(request)) {
    return (mapping.findForward("poststory.success"));
  }


  DynaActionForm postStoryForm = (DynaActionForm) form;

  HttpSession session = request.getSession();

  MemberVO memberVO  = (MemberVO) session.getAttribute("memberVO");

  try{
    StoryVO storyVO = new StoryVO();

    storyVO.setStoryIntro((String)postStoryForm.get("storyIntro"));
    storyVO.setStoryTitle((String)postStoryForm.get("storyTitle"));
    storyVO.setStoryBody((String)postStoryForm.get("storyBody"));
    storyVO.setStoryAuthor(memberVO);
    storyVO.setSubmissionDate(new
                              java.sql.Date(System.currentTimeMillis()));
    storyVO.setComments(new Vector());

    StoryManagerBD storyManager = new StoryManagerBD();
    storyManager.addStory(storyVO);
  } catch (Exception e) {
    System.err.println("An application exception has been raised in
                        PostStory.perform(): " + e.toString());
    return (mapping.findForward("system.failure"));
  }

  return (mapping.findForward("poststory.success"));
 }
}
```

The difference between the above PostStory class and the PostStoryForm class shown earlier is subtle. First, the above PostStory class no longer casts the ActionForm being passed into the perform() method in the PostStoryForm class shown earlier in the chapter. Instead, it casts the incoming ActionForm parameter to be of type DynaActionForm:

```
DynaActionForm postStoryForm = (DynaActionForm) form;
```

Then, while retrieving the data from the form, it does not call an individual getXXX() method for each property in the ActionForm. Instead, it invokes the get() method in the class by passing in the name of the property it wants to retrieve:

```
storyVO.setStoryIntro((String)postStoryForm.get("storyIntro"));
storyVO.setStoryTitle((String)postStoryForm.get("storyTitle"));
storyVO.setStoryBody((String)postStoryForm.get("storyBody"));
```

The code then casts the individual properties retrieved to the Java data types that were defined in the `<form-bean>` tag in the `struts-config.xml` file.

The dynamic form bean is a powerful feature of Struts v1.1b. It allows you to easily implement and change the form beans without having to write a single line of code. This new feature keeps very much in line with the philosophy of Struts which is to let the framework do as much of the work as possible, while allowing the developer to focus on building the business code rather than the infrastructure code.

However, the real power of dynamic form beans comes into play when they are combined with another new Struts v1.1.b feature, the Validator framework.

The Validator Framework

After building several Struts-based applications, you will often find that you are performing the same types of validation over and over again. Some common validations include the following checks:

- ❑ If the user has entered all required fields
- ❑ If the data is within a minimum or maximum size
- ❑ If the data entered is of the right type

Struts release v1.1b now provides a framework that allows you to reuse a set of common validation routines without having to write the code. This framework, called the Validator framework, allows you to write your own validation routines that can be plugged in and used across all of your own form bean classes. We are not going to discuss this framework in depth. For the purposes of this chapter, we will look at how to use it to mimic the `validate()` method of the `PostStoryForm` class shown earlier. Specifically, we are going to use a dynamic form bean to collect the form data and apply the following validation rules:

- ❑ Check if the story title, story body, and story introduction fields, in the Post a Story page, are filled in by the end user
- ❑ Check that each field entered by the user does not exceed a certain character length

The third validation, checking for vulgarity, will not be implemented here. Writing your own validation rules requires much more explanation. For the details on extending the validation framework with your own validation rules, please refer to the Struts documentation (http://www. jakarta.apache.org/struts).

Let's begin our discussion by looking at how the Validator framework is set up and configured.

Validator Framework Setup

The Validator framework requires a modification in the `struts-config.xml` file and the addition of two new configuration files: `validator-rules.xml` and `validation.xml`. Struts v1.1b allows new functionality to be added to the framework via a plug-in. The Validator framework is one such plug-in. We are not going to discuss the Struts v1.1b framework in any detail. For further information on the plug-in architecture, please refer to the Struts v1.1b documentation (http://jakarta.apache.org/struts/userGuide).

To make Struts aware of the Validator framework, we need to add the following entry (that is, `<plug-in>`) at the end of the JavaEdge `struts-config.xml` file:

```
<plug-in className="org.apache.struts.validator.ValidatorPlugIn">
  <set-property property="pathnames" value="/WEB-INF/validator-rules.xml,
                                  /WEB-INF/validation.xml"/>
</plug-in>
```

This defines the fully-qualified Java class that represents the plug-in point between Struts and the third-party software. The `<set-property>` tag is used to set a plug-in specific property. In the above example, the `pathnames` property contains a comma-separated list telling the Validator framework where to find the `validator-rules.xml` file and the `validation.xml` file.

The `validator-rules.xml` file contains individual rule entries for the pre-defined validation rules that come as part of the Validator framework. A partial listing of the validation rules defined in the `validator-rules.xml` is shown below:

Rule Name	Rule Description
required	Checks if the field has been filled in by the end user.
minlength	Ensures that the value entered is of a minimum length.
maxlength	Ensures that the value entered is of a maximum length.
range	Validates that the field entered by the user falls into a certain range.
mask	Validates that the field entered is of a particular format.
byte	Validates that the field entered is of type byte.
short	Validates that the field entered is of type short.
integer	Validates that the field entered is of type integer.
long	Validates that the field entered is of type long.
float	Validates that the field entered is of type float.
double	Validates that the field entered is of type double.
date	Validates that the field entered is of type date.
email	Validates that the field entered is a properly formatted e-mail address.

The `validation.xml` file contains the mappings to each form bean in that application that is going to use the Validator framework. It maps each field of the form bean to the validation rule that is going to be invoked against it. We will be going through some of the `validation.xml` details in the following section.

Implementing the Required Field Validation

In the Post a Story page, the story title, story introduction, and story body are all required fields. To use the Validator framework to enforce these rules, we must create a file called `validation.xml`. The following code shows the `validation.xml` file that is used to enforce the validation of the required fields:

```
<form-validation>
  <formset>
    <form name="postStoryForm">
      <field property="storyTitle" depends="required">
        <msg name="required" key="error.poststory.field.null"/>
        <arg0 key="javaedge.poststory.form.titlelabel"/>
      </field>
      <field property="storyIntro" depends="required">
        <msg name="required" key="error.poststory.field.null"/>
        <arg0 key="javaedge.poststory.form.introlabel"/>
      </field>
      <field property="storyBody" depends="required">
        <msg name="required" key="error.poststory.field.null"/>
        <arg0 key="javaedge.poststory.form.bodylabel"/>
      </field>
    </form>
  </formset>
</form-validation>
```

The `<form-validation>` tag is the root element for the `validation.xml` file. It represents a
collection of forms for the application. A `<formset>` tag can contain one or more `<form>` tags. A
`<form>` tag represents a particular form bean in the application:

```
<form name="postStoryForm">
```

The name attribute in the `<form>` tag is the name of the form bean defined in the `struts-config.xml` file. Each `<form>` tag has one or more `<field>` tags associated with it.

```
<field property="storyTitle" depends="required">
   <msg name="required" key="error.poststory.field.null"/>
   <arg0 key="javaedge.poststory.form.titlelabel"/>
</field>
```

The `<field>` tag represents a single element of the `<form>` that is going to be validated by the
Validator framework. It has two attributes in it. These attributes are:

❑   property
    The name of the field that is going to be validated. This must match the name of a field
    defined in the `<form-bean>` in the `struts-config.xml`. This is a mandatory attribute.

❑   depends
    This lists, from left to right, all of the validation rules that are going to be invoked on the field.
    These rules will be fired in the order in which they are listed. In our example above, we are
    only applying the `required` rule against the field. This is a mandatory attribute.

A `<field>` tag can contain one or more `<msg>` tags. The `<msg>` tag is used by the Validator
framework to determine which message should be displayed to the end user, when a rule is violated:

```
<msg name="required" key="error.poststory.field.null"/>
```

A <msg> tag has three attributes:

- ❑ name
  The name of the rule with which the message is associated. In our above example, the value of name points to the `required` rule.

- ❑ key
  The key for the message in the Struts resource bundle (that is, `ApplicationResources.properties`) file. In our above example, the value of `error.poststory.field.null` would be pulled from the `ApplicationResources.properties` file as:

  ```
  The following field: {0} is a required field. Please provide a value for {0}.
  ```

  The key attribute is a required attribute in the <msg> tag.

- ❑ resource
  Tells the Validator framework that it should use the resource bundle to look up an error message, based on the value of the `key` attribute. If the value of `resource` is set to `true`, the resource bundle is used. If it is set to `false`, the default Struts resource bundle will not be used and the value in the `key` attribute will be taken as a literal string. The default value of the resource attribute is `true`.

A <field> tag can also contain argument tags called <arg0>, <arg1>, <arg2>, <arg3>, and <arg4>. These tags are used to pass arguments into the <msg> tags. The <argX> allows a developer to pass in the values to a message defined in the Struts resource bundle. The postStoryForm validation has one argument being passed into each of the messages in the field.

For example, the storyTitle uses the following <arg0> tag. It indicate that whenever a validation error occurs in the storyValidation field of the postStoryForm, the following key will be used to look up a value from the `ApplicationResources.properties` file and perform a string substitution on the message:

```
<arg0 key="javaedge.poststory.form.titlelabel" />
```

So, if the users did not enter a value into the storyTitle field, they would get the following error message:

```
The following field: Story Title is a required field.  Please provide a value for
Story Title.
```

The <argX> tags have three attributes:

- ❑ name:
  Defines the name of the validation rule with which this argument is associated. For example, if we wanted only the first argument of the message to be available when the required rule is invoked for the storyTitle field, we would write the <arg0> tag as follows:

  ```
  <arg0 name="required" key="javaedge.poststory.form.titlelabel"/>
  ```

  If the name is not provided, this argument will be available to every validation rule that fires off a validation exception for that particular field.

117

❑ key:
The key for the message in the Struts resource bundle (that is,
ApplicationResources.properties) file.

❑ resource:
Tells the Validator framework that it should use the resource bundle to look up an argument
based on the value in the key attribute. If the value of resource is set to true, the resource
bundle is used. If it is set to false, the default Struts resource bundle will not be used and the
value of the key attribute will be taken as a literal string value. The default value of the
resource attribute is true.

Once we have defined all the form and field mappings in the validation.xml file, we need to make
one last change to validate our dynamic form bean against the rules we have defined. Any dynamic
form bean using the Validator framework must have its <form-bean> entry modified in the struts-
config.xml file. In this entry, the type attribute for the form bean must be set to use the
org.apache.struts.validator.DynaValidatorForm class:

```
<form-bean name="postStoryForm"
           type="org.apache.struts.validator.DynaValidatorForm">
```

Now, let's look at setting up a slightly more complicated rule, the maxlength validation rule.

The maxlength Validation Rule

The next rule that we are going to implement, for our rewritten Post a Story page, puts some maximum
size limit on the data entered by the user in each field. It is the maxlength validation rule.

The following code shows the revised validation.xml file, containing the new definitions of the rules:

```
<form-validation>
  <formset>
    <form name="postStoryForm">

      <field property="storyTitle" depends="required,maxlength">
        <msg name="required" key="error.poststory.field.null"/>
        <msg name="maxlength" key="error.poststory.field.length"/>
        <arg0 key="javaedge.poststory.form.titlelabel"/>
        <arg1 name="maxlength" key="${var:maxlength}" resource="false"/>
        <var>
          <var-name>maxlength</var-name>
          <var-value>100</var-value>
        </var>
      </field>

      <field property="storyIntro" depends="required,maxlength">
        <msg name="required" key="error.poststory.field.null"/>
        <msg name="maxlength" key="error.poststory.field.length"/>
        <arg0 key="javaedge.poststory.form.introlabel"/>
        <arg1 name="maxlength" key="${var:maxlength}" resource="false"/>
        <var>
          <var-name>maxlength</var-name>
          <var-value>2048</var-value>
```

```
      </var>
    </field>

    <field property="storyBody" depends="required,maxlength">
      <msg name="required" key="error.poststory.field.null"/>
      <msg name="maxlength" key="error.poststory.field.length"/>
      <arg0 key="javaedge.poststory.form.bodylabel"/>
      <arg1 name="maxlength" key="${var:maxlength}" resource="false"/>
      <var>
        <var-name>maxlength</var-name>
        <var-value>100000</var-value>
      </var>
    </field>

  </form>
 </formset>
</form-validation>
```

To set up each field with the maxlength validation rule, we need to add the rule to the value of the depends attribute in each `<field>` tag. For the storyTitle field, this would look like:

```
<field property="storyIntro" depends="required,maxlength">
```

The rules are always invoked from left to right. In the above validation.xml file, the required validation rule will be invoked before the maxlength rule.

For the two rules associated with each field, we need to add `<msg>` tags that will reflect the different messages for each rule. In the storyTitle, we have two `<msg>` tags with the name attribute of each being the same as one of the names defined in the depends attribute:

```
<msg name="required" key="error.poststory.field.null"/>
<msg name="maxlength" key="error.poststory.field.length"/>
```

In addition, each message has two arguments passed to it. Thus, there are `<arg0>` and `<arg1>` tags defined in each `<field>` tag. For the storyTitle field, it is as shown below:

```
<arg0 key="javaedge.poststory.form.titlelabel"/>
<arg1 name="maxlength" key="${var:maxlength}" resource="false"/>
```

The first argument, `<arg0>`, is going to be shared across all the messages being thrown by the validation field. To do this, we do not define the name attribute in the `<arg0>` tag. However, the second argument, `<arg1>` is going to be available only to the maxlength validation rule. We indicate this by setting the name attribute in the `<arg1>` tag to maxlength.

We need to define the constraints for the validation rule to take effect. For instance, for the maxlength validation rule, we need to specify the acceptable maximum length of the field being validated. This value can be set by using the `<var>` tag. The maxlength validation rule takes a single parameter, maxlength, as an input value:

```
<var>
    <var-name>maxlength</var-name>
    <var-value>100000</var-var>
</var>
```

The `<var>` tag contains two elements, `<var-name>` and `<var-value>`. The `<var-name>` element holds the name of the input parameter being passed into the validation rule. The `<var-value>` element holds the value that is to be set for that variable.

The table below lists all of the validation rules that accept the input parameters:

Rule Name	Parameters	Parameter Description
minlength	Min	Integer value representing the minimum size of the field.
maxlength	Max	Integer value representing the maximum size of the field.
Range	Min, max	Integer value representing the minimum and maximum size for the field.
Mask	Mask	Regular expression indicating the mask to be applied to the field.
Date	Datepattern	Date pattern that is to be applied against the field to determine whether or not the user has entered a proper date.

In the `<arg1>` tag you would have noticed the unusual syntax of the key attribute. The key attribute is set to the value `${var:maxlength}`. This value will pull the value defined for the `<var>` tag whose `<var-name>` is equal to `maxlength`. However, the value of this variable will be pulled only if the resource attribute in the `<arg1>` tag is set to `false`.

Some Final Thoughts

Discussing how to use the Struts development framework is out of the scope of this book. The next release of Struts promises to offer many new features and enhancements, which will make the form processing and validation extremely automated. The section *Dynamic Forms and Validation* of this chapter has discussed these new features very briefly, particularly the Validator framework.

There are some other important topics on the Validator framework such as:

❑ Retrofitting the Validator framework into earlier versions of Struts

❑ Extending the Validator framework to include custom validation rules

The discussion on these topics is out of the scope of this book. For more information on these topics, you can visit the Struts web site (http://jakarta.apache.org/struts).

Summary

This chapter focused on how to use Struts to collect and process the data submitted in an HTML form. The following four pieces must be present to use the Struts-based form processing:

- ❑ `ActionForm` class
- ❑ `Action` class
- ❑ JSP page that uses the Struts HTML tag library to generate the HTML `<input>` fields used to collect the user information
- ❑ name attribute in an `<action>` tag in the `struts-config.xml` file

The `ActionForm` class acts as a wrapper class for the form data submitted by the user. The `ActionServlet` will use the `ActionForm` class defined for an action to pull the submitted form data out of the user's HTTP request. Each piece of data sent from a form will correspond to a `get()` or `set()` method that will be used to retrieve and populate the `ActionForm`. The `ActionForm` class has two methods that can be overridden by the developer, `reset()` and `validate()`. The `reset()` method is used to clear the properties in `ActionForm` to ensure that they are always in a predetermined state. To pre-populate a form with data, you can use the `reset()` method.

The `validate()` method in the `ActionForm` class will contain any validation rules that need to be applied against the submitted data. This method should contain only the lightweight validation rules that check the constraints on the data. If any validation errors are found, an `ActionError` class will be added to the `ActionErrors` class, which is passed back by the `validate()` method. If the `ActionServlet` finds that the `ActionErrors` contains errors, it will redirect the users back to the JSP page where they submitted the data. The validation errors will then be displayed using the `<html:errors>` tag.

The `Action` class is used to process the user's request. Its `perform()` method holds all the business logic used to process the user's request. We did not discuss the `Action` class in detail in this chapter. We are going to explore the handling business logic in the next chapter.

To map the data submitted in the HTML form to the `ActionForm` class, you need to use a JSP page that uses the Struts HTML tag library. The Struts HTML tag library contains a number of tags used for the rendering HTML input tags. Some of the tags that were covered in this chapter include:

- ❑ Tags used for building the base HTML form:
  - ❑ `<html:form>`: Used to render a `<form>` tag
  - ❑ `<html:submit>`: Renders a submit button
  - ❑ `<html:cancel>`: Renders a cancel button
- ❑ Tags used for entering information:
  - ❑ `<html:text>`: Renders a text field
  - ❑ `<html:textarea>`: Renders a textarea field
  - ❑ `<html:select>`: Renders a drop-down box
  - ❑ `<html:option>`: Renders one selection in a drop-down box
  - ❑ `<html:checkbox>`: Renders a checkbox control
  - ❑ `<html:radio>`: Renders a radio button control

These three pieces (ActionForm class, Action class, and JSP page) together are all associated with an <action> tag in the struts-config.xml file. Each ActionForm used in the application must be declared as a <form-bean> tag. Once it is declared, the ActionForm can be associated with an <action> tag. The name attribute of the <action> tag tells the ActionServlet class processing a user request that there is an ActionForm class that will be used to collect the data. If the <action> tag contains a validate attribute set to true, the ActionServlet will invoke the validate() method in the ActionForm class.

Finally, the chapter discussed some of the new form processing features in Struts v1.1b, in short. This chapter gave an overview of the following:

❏ Building dynamic forms using the DynaActionForm feature. We looked at how dynamic forms were configured and how an Action class uses the dynamic forms to retrieve the data submitted by the end user.

❏ Leveraging the Validator framework to automate many of the common form validations. We looked at setting up Struts to use the Validator framework. We also looked at how to implement two inbuilt Validator rules:

    ❏ required: Checks if a field is filled in or not

    ❏ maxlength: Determines whether or not the field length is exceeded

In the next chapter, we are going to look at how to build the business logic in Struts. The Struts development framework, with the help of the Action class, provides a clean mechanism for encapsulating the business logic. However, if you are not careful, you can limit the long-term reusability of your application code. The next chapter demonstrates the use of the several core design patterns, which when coupled with the Struts provide optimal code reusability.

Managing Business Logic with Struts

So far we've seen how to use the Struts framework to facilitate the construction of an application. We've also examined the basic workflow of a Struts-based request along with the different components needed to carry out a user's requested action. However, while the Struts framework is a powerful tool for building applications, it is still only a tool. Using the Struts framework does not relieve you of the responsibility for architecting the application.

A framework like Struts is meant to promote rapid application development as well as ease the maintenance and extensibility of an application. However, if there is no forethought on how the business logic for an application is going to be built, it becomes very easy to "lock" an application's business logic into the Struts framework.

As a result, a development team using Struts might be able to quickly build the initial applications, but later, they will find that they cannot easily reuse the functionality in a non-Struts framework. A framework provides structure, but it also defines boundaries, constraints, and dependencies, which will cause a significant amount of problems, if they are not considered early on.

This chapter is going to demonstrate how to use several common J2EE design patterns, to ensure that the application's business logic is not too tightly coupled with the Struts framework. Specifically we are going to look at:

- ❑ Common implementation mistakes made while implementing a Struts Action class. We will examine how, even with the use of the Struts development framework, the Concern Slush and Tier Leakage antipatterns can still form (Refer to Chapter 1 for the discussion on the various antipatterns).

- ❑ How to refactor these antipatterns into a more maintainable framework, which will allow us to reuse business logic across both Struts and non-Struts applications.

The design patterns that will be covered in this chapter include:

❑ The Business Delegate pattern

❑ The Service Locator pattern

❑ The Session Façade pattern

All these design patterns will be implemented with the help of the JavaEdge application code.

Business-Logic Antipatterns and Struts

The Struts framework's Model-View-Controller implementation significantly reduces the chance that the Concern Slush or Tier Leakage antipattern will form. Recollecting the discussion from Chapter 1, the Concern Slush antipattern forms when the system architect does not provide a framework separating the presentation, business, and data access logic into well-defined application tiers. As a result, it becomes difficult to reuse and support the code.

The Tier Leakage antipattern occurs when an application developer exposes the implementation details of one application tier to another tier. For example, when the presentation logic of the application, which is a JSP page, creates an EJB to invoke some business logic on its behalf. While the business logic for the page has been cleanly separated from the JSP code, the JSP page is exposed to the complexities of locating and instantiating the EJB. This creates a tight dependency between the presentation tier and the business tier.

The Struts framework does an excellent job of enforcing a clean separation of presentation and business logic within an application. All the presentation logic is encapsulated in JSP pages using Struts tag libraries to simplify the development effort. All business logic is placed in a Struts `Action` class. The JSP pages in the application are never allowed to invoke the business logic directly; it's the responsibility of the `ActionServlet`.

However, in a Struts-based application, the way in which the business logic is implemented is still decided by the application developer. Often, a developer who is new to the Struts framework will place all of the business and data-access logic into a Struts `Action` class. They need to consider the long-term architectural consequences of doing this. Without careful forethought and planning, antipatterns such as Concern Slush and Tier Leakage can still manifest themselves within an application.

At this point, you might be asking the question, "I thought the Struts development framework was supposed to refactor these antipatterns?" The answer is yes, to a point.

> **Using a development framework does not relieve the development team of the responsibility of architecting the application. A development team needs to ensure that its use of a framework does not create dependencies that make it difficult to reuse application logic outside of the framework. The application architect is still responsible for enforcing the overall integrity of the application's architecture. A development framework is a tool, not a magic bullet.**

When development teams make the decision to adopt a development framework they often rush in and immediately begin writing code. They have not cleanly separated the "core" business logic from the framework itself. As a result, they often find themselves going through all sorts of contortions to reuse the code in non-framework-based applications.

Let's look at two code examples that can be precursors to the formation of the Concern Slush and Tier Leakage antipatterns in Struts.

Concern Slush and Struts

The Concern Slush antipattern can manifest itself in a Struts-based application, when the developer fails to cleanly separate the business and data access logic from the Struts Action class. Let's revisit the Post a Story page that was explored in the Chapter 3. The following is an example of how the PostStory.java action could be implemented:

```
package com.wrox.javaedge.struts.poststory;

import org.apache.struts.action.*;
import javax.servlet.http.*;
import javax.naming.*;
import java.sql.*;
import javax.sql.*;

import com.wrox.javaedge.story.*;
import com.wrox.javaedge.member.*;
import com.wrox.javaedge.story.ejb.PrizeManager;

public class PostStory extends Action {

  public ActionForward perform(ActionMapping mapping,
                               ActionForm form,
                               HttpServletRequest request,
                               HttpServletResponse response) {

    PostStoryForm postStoryForm = (PostStoryForm) form;
    HttpSession session = request.getSession();

    MemberVO memberVO = (MemberVO) session.getAttribute("memberVO");

    if (this.isCancelled(request)) {
      return (mapping.findForward("poststory.success"));
    }

    Connection conn = null;
    PreparedStatement ps = null;

    try {
      Context ctx = new InitialContext();
      DataSource ds = (DataSource) ctx.lookup("java:/MySQLDS");
      conn = ds.getConnection();
      conn.setAutoCommit(false);

      StringBuffer insertSQL = new StringBuffer();

      /*
       * Please note that this code is only an example. The SQL code assumes
       * that the story table is using an auto-generated key.  However, in
       * the JavaEdge application we use ObjectRelationalBridges Sequence
```

```
                   * capabilities to generate a key. This code will not work unless you
                   * modify the story table to use an auto-generated key for the
                   * story_id column
                   */
                 insertSQL.append("INSERT INTO story(              ");
                 insertSQL.append("   member_id               ,    ");
                 insertSQL.append("   story_title             ,    ");
                 insertSQL.append("   story_into              ,    ");
                 insertSQL.append("   story_body              ,    ");
                 insertSQL.append("   submission_date              ");
                 insertSQL.append(")                               ");
                 insertSQL.append("VALUES(                         ");
                 insertSQL.append("   ?                       ,    ");
                 insertSQL.append("   ?                       ,    ");
                 insertSQL.append("   ?                       ,    ");
                 insertSQL.append("   ?                       ,    ");
                 insertSQL.append("   CURDATE()               )    ");

                 ps = conn.prepareStatement(insertSQL.toString());

                 ps.setLong(1, memberVO.getMemberId().longValue());
                 ps.setString(2, postStoryForm.getStoryTitle());
                 ps.setString(3, postStoryForm.getStoryIntro());
                 ps.setString(4, postStoryForm.getStoryBody());

                 ps.execute();
                 conn.commit();

                 checkStoryCount(memberVO);

             } catch(SQLException e) {
                 try{
                     if (conn != null) conn.rollback();

                 } catch(SQLException ex) {}

                 System.err.println("A SQL exception has been raised in " +
                                    "PostStory.perform(): " + e.toString());

                 return (mapping.findForward("system.failure"));
             } catch(NamingException e) {
                 System.err.println("A Naming exception has been raised in " +
                                    "PostStory.perform(): " + e.toString());
                 return (mapping.findForward("system.failure"));
             } finally {
                 try {
                     if (ps != null) ps.close();
                     if (conn != null) conn.close();
                 } catch(SQLException e) {}

             }

         return (mapping.findForward("poststory.success"));
     }
```

```java
    private void checkStoryCount(MemberVO memberVO)
        throws SQLException, NamingException {
    Connection conn = null;
    PreparedStatement ps = null;
    ResultSet rs = null;

    try {
      Context ctx = new InitialContext();
      DataSource  ds = (DataSource) ctx.lookup("java:/MySQLDS");
      conn = ds.getConnection();

      StringBuffer selectSQL = new StringBuffer();

      selectSQL.append("SELECT                        ");
      selectSQL.append("  count(*) total_count        ");
      selectSQL.append("FROM                           ");
      selectSQL.append("  story where member_id=?  ");

      ps = conn.prepareStatement(selectSQL.toString());
      ps.setLong(1, memberVO.getMemberId().longValue());

      rs = ps.executeQuery();
      int totalCount = 0;

      if (rs.next()) {
        totalCount = rs.getInt("total_count");
      }

      boolean TOTAL_COUNT_EQUAL_1000 = (totalCount==1000);
      boolean TOTAL_COUNT_EQUAL_5000 = (totalCount==5000);

      if (TOTAL_COUNT_EQUAL_1000 || TOTAL_COUNT_EQUAL_5000) {
      //Notify Prize Manager
        PrizeManager prizeManager = new PrizeManager();
        prizeManager.notifyMarketing(memberVO, totalCount);
      }
    } catch(SQLException e) {
      System.err.println("A SQL exception has been raised in " +
                        " PostStory.checkStoryCount(): " + e.toString());

      throw e;
    } catch(NamingException e) {
      System.err.println("A Naming exception has been raised in " +
                        " PostStory.checkStoryCount(): " +
                        e.toString());
      throw e;
    } finally {
      try {
        if (rs != null) rs.close();
            if (ps != null) ps.close();
            if (conn != null) conn.close();
      } catch(SQLException e) {}
    }
  }
}
```

The above `perform()` method performs two very simple functions:

❑ It inserts the data submitted by the user on the Post a Story page using the standard JDBC and SQL calls. From our discussions in Chapter 3, we know that the submitted data has already been validated by the `validate()` method on the `PostForm` class.

❑ It checks, via a call to `checkStoryCount()`, if the total number of stories submitted by a JavaEdge member is at the 1000 or 5000 mark. On the 1000th and 5000th story submitted by the user, the marketing department is notified via the `PrizeManager` class.

The `PrizeManager` class integrates several legacy systems throughout the organization and ultimately sends the user $100 dollars to spend at the bookstore on the JavaEdge site.

From a functional perspective, the code for the `perform()` method works well. However, from an architectural viewpoint, the implementation for the `PostStory` class shown above is a mess. There are several problems present in the above code that will eventually cause significant long-term maintenance and extensibility problems. These problems include:

❑ The entire business logic for adding a story and checking the total number of stories submitted by a user is embedded in the Struts `Action` class. This has several architectural consequences:

    ❑ If the development team wants to reuse this logic, it must use the `PostStory` class (even if it does not really fit into the other application); refactor the business logic into a new Java class; or perform the oldest form of reuse: cut and paste.

    ❑ The business logic for the application is tied directly to the Struts framework. If the development team decides to move the application from the Struts framework, it is looking at a significant amount of work.

❑ There is no clean separation of the business and data access logic. While these two pieces of logic are cleanly separated by Struts from the presentation tier, there is still a significant amount of dependency being created between the business logic and the data access logic:

    ❑ The `Action` class has intimate knowledge of which data access technology is being used to access the data used by JavaEdge application. If the development team wants to switch to a new data access technology at some point, it must revisit every single place in the application that is interacting with a database.

    ❑ The `Action` class has SQL Data Definition Language (DDL) embedded in it. Any changes to the underlying table structures that the JavaEdge application is using can send ripple effects throughout the system.

> **A ripple effect is when there is such tight dependency between application modules or application code and data structures that a change to one piece of code sends you hunting throughout the rest of application for other areas that must be modified to reflect that change.**

For example, if a data relationship between two tables were to change, such as a one-to-many relationship being refactored into a many-to-many relationship, any SQL code embedded in the application that accessed these tables would need to be visited and probably refactored.

Abstraction is the key to avoiding a ripple effect. If the SQL logic for the application is cleanly hidden behind a set of interfaces that did not expose the actual structure of the database table to the application, the chance of a ripple effect occurring is much less. In the next chapter we will demonstrate how to use some basic design patterns to achieve this goal.

The code shown above is difficult to follow and maintain. Even though the business logic for the Post A Story page is very simplistic, it still took almost two pages of code to implement. Keep the following in mind, while building your first Struts-based application:

> **Development frameworks like Struts are used for building applications. However, the business logic in applications often belongs to the enterprise and not just a single application. How many times have you seen the business logic cut across multiple applications within an organization? Be wary of embedding too much business logic directly within Struts. Otherwise you might find that reuse of business logic becomes extremely difficult.**

Tier Leakage and Struts

Many development teams will get an uneasy feeling about the amount of business logic being placed in the Struts `Action` class. They might have already run into situations where they have the same business logic being reused in many of their applications.

The natural tendency is to refactor the Struts code and move it into a component-based architecture (such as Enterprise JavaBeans) or services-based architecture (such as web services). This moves the business logic out of the Struts `Action` class and makes it easily available to the other applications. Let's refactor the `PostStory` class and move all of the business logic into an Enterprise JavaBean called `StoryManager`. The code for the rewritten `PostStory` class is shown below:

```
package com.wrox.javaedge.struts.poststory;

import org.apache.struts.action.*;
import javax.servlet.http.*;
import javax.naming.*;
import javax.ejb.*;
import java.rmi.*;
import javax.rmi.*;

import com.wrox.javaedge.common.*;
import com.wrox.javaedge.story.*;
import com.wrox.javaedge.member.*;
import com.wrox.javaedge.story.ejb.*;

public class PostStory extends Action {

    public ActionForward perform(ActionMapping mapping,
                      ActionForm form,
                      HttpServletRequest request,
                      HttpServletResponse response){
```

```
    if (this.isCancelled(request)) {
      return (mapping.findForward("poststory.success"));
    }

    PostStoryForm postStoryForm = (PostStoryForm) form;
    HttpSession session = request.getSession();

    MemberVO memberVO = (MemberVO) session.getAttribute("memberVO");

    try {
      Context ctx = new InitialContext();
      Object ref = ctx.lookup("storyManager/StoryManager");

      StoryManagerHome storyManagerHome =
        (StoryManagerHome) PortableRemoteObject.narrow(ref,
          StoryManagerHome.class);
      StoryManager storyManager = storyManagerHome.create();
      storyManager.addStory(postStoryForm, memberVO);

    } catch(ApplicationException e){
      System.err.println("An Application exception has been raised in " +
                    "PostStory.perform(): " + e.toString());
      return (mapping.findForward("system.failure"));

    } catch(NamingException e) {
      System.err.println("A Naming exception has been raised in " +
                    "PostStory.perform(): " + e.toString());
      return (mapping.findForward("system.failure"));

    } catch(RemoteException e) {
      System.err.println("A Remote exception has been raised in " +
                    "PostStory.perform(): " + e.toString());
      return (mapping.findForward("system.failure"));

    } catch(CreateException e) {
      System.err.println("A Create exception has been raised in " +
                    "PostStory.perform(): " + e.toString());
      return (mapping.findForward("system.failure"));
    }

    return (mapping.findForward("poststory.success"));
  }
}
```

The above code appears to solve all the problems defined earlier. It is much easier to read and understand. The Concern Slush antipattern, which was present earlier, has been refactored. By moving the business logic out of the `PostStory.perform()` method and into the `StoryManager` EJB, it can be reused more easily across multiple applications.

However, the rewritten `PostStory` class shown above still has flaws in it that can lead to a Tier Leakage antipattern. The refactored `perform()` method has intimate knowledge of how the business logic is being invoked. The entire business logic is contained within the EJB, and the application developer has to perform a JNDI lookup and then retrieve a reference to the EJB by invoking its `create()` method.

What happens if the development team later wants to rewrite the business logic and wrap it to use a web service instead of an EJB? Since the PostStory action class has direct knowledge that the business logic it needs is contained within an EJB, the class must be rewritten to now invoke a web service instead of an EJB.

As you will see shortly, what is needed here is some kind of proxy that will sit between the framework class (the PostStory class) and the actual business logic (the EJB). The proxy should completely abstract how the business logic is being invoked. This proxy, also known as the Business Delegate pattern, will be discussed shortly.

Another problem with the code shown above is that the addStory() method is taking the PostStoryForm class as an input parameter:

```
storyManager.addStory(postStoryForm, memberVO);
```

This creates a dependency between the business logic, which is responsible for adding a story to the JavaEdge application, and the Struts framework in which the application is built. If the developers want to use the StoryManager EJB in a non-Struts-based application, they would not be able to do so easily.

> **Even when choosing to use a Java open source development framework it is important not to create tight dependencies between the framework and business logic. Applications rarely exist in a vacuum. They often have to be integrated with the other systems being maintained by the IT department. This integration often means reusing code that has already been written. Tight-coupling of business logic with framework can limit your ability to reuse that business logic in applications that are not built with your chosen framework.**

This is why it is still extremely important to apply the architectural principals of abstraction and encapsulation, even when building Struts-based applications. Antipatterns are subtle beasts. It is rare for developers to feel the full impact of an antipattern in the first application that they build. Instead, the problems caused by an antipattern will suddenly manifest themselves, when the development team has already deployed several applications and needs to integrate or reuse the code in these applications. That is when the antipattern and the full scope of the necessary rework is revealed.

Separating Business Logic from Struts

The challenge is to build our Struts application in such a way that the business logic for the application becomes independent of the actual Struts framework. The Action classes in our Struts application should only be a plug-in point for the business logic.

Fortunately, common J2EE design patterns provide a readily available solution. These patterns are particularly well suited for solving many of the dependencies between the framework and the business logic as were discussed earlier. In this chapter, we are not going to cover all the J2EE design patterns, in great detail. Instead, we are going to discuss the patterns that are most appropriate for use in building Struts-based applications.

The design patterns that are going to be discussed include:

- ❏ The Business Delegate pattern
- ❏ The Service Locator pattern
- ❏ The Session Façade pattern

The diagram below demonstrates how the above J2EE design patterns can be assembled to partition the business logic used in the application from the Struts development framework:

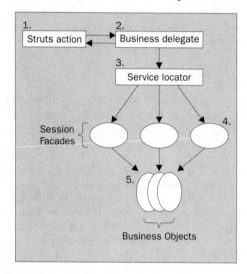

Let's revisit the whole process of how an end user adds a new story to the JavaEdge application, using the architectural model shown above:

1. The user makes a request to add a story. The `perform()` method in the `PostStory` action class is invoked. However, in the above model, the `PostStory` action does not contain the actual code for adding the user's story and checking the number of stories submitted by the user. Instead, the `PostStory` class instantiates a Business Delegate that carries out this business logic.

2. The Business Delegate is a Java class that shields the `PostStory` action class from knowing how the business logic is created and executed. In the section on *Tier Leakage and Struts* earlier, the code for adding a story was moved to the `StoryManager` EJB. The Business Delegate class would be responsible for looking up this EJB via JNDI. All the public methods in the `StoryManager` EJB should be available to the Business Delegate. All the public method calls in the Business Delegate would be forwarded to the `StoryManager` EJB.

3. The Business Delegate does not have the direct knowledge of how to look up the `StoryManager` EJB. Instead, it uses a class called the `ServiceLocator`. The `ServiceLocator` is used to look up the various resources within the application. Examples of resources looked up and returned by a `ServiceLocator` class include the home interface for EJBs and `DataSource` objects for retrieving JDBC connections.

4. The EJBs returned by the `ServiceLocator` class are known as Session Façades. A Session Façade is an EJB that wraps a complex business process involving multiple Java objects behind a simple-to-use coarse-grained interface. In the `PostStory` example, the `StoryManager` EJB is a Session Façade that hides all of the steps involved in adding a story to the JavaEdge application.

5. The business objects are responsible for carrying out the individual steps in the business action requested by the end user. Business-logic classes should never be allowed to talk directly to any of the databases used by the application. Instead, theses classes should interact with the database via a data-persistence façade.

At a first glance, this might seem like a significant of work for carrying out even the simplest task. However, the abstraction provided by these design patterns is tremendous.

> **The effects of good architecture (and bad) are not immediately apparent. However, the time spent in properly abstracting your applications can have huge pay offs in terms of the maintainability and extensibility of your code.**

The J2EE design patterns, demonstrated in the above diagram, completely separate the business logic from the Struts framework and ensure that the business logic for the whole application has no intimate knowledge of the data-access code being used.

Implementing the Design Patterns

The remaining sections of this chapter are going to discuss the implementations of the J2EE design patterns discussed so far. We will be refactoring the `PostStory` action class so that it uses a Business Delegate to invoke the logic that it needs to carry out the user request.

The diagram below, which looks similar to the previous one, demonstrates the actions that takes place when the `perform()` method of the `PostStory` class is invoked:

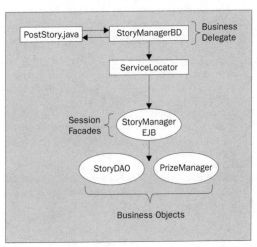

Implementing the Business Delegate Pattern

A Business Delegate pattern hides the complexity of instantiating and using the enterprise services such as EJBs or web services from the application consuming the service. A Business Delegate pattern is very straightforward. It is implemented by wrapping an already existing service behind a plain Java class. Each public method available in the service is mapped to a public method in the Business Delegate.

The code below, called `StoryManagerBD.java`, demonstrates how to wrap an EJB called `StoryManager`. The `StoryManager` EJB is responsible for adding the stories and comments submitted by JavaEdge users to the JavaEdge database.

The details of the JavaEdge database will be covered in the next chapter.

```
package com.wrox.javaedge.ejb;

import javax.naming.*;
import javax.rmi.*;
import java.rmi.*;
import javax.ejb.*;
import com.wrox.javaedge.story.*;
import com.wrox.javaedge.member.*;
import com.wrox.javaedge.common.*;
import com.wrox.javaedge.story.ejb.*;

public class StoryManagerBD {
  StoryManager storyManager = null;

  public StoryManagerBD() throws ApplicationException {

    try {
      Context ctx = new InitialContext();
      Object ref = ctx.lookup("storyManager/StoryManager");

      StoryManagerHome storyManagerHome = (StoryManagerHome)
          PortableRemoteObject.narrow(ref, StoryManagerHome.class);
      storyManager = storyManagerHome.create();

    } catch(NamingException e) {
      throw new ApplicationException("A Naming exception has been raised in " +
                              "StoryManagerBD constructor: " +
                              e.toString());
    } catch(RemoteException e) {
      throw new ApplicationException("A Remote exception has been raised in " +
                              "StoryManagerBD constructor: " +
                              e.toString());
    } catch(CreateException e) {
      throw new ApplicationException("A Create exception has been raised in " +
                              "StoryManagerBD constructor: " +
                              e.toString());
    }
  }
```

```
    public void addStory(StoryVO storyVO) throws ApplicationException {
      try {
        storyManager.addStory(storyVO);
      } catch(RemoteException e) {
        throw new ApplicationException("A Remote exception has been raised in " +
                                "StoryManagerBD.addStory(): " +
                                e.toString());
      }
    }

    public void addComment(StoryVO storyVO, StoryCommentVO storyCommentVO)
        throws ApplicationException{
      try {
        storyManager.addComment(storyVO, storyCommentVO);
      } catch(RemoteException e) {
        throw new ApplicationException("A Remote exception has been raised in "+
                                "StoryManagerBD.addComment(): " +
                                e.toString());
      }
    }
  }
```

The `StoryManagerBD` class looks up the home interface of the `StoryManager` EJB in its constructor. Using the retrieved home interface, the `StoryManager` EJB is created. A reference to the newly created bean will be stored in the private attribute, called `storyManager`, of the `StoryManagerBD` class:

```
    public StoryManagerBD() throws ApplicationException{
      try{
        Context ctx = new InitialContext();
        Object ref = ctx.lookup("storyManager/StoryManager");

        StoryManagerHome storyManagerHome = (StoryManagerHome)
          PortableRemoteObject.narrow(ref, StoryManagerHome.class);
        storyManager = storyManagerHome.create();
      }
```

Handling Exceptions in the Business Delegate

While looking up and creating a reference to the `StoryManager` EJB, any exceptions that are raised will be caught and thrown back as an `ApplicationException`:

```
      } catch(NamingException e) {
        throw new ApplicationException("A Naming exception has been raised in "+
                                "StoryManagerBD constructor: " +
                                e.toString());
      }
```

An `ApplicationException` is a generic exception that will be used to wrap any exceptions raised while the Business Delegate is processing a request.

It is extremely important that any raised exception be caught and thrown back as an `ApplicationException`. The Business Delegate design pattern is supposed to simplify the process of invoking the business logic for an application and hide the underlying implementation details.

The `ApplicationException` class is used to "level" all exceptions thrown by the business logic tier to a single type of exception. By doing this, classes such as `PostStory` only need to know how to deal with one type of exception and will not be unnecessarily exposed to implementation details of the business tier (that the business logic is implemented using EJBs or web services, etc.).

In our example, this means that the `PostStory` class would have to capture `CreateException`, `RemoteException`, and `NamingException`, which could be thrown while using the Business Delegate pattern. This would give the `PostStory` class intimate knowledge of how the business logic for the request was being carried out.

> **Never expose an application that uses a Business Delegate to any of the implementation details wrapped by the delegate. This includes any exceptions that might be raised during the course of processing a request.**

The `ApplicationException` is used to notify the application, which consumes a service provided by the Business Delegate, that some kind of error has occurred. It is up to the application to decide how it will respond to an unexpected exception.

Avoiding Dependencies

Another noticeable part of our implementation of the `StoryManagerBD` class is that each of the public methods is just a simple pass through to the underlying service (in this case, a stateless EJB). However, none of these public methods takes a class that can tie the business logic to a particular front-end technology or development framework.

A very common mistake while implementing the first Struts application is to pass an `ActionForm` or `HttpServletRequest` object to the code executing the business logic. Passing in a Struts-based class, such as `ActionForm`, ties the business logic directly to the Struts framework. Passing in an `HttpServletRequest` object creates a dependency where the business logic is only usable by a web application. Both of these situations can be easily avoided by allowing "neutral" objects, which do not create these dependencies, to be passed into a Business Delegate implementation.

After the `StoryManagerBD` has been implemented, let's look at how the `PostStory` class has changed:

```
package com.wrox.javaedge.struts.poststory;

import java.util.Vector;

import org.apache.struts.action.*;
import javax.servlet.http.*;

import com.wrox.javaedge.common.*;
import com.wrox.javaedge.story.*;
import com.wrox.javaedge.member.*;
import com.wrox.javaedge.story.*;

public class PostStory extends Action {

    public ActionForward perform(ActionMapping mapping,
                                 ActionForm form,
```

```
                            HttpServletRequest request,
                            HttpServletResponse response) {

    if (this.isCancelled(request)){
      return (mapping.findForward("poststory.success"));
    }

    PostStoryForm postStoryForm = (PostStoryForm) form;
    HttpSession session = request.getSession();

    MemberVO memberVO = (MemberVO) session.getAttribute("memberVO");

    try {
        StoryVO storyVO = new StoryVO();

        storyVO.setStoryIntro(postStoryForm.getStoryIntro());
        storyVO.setStoryTitle(postStoryForm.getStoryTitle());
        storyVO.setStoryBody(postStoryForm.getStoryBody());

        storyVO.setStoryAuthor(memberVO);
        storyVO.setSubmissionDate(new java.sql.Date(System.currentTimeMillis()));
        storyVO.setComments(new Vector());

        StoryManagerBD storyManager = new StoryManagerBD();
        storyManager.addStory(storyVO);

    } catch(Exception e) {
      System.err.println("An application exception has been raised in " +
                    "PostStory.perform(): " + e.toString());
      return (mapping.findForward("system.failure"));
    }

    return (mapping.findForward("poststory.success"));
  }
}
```

In the redesigned `PostStory` class we do introduce a little bit more code because we have to copy the data from the `PostStoryForm` class to a `StoryVO` and then pass that value object into the `StoryManagerBD`'s `addStory()` method. However, even though we are writing more code we have broken a dependency between our Struts `Action` class and a piece of business logic.

The `StoryManagerBD`, as it no longer has the `PostStoryForm` class passed in as a parameter, can be reused in a non-Struts based application. This small piece of abstraction avoids creating a dependency on a Struts-specific class.

> **Abstraction, when applied appropriately, gives our applications the ability to evolve gracefully as the business and technical requirements of the application change over time.**

Implementing the Service Locator Pattern

Implementing a Business Delegate can involve a significant amount of repetitive coding. Every Business Delegate constructor has to look up the service that it is going to wrap, via a JNDI call. The Service Locator pattern mitigates the need for this coding and, more importantly, allows the developer to hide the implementation details associated with looking up a service. A Service Locator can be used to hide a variety of different resources such as:

- ❏   JNDI lookups for an EJBHome interface

- ❏   JNDI lookups associated with finding a JDBC DataSource for retrieving a database connection

- ❏   Object creation associated with:

    - ❏   Looking up an Apache Axis Call class for invoking a web service

    - ❏   Retrieving a Persistence Broker/Manager for ObjectRelational Management tools, such as the open source package ObjectRelationalBridge (OJB), Oracle's TopLink, etc.

In addition, the implementation of a Service Locator pattern allows you to implement optimizations to your code without having to revisit the multiple places in your application.

For instance, performing a JNDI lookup is expensive. If you allow your Business Delegate classes to directly invoke a JNDI, to implement a caching mechanism that minimizes the number of JNDI calls would involve a significant amount of rework. However, if you centralize all of your JNDI lookup calls behind a Service Locator pattern, you would be able to implement the optimizations and caching and only have to touch one piece of code. A Service Locator pattern is easy to implement. For the time it takes to implement the pattern, the reduction in overall maintenance costs of the application can easily exceed the costs of writing the class.

The Business Delegate class also allows you to isolate vendor-specific options for looking up JNDI components; thereby limiting the effects of "vendor lock-in".

Shown below is a sample Service Locator implementation that abstracts how an EJB home interface is looked up via JNDI. The Service Locator implementation for the JavaEdge application provides the methods for looking up EJBHome interfaces and JDBC database connections:

```java
package com.wrox.javaedge.story.ejb;

import java.sql.*;
import javax.sql.DataSource;
import java.util.Hashtable;
import javax.naming.*;
import javax.ejb.*;
import javax.rmi.*;
import org.apache.ojb.broker.*;

import com.wrox.javaedge.story.ejb.StoryManagerHome;
import com.wrox.javaedge.common.*;

public class ServiceLocator {
```

```
private static ServiceLocator serviceLocatorRef = null;
private static Hashtable ejbHomeCache = null;
private static Hashtable dataSourceCache = null;

//Enumerating the different services available from the Service Locator
public static final int STORYMANAGER = 0;
public static final int JAVAEDGEDB = 1;

//The JNDI Names used to lookup a service
private static final String STORYMANAGER_JNDINAME =
  "storyManager/StoryManager";

private static final String JAVAEDGEDB_JNDINAME="java:/MySQLDS";

//References to each of the different EJB Home Interfaces
private static final Class STORYMANAGERCLASSREF = StoryManagerHome.class;

static {
  serviceLocatorRef = new ServiceLocator();
}

//Private Constructor for the ServiceLocator
private ServiceLocator() {
  ejbHomeCache    = new Hashtable();
  dataSourceCache = new Hashtable();
}

/*
 * The Service Locator is implemented as a Singleton. The getInstance()
 * method will return the static reference to the Service Locator stored
 * inside the ServiceLocator Class.
 */
public static ServiceLocator getInstance() {
  return serviceLocatorRef;
}

/*
 * The getServiceName will retrieve the JNDI name for a requested
 * service. The service is indicated by the ServiceId passed into
 * the method.
 */
static private String getServiceName(int pServiceId)
    throws ServiceLocatorException {

  String serviceName = null;
  switch (pServiceId) {
    case STORYMANAGER:      serviceName = STORYMANAGER_JNDINAME;
                            break;
    case JAVAEDGEDB:        serviceName = JAVAEDGEDB_JNDINAME;
                            break;
    default:                throw new ServiceLocatorException(
                              "Unable to locate the service requested in " +
                              "ServiceLocator.getServiceName() method.  ");
  }
```

```
      return serviceName;
    }

    /*
     * Returns the EJBHome class reference for a requested service.
     * If the method cannot make a match, it will throw a ServiceLocatorException.
     */
    static private Class getEJBHomeRef(int pServiceId)
        throws ServiceLocatorException {

      Class homeRef = null;
      switch (pServiceId) {
        case STORYMANAGER:         homeRef = STORYMANAGERCLASSREF;
                                   break;
        default:                   throw new ServiceLocatorException(
                                     "Unable to locate the service requested in " +
                                     "ServiceLocator.getEJBHomeRef() method.  ");
      }
      return homeRef;
    }

    /*
     * The getEJBHome() method will return an EJBHome interface for a requested
     * service. If it cannot find the requested EJB, it will throw a
     * ServiceLocator exception.
     *
     * The getEJBHome() method caches a requested EJBHome so that the first
     * time an EJB is requested, a home interface will be retrieved and then
     * be placed into a cache.
     */
    public EJBHome getEJBHome(int pServiceId)
        throws ServiceLocatorException {

      //Trying to find the JNDI Name for the requested service
      String serviceName = getServiceName(pServiceId);
      EJBHome ejbHome = null;

      try {
        //Checking to see if I can find the EJBHome interface in cache
        if (ejbHomeCache.containsKey(serviceName)) {
          ejbHome = (EJBHome) ejbHomeCache.get(serviceName);
          return ejbHome;
        } else {
          //If I could not find the EJBHome interface in the cache, look it
          //up and then cache it.
          Context ctx = new InitialContext();
          Object jndiRef = ctx.lookup(serviceName);

          Object portableObj =
            PortableRemoteObject.narrow(jndiRef, getEJBHomeRef(pServiceId));

          ejbHome = (EJBHome) portableObj;
```

```
            ejbHomeCache.put(serviceName, ejbHome);
            return ejbHome;
        }

    } catch(NamingException e) {
        throw new ServiceLocatorException("Naming exception error in " +
                                "ServiceLocator.getEJBHome()", e);
    } catch(Exception e) {
        throw new ServiceLocatorException("General exception in " +
                                "ServiceLocator.getEJBHome", e);

    }
}


/*
 * The getDBConn() method will create a JDBC connection for the
 * requested database. It too uses a caching algorithm to minimize
 * the number of JNDI hits that it must perform.
 */
public Connection getDBConn(int pServiceId) throws ServiceLocatorException {
    //Getting the JNDI Service Name
    String serviceName = getServiceName(pServiceId);
    Connection conn = null;
    try {
        // Check to see if the requested DataSource is in the cache
        if (dataSourceCache.containsKey(serviceName)) {
            DataSource ds = (DataSource) dataSourceCache.get(serviceName);
            conn = ((DataSource)ds).getConnection();

            return conn;
        } else {
            // The DataSource was not in the cache. Retrieve it from JNDI
            // and put it in the cache.
            Context ctx = new InitialContext();
            DataSource newDataSource = (DataSource) ctx.lookup(serviceName);
            dataSourceCache.put(serviceName, newDataSource);
            conn = newDataSource.getConnection();
            return conn;
        }

    } catch(SQLException e) {
        throw new ServiceLocatorException("A SQL error has occurred in " +
                                "ServiceLocator.getDBConn()", e);
    } catch(NamingException e) {
        throw new ServiceLocatorException("A JNDI Naming exception has "+
                                "occurred in " +
                                "ServiceLocator.getDBConn()", e);
    } catch(Exception e) {
        throw new ServiceLocatorException("An exception has occurred " +
                                "in ServiceLocator.getDBConn()", e);

    }
  }
}
```

143

The Service Locator implementation shown above is built using the Singleton design pattern. This design pattern allows us to keep only one instance of a class per Java Virtual Machine (JVM). This instance is used to service all the requests for the entire JVM.

Since looking up the resources such as EJBs or `DataSource` objects is a common activity, implementing the `ServiceLocator` class pattern as a Singleton pattern prevents the needless creation of multiple copies of the same object doing the same thing. To implement the Service Locator as a Singleton, we need to first have a private constructor that will instantiate any resources being used by the `ServiceLocator` class:

```
private ServiceLocator() {
   ejbHomeCache = new Hashtable();
   dataSourceCache = new Hashtable();
}
```

The default constructor for the `ServiceLocator` class shown above is declared as private so that a developer cannot directly instantiate an instance of the `ServiceLocator` class. (We can have only one instance of the class per JVM.)

A Singleton pattern ensures that only one instance of an object is present within the virtual machine. The Singleton pattern is used to minimize the proliferation of large numbers of objects that serve a very narrow purpose. In the case of the Service Locator pattern, its sole job is to look up or create objects for other classes. It does not make sense to have a new Service Locator instance being created every time a user needs to carry out one of these tasks.

> **The Service Locator pattern is a very powerful design pattern, but it tends to be overused. Inexperienced architects will make everything a Singleton implementation. Using a Singleton pattern can introduce re-entrancy problems in applications that are multi-threaded.**
>
> **One thread can alter the state of Singleton implementation while another thread is working. Now, a Singleton pattern can be made thread-safe through the use of Java synchronization blocks. However, synchronization blocks represent potential bottlenecks within an application as only one thread at a time can execute the code surrounded by a synchronization block.**

Our Service Locator implementation is going to use two `Hashtables`, `ejbHomeCache` and `dataSourceCache`, which respectively store `EJBHome` and `DataSource` interfaces. So, we initialize them in the default constructor of the `ServiceLocator`.

The constructor is called via an anonymous static block that is invoked the first time the `ServiceLocator` class is loaded by the JVM:

```
static {
   serviceLocatorRef = new ServiceLocator();
}
```

This anonymous static code block invokes the constructor and sets a reference to a `ServiceLocator` instance, which is declared as a private attribute in the `ServiceLocator` class.

We use a method called `getInstance()` to retrieve an instance of `ServiceLocator` class stored in the `serviceLocatorRef` variable:

```
public static ServiceLocator getInstance(){
  return serviceLocatorRef;
}
```

To retrieve an `EJBHome` interface, the `getEJBHome()` method in the `ServiceLocator` class is invoked. This method takes an integer value (`pServiceId`) that represents the EJB being requested. For our Service Locator implementation, all the available EJBs have a public static constant defined in the `ServiceLocator` class. For instance, the `StoryManager` EJB has the following constant value:

```
public static final int STORYMANAGER = 0;
```

The first action taken by the `getEJBHome()` method is to look up the JNDI name that will be used to retrieve a resource, managed by the Service Locator. The JNDI name is looked up by calling the `getServiceName()` method, into which the `pServiceId` parameter is passed.

```
String serviceName = getServiceName(pServiceId);
```

Once the JNDI service name is retrieved, the `ejbHomeCache` is checked to see if that `EJBHome` interface is already cached. If a hit is found, the method immediately returns with the `EJBHome` interface stored in the cache:

```
if (ejbHomeCache.containsKey(serviceName)) {
    ejbHome = (EJBHome) ejbHomeCache.get(serviceName);
    return ejbHome;
```

If the requested `EJBHome` interface is not located in the `ejbHomeCache` Hashtable, the `getEJBHome()` method will look up the interface, add it to the `ejbHomeCache`, and then return the newly retrieved interface back to the calling application code:

```
} else {
  Context ctx = new InitialContext();
  Object jndiRef = ctx.lookup(serviceName);

  Object portableObj =
    PortableRemoteObject.narrow(jndiRef, getEJBHomeRef(pServiceId));

  ejbHome = (EJBHome) portableObj;
  ejbHomeCache.put(serviceName, ejbHome);
  return ejbHome;
}
```

The `getDBConn()` method is designed in a very similar fashion. When the user requests a JDBC connection via the `getDBConn()` method, the method checks the `dataSourceCache` for a `DataSource` object before doing a JNDI lookup. If the requested `DataSource` object is found in the cache, it is returned to the method caller, otherwise, a JNDI lookup takes place.

Let's revisit the constructor of the `StoryManagerBD` and see how using a Service Locator can significantly lower the amount of work involved in instantiating the `StoryManager` EJB:

```
public StoryManagerBD() throws ApplicationException {
  try {
    ServiceLocator serviceLocator = ServiceLocatory.getInstance();
    StoryManagerHome storyManagerHome = (StoryManagerHome)
      serviceLocator.getEJBHome(ServiceLocator.STORYMANAGER);
    storyManager = storyManagerHome.create();

  } catch(ServiceLocatorException e) {
    throw new ApplicationException("A ServiceLocator exception has been " +
                                   "raised in StoryManagerBD constructor: "
                                   + e.toString());
  }
}
```

Our Service Locator implementation has significantly simplified the process of looking up and creating an EJB.

The Service Locator Pattern to the Rescue

The author ran into a situation just this past year in which he was building a web-based application that integrated to a third-party Customer Relationship Management (CRM) system.

The application had a significant amount of business logic, embedded as PL/SQL stored procedures and triggers, in the Oracle database it was built on. Unfortunately, they had used an Oracle package, called DBMS_OUTPUT, to put the trace code through all of their PL/SQL code. This packaged never caused any problems because the end-users of the CRM package used to enter the database data via a "fat" GUI interface, which always kept the database transactions very short.

However, the author needed to build a web application that would collect all of the user's data and commit it all at once. The transaction length was significantly longer than what the CRM vendors had anticipated. As a result, the message buffer that the DBMS_OUTPUT package used for writing out the log, would run out of space and the web application would fail at what appeared to be random intervals.

At this point the author and his team were faced with the choice of going through every PL/SQL package and trigger and stripping out the DBMS_OUTPUT code (which should have never been put in production code). However, the DBA informed them that if they started every session with a call to DBMS_OUTPUT.DISABLE, they would be able to disable the DBMS_OUTPUT package. This would disable the DBMS_OUTPUT package for that particular session, but would not cause any problems for other application users.

If the developers had allowed a direct JNDI lookup to retrieve DataSource objects for getting a JDBC connection, they would have had the daunting task of going through every line of in the application and making the call to the DBMS_OUTPUT.DISABLE. However, since the team had implemented a Service Locator pattern and used it to retrieve all the database connections, there was only one place in which the code had to be modified.

This indicates that you might not appreciate the abstraction that the Service Locator pattern provides until you need to make a change in how a resource is requested that will affect a significant amount of your code base.

EJBs and Struts

Since the release of the J2EE specifications, it has been incessantly drilled into every J2EE developer that all business logic for an application should be placed in the middle tier as session-based Enterprise JavaBeans (EJB). Unfortunately, many developers believe that by putting their business logic in EJBs they have successfully designed their application's middle tier.

The middle tier of an application often captures some of the core business processes used throughout the enterprise. Without careful forethought and planning, many applications end up with a middle tier that is too tightly coupled to a specific application. The business logic contained within the application cannot easily be reused elsewhere and can become so complex that is not maintainable.

Two symptoms of a poorly designed middle tier are when EJBs for the application are:

❑ **Too fine-grained**
A very common mistake, when building Struts-based applications with EJBs, is to have each Action class have a corresponding EJB. This results in a proliferation of EJBs and can cause serious performance problems in a high-transaction application. The root cause of this is that the application developer is treating a component-based technology (that is, EJB) like an object-oriented technology (that is, plain old Java classes).

In a Struts application, you can often have a small number of EJBs carrying out the requests for a much larger number of Action classes. If you find a one-to-one mapping between Action classes and EJBs, the design of the application needs to be revisited.

❑ **Too fat**
Conversely, some developers end up placing too much of their business logic in an EJB. Putting too much business logic into a single EJB makes it difficult to maintain it and reuse it in other applications. "Fat" EJBs are often implemented by the developers who are used to programming with a module development language, such as C or Pascal, and are new to object-oriented analysis and design.

The author has encountered far more of the latter design problem: "fat" EJBs when building Struts-based applications. Let's look at the "fat" EJB problem in more detail.

On "Fat" EJBs

"Fat" EJBs are monolithic "blobs" of code that do not take advantage of object-oriented design.

> The term "blob" is not the author's term. It is actually an antipattern that was first defined in the text: *AntiPatterns: Refactoring Software, Architectures, and Projects in Crisis*, Brown, Malveau, McCorkmick, Mowbray; John Wiley & Sons, ISBN 0-471-19713-0. The Blob antipattern is an antipattern that forms when a developer takes an object-oriented language like C++ or Java and uses it in a procedural manner.

In a Struts application an extreme example of this might be manifested by a single EJB that contains one method for each of the Action classes present in the Struts application. The perform() method for each Action class would invoke a corresponding method on the EJB to carry out the business logic for the action.

This is an extreme example of a "fat" EJB. A more typical example of a "fat" EJB is one in which the EJBs are designed along functional breakdowns within the application. In the JavaEdge application, you might have a `Member` EJB and a `Story` EJB that encapsulate all of the functionality for that specific set of application tasks.

This kind of functional breakdown into individual EJBs makes sense. EJBs are coarse-grained components that wrap processes. The EJB model does offer the same type of object-oriented features (polymorphism, encapsulation, etc.) as its more fine-grained counterparts: plain java classes. The problem arises when the EJB developer does not use the EJB as a wrapper around more fine-grained objects but instead puts all of the business logic for a particular process *inside* the EJB.

For example, if you remember earlier in the chapter we talked about how many developers will push all of their business logic from their Struts `Action` class to an EJB. We demonstrated how if you did not use a Business Delegate pattern to hide the fact you were using EJBs, you could end up creating tight dependencies between Struts and the EJB APIs.

What we did not talk about is how blindly moving your business logic out of the `PostStory Action` class and into an EJB can result in a "fat" EJB. Shown below is the `StoryManagerBean.java` class:

```java
package com.wrox.javaedge.story.ejb;

import javax.naming.*;
import java.rmi.*;
import javax.ejb.*;
import java.sql.*;

import com.wrox.javaedge.common.*;
import com.wrox.javaedge.story.*;
import com.wrox.javaedge.member.*;
import com.wrox.javaedge.story.dao.*;
import com.wrox.javaedge.struts.poststory.*;

public class StoryManagerBean implements SessionBean {
  private SessionContext ctx;

  public void setSessionContext(SessionContext sessionCtx) {
    this.ctx = sessionCtx;
  }

  public void addStory(StoryVO storyVO)
      throws ApplicationException, RemoteException{
    Connection conn = null;
    PreparedStatement ps = null;

    try {
      conn = ServiceLocator.getInstance().getDBConn(ServiceLocator.JAVAEDGEDB);
      conn.setAutoCommit(false);

      StringBuffer insertSQL = new StringBuffer();

      insertSQL.append("INSERT INTO story(          ");
      insertSQL.append("  member_id              ,  ");
```

```
          insertSQL.append(" story_title           ,      ");
          insertSQL.append(" story_into             ,      ");
          insertSQL.append(" story_body             ,      ");
          insertSQL.append(" submission_date               ");
          insertSQL.append(")                              ");
          insertSQL.append("VALUES(                        ");
          insertSQL.append("  ?                     ,      ");
          insertSQL.append("  ?                     ,      ");
          insertSQL.append("  ?                     ,      ");
          insertSQL.append("  ?                     ,      ");
          insertSQL.append("  CURDATE()                  ) ");

          ps = conn.prepareStatement(insertSQL.toString());

          ps.setLong(1, storyVO.getStoryAuthor().getMemberId().longValue());
          ps.setString(2, storyVO.getStoryTitle());
          ps.setString(3, storyVO.getStoryIntro());
          ps.setString(4, storyVO.getStoryBody());

          ps.execute();
          checkStoryCount(storyVO.getStoryAuthor());

    } catch(SQLException e) {
       throw new ApplicationException("SQL Exception occurred in " +
                                "StoryManagerBean.addStory()", e);

    } catch(ServiceLocatorException e) {
       throw new ApplicationException("Service Locator Exception occurred in " +
                                "StoryManagerBean.addStory()", e);

    } finally {
       try {
          if (ps != null) ps.close();
          if (conn != null) conn.close();
       } catch(SQLException e) {}

    }
}

private void checkStoryCount(MemberVO memberVO)
     throws SQLException, NamingException {
  ...
}

public void addComment(StoryVO storyVO, StoryCommentVO storyCommentVO)
    throws ApplicationException, RemoteException{
  ...
}

public void addStory(PostStoryForm postStoryForm, MemberVO memberVO)
    throws ApplicationException, RemoteException{
  ...
}
```

```
    public void ejbCreate() { }
    public void ejbRemove() { }
    public void ejbActivate() { }
    public void ejbPassivate(){ }


}
```

We have not included the full listing of the `StoryManagerBean` class for the sake of brevity. However, you should be able to tell that this EJB is going to be huge if all of the business logic associated with managing stories is put into it.

The JavaEdge application is an extremely simple application. In more real-world EJB implementations, the amount of business logic that is put into the EJB can become staggering. Let's look at how the Session Façade design pattern can help us manage the business logic contained within an EJB.

The Session Façade Pattern

The Session Façade pattern is implemented as a stateless session EJB, which acts as a coarse-grained wrapper around finer-grained pieces of code. Typically, these finer-grained pieces of code are going to be plain old Java classes rather than the more component-oriented EJB architecture. In a component-based architecture, a component wraps the business processes behind immutable interfaces. The implementation of the business process may change, but the interface that the component presents to the applications (which invoke the business process) does not change.

Instead the methods on an EJB implemented as a Session Façade should act as entry point through which the business process is carried by more fine-grained Java classes.

The diagram below illustrates this:

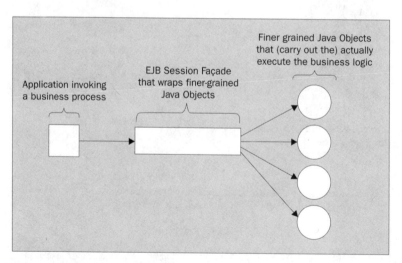

So if we were going to re-write the `StoryManagerBean`'s `addStory()` method to be less monolithic and be more fine-grained it might be rewritten to look something like this:

```
public void addStory(StoryVO storyVO)
    throws ApplicationException, RemoteException {

  try {
    StoryDAO storyDAO = new StoryDAO();
    storyDAO.insert(storyVO);

    PrizeManager prizeManager = new PrizeManager();
    int numberOfStories =
      prizeManager.checkStoryCount(storyVO.getStoryAuthor());

    boolean TOTAL_COUNT_EQUAL_1000 = (numberOfStories==1000);
    boolean TOTAL_COUNT_EQUAL_5000 = (numberOfStories==5000);

    if (TOTAL_COUNT_EQUAL_1000 || TOTAL_COUNT_EQUAL_5000) {
      prizeManager.notifyMarketing(storyVO.getStoryAuthor(), numberOfStories);
    }

  } catch (DataAccessException e){
    throw new ApplicationException("DataAccessException Error in " +
                                   StoryManagerBean.addStory(): " +
                                   e.toString(), e);
  }
}
```

The addStory() method is much more manageable and extensible. All of the data-access logic for adding a story has been moved to the StoryDAO class (which will be covered in more detail in the next chapter). All of the logic associated with prize management has been moved to the PrizeManager class.

As you can see, we've also refactored the code associated with the checkStoryCount() method. The checkStoryCount() method is only used when trying to determine whether or not the individual qualifies for a prize. So we moved the checkStoryCount() method to the PrizeManager. We could also have moved this method to the StoryDAO class. By moving it out of the StoryManager EJB we avoid having "extraneous" code in the Session Façade implementation.

Implementing the Session Façade pattern is not difficult. It involves looking at your EJBs and ensuring that the individual steps for carrying out a business process are captured in fine-grained Java objects. The code inside of the Session Façade implementation should act as the "glue" that strings these individual steps together into a complete process.

Any method on a Session Façade EJB should be short. If its over 20-30 lines, you need to go back and revisit the logic contained within the method to see if it can be refactored out into smaller individual classes. Remember, one of the core concepts behind object-oriented design is division of responsibility. Always keep this in mind as you are building your EJBs.

What about Non-EJB Applications?

All of the examples presented so far in this chapter have made the assumption that we are using EJB-based J2EE to gain the benefits offered by these design patterns. However, it is very easy to adapt these patterns to a non-EJB Struts-based application. The author has worked on many successful Struts applications using these patterns and just a web container.

For non-EJB Struts implementations, you should still use the Business Delegate pattern to separate the Struts `Action` class from the Java classes that carry out the business logic. You need not implement a Session Façade pattern in these situations. Instead, your Business Delegate class will perform the same function as the Session Façade class. The Business Delegate would act as a thin wrapper around the other Java objects carrying out a business process.

You might ask the question, "Why go through all of this extra work even in a non-J2EE application?" The reason is simple; by cleanly separating your `Action` class from the application's business logic (using a Business Delegate pattern), you provide a migration path for moving your applications to a full J2EE environment.

At some point, you might need to move the Struts applications to a full-blown J2EE application server and not just a JSP/servlet container. You can very easily move your business logic to Session Façades and EJBs, without rewriting any of your Struts applications. This is because you have separated your Struts applications from your business logic.

Your Struts applications only invoke the business logic through a plain Java interface. This abstraction allows you to completely refactor the business tier of your applications without affecting the applications themselves.

The authors of this book struggled when trying to determine whether or not they should build the JavaEdge application as an EJB-based application. In the end, we decided not, because JavaEdge is such a simple application, that it did require the power (and the complexity) that came with implementing an EJB solution.

Since the logic for the JavaEdge application was simple we embedded most of it as calls to Data Access Objects (covered in the next chapter) directly inside the Business Delegate implementations. The business logic was not broken out into Session Façade and was instead kept inside the Business Delegate classes.

However, even though the JavaEdge application does not use EJBs in its implementation, the author of this chapter felt that this material was an important piece when looking at using Struts for your own EJB-based applications.

As the Struts `Action` classes only talked to Business Delegates we could have easily refactored the code into an EJB-based solution without having to touch any of the Struts code.

The design patterns talked about in this chapter cleanly separate the Struts framework from how the business logic for the application is being invoked. This allows us to evolve the application over time while minimizing the effects of these changes on the application.

Summary

Often, in an object-oriented and component-based environment, more value is gained from interface reuse and the abstraction it provides than the actual code reuse. The business logic for an application changes regularly. Well-defined interfaces that abstract away the implementation details help shield an application from this uncertainty. This chapter explored how to use common J2EE design patterns to cleanly separate the business logic from the Struts framework on which the application is built. This promotes code reuse and also gives the developer more flexibility in refactoring business logic at a later date.

This chapter covered the following J2EE design patterns:

❑ **Business Delegate Pattern**
Hides the details of how the business logic used by the Struts application is actually invoked. It allows the development team to refactor the business tier while minimizing its impact on the applications that use the business logic. It also hides the technology (EJBs, web services, or just plain Java classes) used to implement the actual business logic.

❑ **Service Locator Pattern**
Simplifies the process of requesting commonly used resources like EJBs and `DataSource` objects within your Business Delegate.

❑ **Session Façade Pattern**
Is an EJB, which provides a coarse-grained interface that wraps a business process. Carrying out the individual steps for the business process, wrapped by the Session Façade, is left to much more fine-grained Java objects.

This chapter focused solely on modeling and implementing the business tier of a Struts-based application. However, we still need to focus on the how data is retrieved and manipulated by the business-logic tier. The next chapter is going to demonstrate how to use an open source object/relational mapping tool, called ObjectRelationalBridge (OJB), to build a data persistence tier. In addition, it will discuss how to use J2EE data-access design patterns to hide the implementation details in the data-persistence tier from the business tier.

5

Building a Data Access Tier with ObjectRelationalBridge

A well defined data access tier, which provides a logical interface for accessing corporate data sources, is one of the most reused pieces of code in any system architecture. This statement, on the surface, may appear to be an over-inflated claim, but it is made with the following two points in mind:

❑ Applications are developed according to the changing needs of the organization. However, the data used by these applications is used for a long time, even after the application has been replaced with some completely new piece of technology. The data possessed by an organization is often the only constant in any IT ecosystem.

❑ Any application does not exist all by itself. Most of the development efforts involve integrating a newly built or bought application with the other existing systems. To maximize their value, most applications must exchange their data with other systems using a consistent interface, which abstracts away the "messy" technology details associated with accessing the data.

The previous three chapters have focused on building the presentation and business layers of the JavaEdge web site using the Struts development framework. In this chapter, we are going to change our perspective and move the focus off the Struts development framework and onto building the JavaEdge data access tier.

Building a data access tier is more than just using a particular technology to retrieve and manipulate data. The requirements of the data access tier are:

❑ To minimize the need to write significant amounts of SQL and JDBC database code. Accessing data from a relational database using SQL is often a tedious and error-prone process. It involves writing a large amount of code that does not map well into the object-oriented model, in which most Java developers are used to working. Furthermore, poorly written data access code can bring the performance of any application to an unpleasant halt.

❑ To abstract away the underlying details of the data store used to hold the application data. These details include the specific database technology used to hold the data, physical details of how the data is stored, and the relationships that might exist within the data. Abstracting away these details provides the developers with more flexibility in changing the underlying data access tier, without having the impact of those changes on the presentation and business tiers of the application.

While building the JavaEdge data access tier, we are going to focus on:

❑ Using the Jakarta group's object/relational (O/R) mapping tool: ObjectRelationalBridge (OJB). OJB allows a developer to transparently map data pulled from a relational database to plain Java objects. Using OJB, you can significantly reduce the amount of data access code that needs to be written and maintained by the application team.

❑ Implementing two core J2EE data access design patterns, which ensure that our business and presentation tiers are never exposed to the underlying data access technology used to retrieve our data. There is no need for a business component to know whether the data it is consuming is retrieved via JDBC, entity beans, or OJB. Specifically, we are going to explore the following J2EE data access patterns:

  ❑ The Data Access Object (DAO) pattern
  ❑ The Value Object (VO) pattern

Developing a Data Access Strategy

While it is difficult to emphasize the importance of a data access tier, the fact is that most development teams do not have a coherent strategy defined for building one. Rather than having a well-defined set of services and interfaces for accessing their data, they will define their data access strategy in one of two ways:

❑ By the particular data access technology that they use to get the data

❑ By the database that they use to hold their data

The problem with the two definitions above is that the focus is on a purely technological solution.

> **A well-designed data access tier should transcend any one particular technology or data store.**

Technologies change at a rapid rate; a new technology that appears to be a cutting-edge technology can quickly become obsolete. Development teams who couple their applications too tightly with a particular technology or technology vendor, will find that their applications are not as responsive when new business requirements force an organization to adopt new data access technologies.

A data access tier should allow the business services to consume data without giving any idea of how or from where it is being retrieved. Specifically, a data access tier should:

❑ Allow a clean separation of data-persistence logic from the presentation and business logic. For instance, a business component should never be passed a Java `ResultSet` object or have to capture a `SQLException`. The entire data access logic should be centralized behind a distinct set of interfaces, which the business logic *must* use to retrieve or manipulate data.

❑ Decouple the application(s) from any knowledge of the database platform in which the data resides. The objects in the business tier requesting the data need not know that they are accessing a relational database such as Oracle, an object-based database such as Poet, or an XML database such as the Apache group's Xindice database.

❑ Abstract away the physical details of how data is stored within the database and the relationships that exist between entities in the database. For instance, a business-tier class should never know that the `Customer` object and the `Address` object have a one-to-many or many-to-many relationship. These details should be handled by the data access tier and be completely hidden from the developer.

❑ Simplify the application development process by hiding the details associated with getting a database connection, issuing a command, or managing transactions. Data access code can be very complicated even though it looks very easy to write. By putting all data access code behind a set of data access services, the development team can give the responsibility of writing that code to one or two developers who thoroughly understand the data access technology being used. All the other developers in the team only have to use the services, provided by the data access tier, to retrieve and manipulate data. They do not have to worry about the underlying details of the data access code. This significantly simplifies application development efforts and reduces the chance that a piece of poorly written data access code will inadvertently affect the application's code base.

As discussed in Chapter 1, the lack of planning for the data access tier results in the formation of the Data Madness antipattern. This antipattern manifests in a number of different manners including:

❑ The creation of tight dependencies between the applications consuming the data and the structures of the underlying data stores. Every time a change is made to the database structure, the developers have to hunt through the application code, identify any code that references the changed database structures (that is, the tables), and then update the code to reflect the changes. This is time-consuming and error-prone.

❑ The inability to easily port an application to another database platform because of the dependencies on the vendor-specific database extensions. Often, neglecting to abstract simple things, such as how a primary key is generated in the application's SQL code, can make it very difficult to port the application to another database platform.

❑ The inability to easily change data access technologies without rewriting a significant amount of application code. Many developers mix their data access code (that is, their SQL/JDBC or entity EJB lookups) directly in their application code. This intermixing will cause tight dependencies and increase in the amount of code that needs to be reworked, when you want to use a new data access technology.

❑ The presence of a 2.5 tier architecture. A 2.5 tier architecture is an architecture in which there is a well-defined presentation tier for the application, but the business logic is not clearly separated from the data access logic of the application. This particular symptom is sometimes very obvious.

You will find this symptom, when you start studying the business logic of an application and find the SQL code scattered throughout the logic. (The code is found anywhere in the business logic and affects the flow. A good sign of this is when a Database Administrator asks the developers to look at all of the SQL code for an application and they have to search the entire application source code to find it.)

The presence of Data Madness can be easily found by knowing how the data access tier is designed. If the development team says that it is using JDBC, entity EJBs, SQLJ, Oracle, SQL Server, and so on, it is likely that there has been no real preplanning for the data access tier.

The JavaEdge Data Access Model

The data model for the JavaEdge application is very simple. It contains three tables: member, story, and story_comment. The diagram below shows the JavaEdge database tables, the data elements contained within them, and the relationships that exist between them.

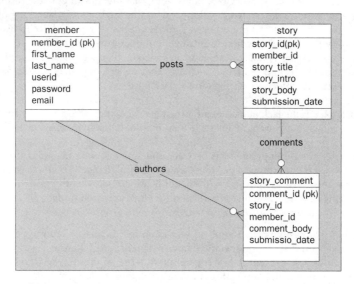

The above diagram illustrates that:

❑ A JavaEdge member can post zero or more stories. A story can belong to one and only one member.

❑ A story can have zero or more comments associated with it. A story_comment can belong to one and only one story.

❑ A JavaEdge member can post zero or more comments on a particular story. A JavaEdge story_comment can be posted only by one member.

The JavaEdge data access tier is going to be built on one tenet:

> **The business code for the application will never be allowed to directly access the JavaEdge database.**

All interactions with the JavaEdge database will be through a set of **Data Access Objects (DAO)**. DAO is a core J2EE design pattern that completely abstracts the **Create, Replace, Update, and Delete (CRUD)** logic, needed to retrieve and manipulate the data behind Java interface. (One of the first examples of the Data Access Objects and Value Objects being articulated in a Java book is in *Core J2EE Patterns: Best Practices and Design Strategies, Prentice Hall, ISBN 0-13-064884-1*)

The JavaEdge database is a relational database. Relational databases are row-oriented and do not map well into an object-oriented environment like Java. Even with the use of DAO classes, the question that needs to be solved is: how to mitigate the need to pass row-oriented Java objects, such as the `ResultSet` class, back and forth between the business tier and DAO classes.

The answer is to use the **Value Object (VO) pattern** to map the data retrieved from and sent to a relational database, to a set of Java classes. These Java classes wrap the retrieved data behind simple `get()` and `set()` methods and minimize the exposure of the physical implementation of the underlying database table to the developer. The underlying database structure can be changed or even moved to an entirely different platform with a very small risk of breaking any applications consuming the data.

Let's look at the diagram below and see how all of these pieces fit together:

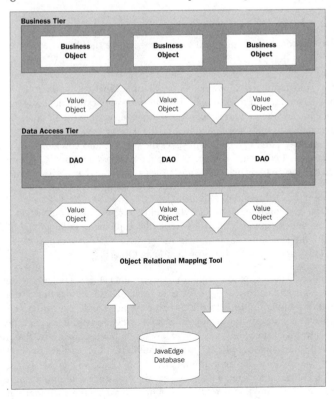

The above diagram lays out the architecture for our data access tier at a high level. As shown, the business tier uses the Data Access Objects to retrieve, insert, update, and delete data from the JavaEdge database. All data coming to and from the DAOs is encapsulated in a Value Object. A Value Object represents a single record residing within the JavaEdge database. It abstracts away the physical database-specific details of the record and provides the Java programmer simple `get()`/`set()` methods for accessing individuals attributes in a record. A Value Object can contain collections of other Value Objects. For example, the `MemberVO` class (in our JavaEdge application) contains a collection of stories. This collection represents the relationship that exists between a member record and its corresponding story records.

The DAOs never talk directly to the JavaEdge database. Instead, all the database access is done through an object/relational (O/R) mapping tool. The introduction of an O/R mapping tool is significantly time saving. This tool allows the developer to define declaratively, rather than programmatically, how data is to be mapped to and from the Value Objects in the application. This means that the developers do not have to write JDBC and SQL code to retrieve the JavaEdge data.

Now, let's cover the Data Access Objects and Value Objects being used for the JavaEdge application, in more detail.

Data Access Object

Data Access Objects are meant to wrap all the CRUD logic associated with entities within the JavaEdge database. DAOs provide an abstraction layer between the business tier and the physical data stores. Specifically, DAOs abstract:

- ❑ The type of data store being accessed
- ❑ The database access technology being used to retrieve the data
- ❑ The physical location of data

Use of a set of DAOs removes the need for a developer to know whether the database is being stored in an Oracle server, a MySQL server, or a mainframe. This keeps the application database independent and minimizes the risk of exposing the vendor-specific database extensions to the business tier. Database vendors provide a number of extensions that often make writing the data access code easy or offer performance enhancements above the standard SQL code. However these extensions come at a price, that is, portability. By abstracting away these database-specific extensions from the business tier, the development team can minimize the impact of vendor locking on their business code. Instead, only the data access tier is exposed to these details.

In addition, DAOs keep the business-tier code from being exposed to the way in which the data is being accessed. This gives the development team lot of flexibility in choosing its data access technology. A beginning team of Java developers may choose to write the application code with JDBC. As they become more comfortable with the Java environment, they may rewrite their data access objects using a much more sophisticated technology such as entity Beans or Java Data Objects (JDO).

In many IT organizations, data is spread throughout various data stores. Hence, the developers have to know where all of this data is located and write the code to access it. DAOs allows the system architect to put together the data that is found in multiple locations and present a single logic interface for retrieving and updating it. The application consuming the data is location-independent. For example, most organizations do not have all of their customer data in one location. They might have some of the data residing in the Customer Relationship Management (CRM) system, some of it in their order entry system, some of it in the contact management used by the sales department, and so on. Using a Data Access Object, a system architect can centralize all CRUD logic associated with accessing the customer data into a single Java object. This relieves the developer from having to know where and how to access the customer data.

DAOs simplify the work for the development team because it relieves the majority of the team from knowing the "dirty" details of data access.

The JavaEdge Data Access Objects

All the DAOs in our JavaEdge application are going to extend a single interface class called `DataAccessObject`. This interface guarantees that all the data access objects in the JavaEdge application have the following four base methods:

- ❏ FindByPK()
- ❏ Insert()
- ❏ Update()
- ❏ Delete()

If you want all of your DAOs to have a particular functionality, make the `DataAccessObject` an abstract class rather than an interface. The code for the `DataAccessObject` interface is shown below:

```
package com.wrox.javaedge.common;

public interface DataAccessObject {

  public ValueObject findByPK(String primaryKey) throws DataAccessException;
  public void insert(ValueObject insertRecord) throws DataAccessException;
  public void update(ValueObject updateRecord) throws DataAccessException;
  public void delete(ValueObject deleteRecord) throws DataAccessException;
}
```

The `findByPK()` method is a **finder** method used to retrieve a record based upon its primary key. This method will perform a database lookup and return a `ValueObject` containing the data. A `ValueObject` is a Java class that wraps the data retrieved using `get()`/`set()` methods. We will discuss more about this class in the next section.

The `DataAccessObject` interface, shown above, supports only primary key lookups using a single key. However often in a data model, the uniqueness of a row of data can be established only by combining two or more keys together. To support this model, you could easily change the above interface to have a `ValueObject` passed in as a parameter. This `ValueObject` could then contain more than one value necessary to perform the database lookup.

The `insert()`, `update()`, and `delete()` methods correspond to different actions that can be taken against the data stored in the JavaEdge database. Each of these three methods has a `ValueObject` passed in as a parameter. The DAO will use the data contained in the `ValueObject` parameter to carry out the requested action (that is, a database insert, update, or delete). All of the four methods in the `DataAccessObject` interface throw an exception called `DataAccessException`. The `DataAccessException` is a user-defined exception, which is used to wrap any exceptions that might be thrown by the data access code contained within the DAO. The whole purpose of a DAO is to hide how the data is accessed. This means the DAO should never allow a data access-specific exception, such as a JDBC `SQLException`, to be thrown.

Often, implementing a solid system architecture that is going to be easily maintainable and extensible, may involve small decisions to be made early on in the design of the architecture. In our data access tier, small things, such as wrapping the technology-specific exceptions with a more generic exception, can have a huge impact. For instance, allowing a JDBC SQLException to be thrown from DAO would unnecessarily expose the way in which the data is being accessed to application code using the DAO. The business code would have to catch the SQLException every time it wanted to access a method in that DAO. Also, if the developers later wanted to rewrite the DAO to use something other than JDBC, they would have to go back to every place in the business tier that used the DAO and refactor the try...catch block for the SQLException. Wrapping the SQLException with the DataAccessException avoids this problem.

> **You often do not feel the pain of poor design decisions until the application has gone into production and you now have to maintain and extend it.**

The JavaEdge application is going to have two DAOs: StoryDAO and MemberDAO. The following class diagram shows the DAOs and their corresponding methods.

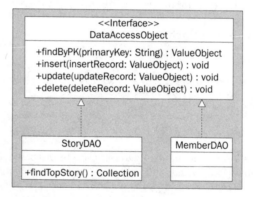

Two observations can be made from the above class diagram. First, the DataAccessObject interface defines only the base methods that all DAO classes must implement. You can add any other methods to the classes implementing the DAO interface. For example, the StoryDAO has an additional finder method called findTopStory(). This method will return a Java Collection of StoryVO Value Objects. A DAO implementation can have as many finder methods in it as needed. The additional methods added in a DAO implementation can do additional tasks, such as perform specialized queries or invoke a stored procedure.

The second observation from the above diagram is that even though there are three database tables (member, story, and story_comment), only two DAOs (StoryDAO and MemberDAO) have been implemented for the JavaEdge application. There is no DAO present for handling the data logic associated with manipulating data in the story_comment table.

A common mistake while implementing a data access tier using a Data Access Object pattern, is to mimic the physical layout of the database. The application designer tends to create a DAO for each of the tables in the database schema. However, the designers have to consider the context in which their data is going to be used while modeling the DAOs.

In the JavaEdge application, the story and the story_comment table have a one-to-many relationship. Story comments have no context other than being associated with a story. So, the StoryDAO is responsible for managing both story and story_comment data. This may seem a little unclear now but as we start discussing Value Objects, we will see that one Value Object can contain collections of other Value Objects.

If you model your DAOs to mirror the physical layout of your database, you might introduce performance problems into the application. This happens because you have to "join" several DAOs to mimic the relationships that might exist in the database. As a result, there are multiple SQL statements being issued to retrieve, update, or delete data, which could have easily been done with one SQL statement.

By modeling your DAO, based on how the application(s) will use the data and not just mimicking the physical layout of the database, you can often avoid unnecessary database calls. This is particularly true for relational databases, where with a little forethought you can leverage SQL "joins" to retrieve data (particularly the data that has a one-to-many relationship) in one SQL call inside one DAO, instead of multiple SQL calls involving multiple DAOs.

Value Objects

The Value Object pattern evolved in response to the performance problems inherent in the EJB 1.1 specification. In the EJB 1.1 specification, entity beans supported only remote interfaces. It was expensive to invoke methods in a remote interface. Each time a method was invoked, a significant amount of data marshaling had to take place, even if the code invoking the entity bean was located in the same Java Virtual Machine (JVM) as the bean. This meant that the fine-grained get() and set() method calls, for retrieving individual data elements from an entity bean, could quickly incur a performance hit.

The solution was to minimize the number of individual get()/set() methods being called on an entity bean. This is how the Value Object pattern evolved. A Value Object pattern is nothing more than a plain old Java class, which originally held the data retrieved from an entity bean lookup. A Value Object contains no business logic and only has get()/set() methods to retrieve and alter data that it contains.

An entity bean populates a Value Object with the data it retrieved and then returns that Value Object to the caller as a serialized object. By putting all of the data in a Value Object, an entity bean developer could avoid the performance costs associated with multiple invocations on a remote interface. The application using the Value Object would use the get() methods in the object to retrieve the data looked up by the entity bean. Conversely, if the application wanted to insert or update via the entity bean, it would populate a new Value Object or update an already existing one and return it back to the entity bean to perform the database write.

The Value Object pattern was evolved to deal with the inherent performance problems in entity beans. With release of the EJB 2.0 specification and the introduction of local interfaces, it would seem that the Value Object pattern would not be needed. However, this pattern is also very useful for abstracting physical database details and moving data back and forth between the data tier and the other tiers in a web-based application.

Value Objects provide a mechanism in which the data being used by the application can be decoupled from the data store that holds the data. By using Value Objects in your data access tier, you can:

❑ Easily pass data to and from the presentation and business tier without ever exposing the details of the underlying data store. The Value Objects become the transport mechanism for moving data between the presentation framework (that is, Struts), the business tier (that is, your business delegates and Session Façades), and the data tier.

❑ Hide the physical details of the underlying data store. Value Objects can be used to hold your data; as a result, the developer would not know the physical data types being used to store data in the database. For instance, one of your database tables may contain a BLOB (Binary Large Object). Rather than forcing the developer to work with the JBDC `Blob` type, you can have the developer work with a `String` data type on the Value Object and make the DAO using that Value Object responsible for converting that `String` to the JDBC `Blob` data type.

❑ Hide the details of the relationships that exist between the entities within your data store. An application, using a Value Object, is exposed to the cardinality between entities only through a `get()` method that returns a `Collection` of objects. It has no idea of whether that cardinality is a one-to-many or many-to-many relationship. In our example, if we want to restructure the `story` and `story_comment` table to have a many-to-many relationship, only the `StoryDAO` would need to be modified. None of the applications using the `Story` data would be affected.

Let's look at the Value Objects that are implemented for the JavaEdge application.

The JavaEdge Value Objects

There are three Value Objects being used in the JavaEdge application: `MemberVO`, `StoryVO`, and `StoryCommentVO`. All of these classes implement an interface called `ValueObject`. (The Value Object pattern can be implemented in a number of ways. For a different implementation of the Value Object pattern, you may want to refer to *J2EE Design Patterns Applied, Wrox Press, ISBN: 1-86100-528-8*). It is common for the Value Object base call to be either an interface or class. If you are going to pass your Value Objects between different Java Virtual Machines, they should at least implement the `Serializable` interface.

In the JavaEdge application, the `ValueObject` interface is used as a **marker** interface to indicate that the class is a Value Object. This interface has no method signatures and provides a generic type for passing data in and out of a DAO. By passing only `ValueObjects` in the `DataAccessObject` interface, we can guarantee that every DAO in our JavaEdge application supports a base set of CRUD functionality. It is the responsibility of the DAO to cast the `ValueObject` to the type it is expecting.

The class diagram below shows the details of the Value Objects used in the JavaEdge application:

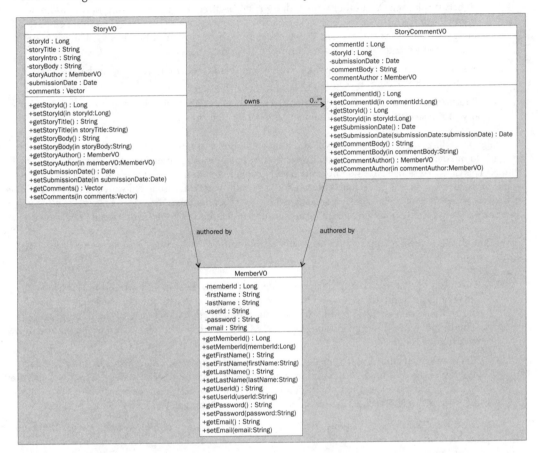

All of the above classes implement the `ValueObject` interface. Based on the class diagram, we can see the following relationships among the classes:

❑ A `StoryVO` class can contain zero or more `StoryCommentVO` objects. The `StoryCommentVO` classes are stored in a `Vector` inside the `StoryVO` class. A `StoryVO` object contains a reference, via the `storyAuthor` property, to the JavaEdge member who authored the original story.

There are number of ways in which child objects can be returned from a parent object. For the JavaEdge application, a `Vector` was chosen to return "groups" of Value Objects because a `Vector` enforces thread-safety, by synchronizing the access to the items stored within the `Vector`. This means two threads cannot simultaneously add or remove items from the `Vector`.

If you are trying to maximize the performance and know that multiple threads in your application are not going to add or remove items from the collection, you can use a non-synchronized `Collection` object like an `ArrayList`.

- ❏ The `StoryVO` class enforces strict navigability between the `StoryCommentVO` and `MemberVO` objects it references. In other words, there is no bi-directional relationship between the `StoryVO` and `StoryCommentVO` class or the `StoryVO` and `MemberVO` class. One cannot navigate from a `StoryCommentVO` object to find the `StoryVO` it belongs to. The same holds true for the `MemberVO` contained within the `StoryVO` class.

- ❏ A `StoryCommentVO` class contains a reference, via the `commentAuthor` to the member property, who wrote the comment.

- ❏ The `MemberVO` class is a standalone object. It does not allow the developer to directly access any of the stories or story comments authored by that member.

From the preceding class diagram, you will also notice that the relationships that exist between the classes do not map to the data relationships in the entity-relationship diagram shown earlier. The reason for this is simple. The class diagram is based on how the data is going to be used by the JavaEdge application. The application does not have a functional requirement to see all the stories associated with a particular member. If we were to retrieve all of the stories associated with a member and map them into a `Vector` in the `MemberVO`, we would be retrieving a significant amount of data into the objects that would never be used.

Even though the JavaEdge application uses only a small number of Value Objects, you will have to keep in mind:

- ❏ The number of values being retrieved from a call to the DAOs. One would not want to retrieve large numbers of Value Objects in one call, as this can quickly consume memory within the Java Virtual Machine. In particular, one needs to be aware of the data that is actually being used in one's Value Objects. Many development teams end up retrieving more data than is required.

- ❏ The numbers of child Value Objects being retrieved by a parent. Often, while building the data access tier, the developers will unknowingly retrieve a large number of Value Objects because they do not realize how deep their object graphs are. For instance, if you retrieve 10 stories in a call to the `StoryDAO` and each `StoryVO` contains 20 `StoryCommentVOs`. You end up retrieving:

  10 stories * 20 story comments + 10 story authors + 20 story comment authors = 230 objects for one call.

The primary design principle that was embraced while designing the Value Objects used in the JavaEdge application was:

> **Understand how the data in your application is going to be used. A Value Object is nothing more than a view of the data and there is nothing inappropriate about having a DAO return different types of Value Objects, all showing a different perspective of the same piece of data.**

Using an O/R Mapping Tool

It has been said that 40-60% of a development team's time is spent writing the data access code. For most Java developers, this means writing significant amount of SQL and JDBC code. The developers of the JavaEdge application (that is, the authors) decided that they wanted to significantly reduce the amount of work needed to implement their data access tier. They decided to use an object/relational (O/R) mapping tool, which would allow them to dynamically generate SQL requests and map any data operations needed from plain Java objects. O/R mapping tools have been available for quite a while and actually have pre-dated Java. Even though these tools offer fine solutions, they are expensive. Hence the developers had to use a single vendor's proprietary toolset.

Fortunately, several open source O/R mapping tools are now available and gaining widespread acceptance in the development community. O/R mapping tools fall into two broad categories in terms of how they are implemented:

- **Code generators**:
  O/R mapping tools in the code generator category require the development team to map out the structure of their database tables and Java objects. These tools then generate all of the Java and JDBC code needed to carry out database transactions. The development team can use these generated classes in the applications. Examples of open source O/R code generators include:

  - **The Apache Jakarta Group's Torque project**
    (http://jakarta.apache.org/turbine/torque)
    Torque originally started as a component of the Apache Jakarta Group's Turbine project. Torque is a very powerful persistence tool, which can convert an existing database into a set of usable persistence-aware Java classes. Torque can even be used to develop a database from scratch and then generate the entire database DDL and Java classes via an Ant Task. Torque uses a proprietary API for performing database queries.

  - **The MiddleGen project** (http://boss.bekk.no/boss/middlegen)
    MiddleGen, another in this category, takes a slightly different approach from Torque. It can take an existing database and generate either container-managed persistence-based entity beans or Java Data Objects (JDO). Both entity beans and JDO are industry-accepted standards and are not solely "owned" by a vendor. MiddleGen can even generate the EJB 2.0 vendor-specific deployment descriptors for many of the leading application servers.

- **Dynamic SQL generators**:
  The other category of O/R mapping tools is the dynamic SQL generators. These O/R tools allow you to define your database according to Java object mappings. However, these tools do not generate the Java classes for you. Instead, the developer is responsible for writing the mapped Java objects (usually implemented as Value Objects). The O/R tools' runtime engine will then transparently map data to and from the Java object.

  An example of a dynamic SQL generator is the Apache Jakarta Group's ObjectRelationalBridge (OJB). Three main reasons for choosing this tool for implementing the JavaEdge project are as follows:

  - OJB is very lightweight and extremely easy to set up and use. A simple data-persistence tier can be implemented by just configuring two files: `repository.xml` and `OJB.properties`. You can start using OJB without having to modify existing Java class files.

❑ Since OJB does not perform the code generation, it makes it extremely easy to use with existing applications. This is a key consideration while evaluating O/R mapping tools. It is better to use O/R mapping tools that generate code, while developing a project from scratch. However, they can be an absolute nightmare to implement while retrofitting the O/R tool into an existing application. If the developers want to tweak the code generated by the tool, they must remember to re-implement their changes every time they regenerate their persistence-tier code.

In addition, code generator O/R mapping tools require you to set up the generation process as part of your development environment and/or build process. This itself can be a time-consuming and error-prone process.

❑ OJB has a unique architecture, which allows it to embrace multiple industry standards for data persistence. As explained in the section called *About ObjectRelationalBridge*, OJB implements a micro-kernel architecture, which allows it to use its own proprietary APIs for making persistence calls and the JDO and Object Data Management Group (ODMG) 3.0 standards. This makes it easier to move the applications away from OJB, if the applications are not favorable to the organization.

In addition, OJB supports a number of features that are normally found in its more expensive commercial cousins. Some of these features are:

❑ An object cache, which greatly enhances the performance and helps guarantee the identities of multiple objects pointing to the same data row.

❑ Transparent persistence. The developer does not need to use OJB-generated classes or extend or implement any additional classes to make the state of the objects persistable to a database.

❑ Automatic persistence of child objects. When a parent object is saved, updates are made to all persistence-aware child objects that the parent references.

❑ An architecture that can run in a single JVM or in a client-server mode that can service the needs of multiple application servers running in a cluster.

❑ The ability to integrate in an application server environment, including participation in container-managed transactions and JNDI data source lookups.

❑ Multiple types of locking support, including support for optimistic locking.

❑ A built-in sequence manager.

This is just a small list of the features currently supported by OJB. Let's discuss OJB in more detail.

About ObjectRelationalBridge (OJB)

ObjectRelationalBridge is one of the newest Apache Jakarta Group projects. It is a fully functional O/R mapping tool. OJB is based on micro-kernel architecture. A micro-kernel architecture is the one in which a core set of functionality is built around a very minimalist and concise set of APIs. Additional functionality is then layered around the kernel APIs. Micro-kernel APIs are very flexible because different implementations of a technology can be built around a single set of APIs.

The following diagram illustrates this architecture:

At the heart of OJB is the **Persistence Broker (PB)** API. This API defines a number of standard calls for interacting with a data store. The PB API supports making calls only against a relational database (as designated by the Persistence Broker Relational Database API shown in the above diagram). It uses JDBC 1.0 database calls and a subset of SQL to guarantee the maximum amount of database support. In future releases, the OJB development team is planning to implement an additional JDBC support along with support for Object, LDAP, and XML-based databases.

Since OJB is designed using micro-kernel architecture, OJB uses a very basic kernel API (that is, the PB API) and then builds on that API to implement multiple data access APIs. OJB currently supports both JDO and the Object Data Management Group's (ODMG) Object Data Standard (version 3.0). Both of these APIs are built on top of OJB's PB API and interact with it.

OJB is an extremely configurable and tunable product. It is built on a set of pluggable components, so that if you find that some feature in OJB does not meet your needs (such as its caching model), you can easily replace that component with your own implementation.

The JavaEdge application uses the following technology to build the data access tier:

- ❏ MySQL-MAX 3.23 – Available at http://mysql.com
- ❏ Connector/J 3.0.2 (A MySQL JDBC Driver) – Available at http://mysql.com
- ❏ OJB 0.9.7 – Available at http://jakarta.apache.org/ojb

  Please use at least OJB version 0.9.7 while running the JavaEdge application source code. Earlier releases of OJB had bugs in them that caused unusual behavior with the JavaEdge application.

Now, we will walk through some of the key files.

The Core OJB Files

OJB is very easy to set up. To begin writing the code using OJB, you need to first place the following JAR files in your classpath. These files are located in the `lib` directory of the unzipped OJB distribution. The required files are:

- ❑ Jakarta-ojb-<version_number>.jar: This is the core OJB JAR file.
- ❑ Several Jakarta Commons JAR files including:
    - ❑ `commons-beanutils.jar`
    - ❑ `commons-collections-2.0.jar`
    - ❑ `commons-lang-0.1.-dev.jar`
    - ❑ `commons-logging.jar`
    - ❑ `commons-pool.jar`

Once these JAR files are included in your classpath, you are ready to begin mapping your Java class files. In the JavaEdge application, these will be the `MemberVO`, `StoryVO`, and `StoryCommentVO` classes, mapping to your database tables.

Setting up the Object/Relational Mappings

Setting up your O/R mappings using OJB is a straightforward process, which involves creating and editing two files: `OJB.properties` and `repository.xml`. The `OJB.properties` file is used to customize the OJB runtime environment.

By modifying the `OJB.properties` file, a developer can control whether OJB is running in single virtual machine or client-server mode, the size of the OJB connection pool, lock management, and the logging level of the OJB runtime engine. We will not be going through a step-by-step description of the `OJB.properties` file. Instead, we are going to review the relevant material.

The `repository.xml` file is responsible for defining the database-related information. It defines the JDBC connection information that is going to be used to connect to a database. In addition, it defines all of the Java class-to-table definitions. This includes mapping the class attributes to the database columns and the cardinality relationships that might exist in the database (such as one-to-one, one-to-many, and many-to-many).

The JavaEdge repository.xml

The JavaEdge `repository.xml` file is quite simple. It only maps three classes to three database tables. A `repository.xml` file for a medium-to-large size database would be huge. Right now, the OJB team is working on a graphical O/R mapping tool, but it could take sometime before it is stable.

The following code is the JavaEdge `repository.xml` file:

```
<?xml version="1.0" encoding="UTF-8"?>

<!-- This is a sample metadata repository for the ObJectBridge System.
     Use this file as a template for building your own mappings-->

<!-- defining entities for include-files -->
```

```xml
<!DOCTYPE descriptor-repository SYSTEM "repository.dtd" [
<!ENTITY internal SYSTEM "repository_internal.xml">
]>

<descriptor-repository version="0.9.6"
                       isolation-level="read-uncommitted">


<!--
     The Default JDBC Connection. If a class-descriptor does not specify
     its own JDBC Connection, the Connection specified here will be used. -->

  <jdbc-connection-descriptor
        platform="MySQL"
        jdbc-level="2.0"
        driver="org.gjt.mm.mysql.Driver"
        protocol="jdbc"
        dbalias="waf"
        username="waf_user"
        password="password"/>

  <class-descriptor class="com.wrox.javaedge.member.MemberVO"
                    table="member">

    <field-descriptor id="1" name="memberId" column="member_id"
                      jdbc-type="BIGINT"  primarykey="true"
                      autoincrement="true"/>
    <field-descriptor id="2" name="firstName" column="first_name"
                      jdbc-type="VARCHAR"/>
    <field-descriptor id="3" name="lastName" column="last_name"
                      jdbc-type="VARCHAR"/>
    <field-descriptor id="4" name="userId" column="userid"
                      jdbc-type="VARCHAR"/>
    <field-descriptor id="5" name="password" column="password"
                      jdbc-type="VARCHAR"/>
    <field-descriptor id="6" name="email" column="email"
                      jdbc-type="VARCHAR"/>
  </class-descriptor>

  <class-descriptor class="com.wrox.javaedge.story.StoryVO"
                    table="story">
    <field-descriptor id="1" name="storyId" column="story_id"
                      jdbc-type="BIGINT"  primarykey="true"
                      autoincrement="true"/>
    <field-descriptor id="2" name="memberId" column="member_id"
                      jdbc-type="BIGINT"/>
    <field-descriptor id="3" name="storyTitle" column="story_title"
                      jdbc-type="VARCHAR"/>
    <field-descriptor id="4" name="storyIntro" column="story_intro"
                      jdbc-type="VARCHAR"/>
    <field-descriptor id="5" name="storyBody" column="story_body"
                      jdbc-type="LONGVARBINARY"/>
    <field-descriptor id="6" name="submissionDate"
                      column="submission_date" jdbc-type="DATE"/>
    <collection-descriptor name ="comments"
                           element-class-ref=
                                  "com.wrox.javaedge.story.StoryCommentVO"
                           auto-retrieve="true" auto-update="true"
                           auto-delete="true">
      <inverse-foreignkey field-id-ref="2"/>
    </collection-descriptor>
```

```
        <reference-descriptor name="storyAuthor"
                       class-ref="com.wrox.javaedge.member.MemberVO"
                       auto-retrieve="true">
     <foreignkey field-id-ref="2"/>
   </reference-descriptor>
 </class-descriptor>

 <class-descriptor class="com.wrox.javaedge.story.StoryCommentVO"
                 table="story_comment">
   <field-descriptor id="1" name="commentId" column="comment_id"
                   jdbc-type="BIGINT" primarykey="true"
                   autoincrement="true"/>
   <field-descriptor id="2" name="storyId" column="story_id"
                   jdbc-type="BIGINT"/>
   <field-descriptor id="3" name="memberId" column="member_id"
                   jdbc-type="BIGINT"/>
   <field-descriptor id="4" name="commentBody" column="comment_body"
                   jdbc-type="LONGVARBINARY"/>
   <field-descriptor id="5" name="submissionDate"
                   column="submission_date" jdbc-type="DATE"/>
   <reference-descriptor name="commentAuthor"
                       class-ref="com.wrox.javaedge.member.MemberVO"
                       auto-retrieve="true">
     <foreignkey field-id-ref="3"/>
   </reference-descriptor
 </class-descriptor>
 <!-- include ojb internal mappings here -->

 &internal;
</descriptor-repository>
```

The root element of the `repository.xml` file is the deployment descriptor called `<descriptor-repository>`. This element has two attributes defined in it: `version` and `isolation-level`. The `version` attribute is a required attribute and indicates the version of the `repository.dtd` file used for validating the `repository.xml` file. The `isolation-level` attribute is used to indicate the default transaction level used by the all of the `class-descriptor` elements in the file. A `class-descriptor` element is used to describe a mapping between a Java class and a database table. It is discussed in the section called *Setting Up a Simple Java Class-to-Table Mapping*.

The values that can be set for the `isolation-level` attribute include:

❑   `read-uncommitted`

❑   `read-committed`

❑   `repeatable-read`

❑   `serializable`

❑   `optimistic`

If no value is set for the `isolation-level` attribute, it will default to `read-uncommitted`.

In the next several sections, we are going to study the individual pieces of the `repository.xml` file. We will start by discussing how to configure OJB to connect to a database. We will then look at how to perform a simple table mapping, and finally, work our way up to the more traditional database relationships, such as one-to-one, one-to-many, and many-to-many.

Setting up the JDBC Connection Information

Setting up OJB to connect to a database is a straightforward process. It involves setting up a <jdbc-connection-descriptor> element in the repository.xml file. The <jdbc-connection-descriptor> for the JavaEdge application is show below:

```
<jdbc-connection-descriptor
      platform="MySql"
      jdbc-level="2.0"
      driver="org.gjt.mm.mysql.Driver"
      protocol="jdbc"
      dbalias="waf"
      username="waf_user"
      password="password"
/>
```

The majority of the above attributes map exactly to the properties that can be set while making a database connection. They are used to open a JDBC connection and authenticate against it. It is not necessary to embed your username and password values in the repository.xml file. The PersistenceBroker class, which is used to open a database connection, can take a username and password as parameters in its open() method call. We will be covering the PersistenceBroker class in the section called *OJB in Action*.

The two attributes that are not standard to JDBC and particular to OJB are the platform and jdbc-level attributes. The platform attribute tells OJB the database platform that the repository.xml file is being run against. OJB uses a pluggable mechanism to handle calls to a specific database platform. The value specified in the platform attribute will map to a PlatformxxxImpl.java (located in the org.apache.ojb.broker.platforms package).

The following databases are supported officially by OJB:

- ❑ DB2
- ❑ Hsqldb (HyperSonic)
- ❑ Informix
- ❑ MsAccess (Microsoft Access)
- ❑ MsSQLServer (Microsoft SQL Servers)
- ❑ MySQL
- ❑ Oracle
- ❑ PostgresSQL
- ❑ Sybase
- ❑ SapDB

The jdbc-level attribute is used to indicate the level of JDBC compliance at which the JDBC driver being used runs. The values currently supported by the jdbc-level attribute are 1.0, 2.0, and 3.0. If it is not set, OJB will use the default value of 1.0.

OJB can integrate with a JNDI-bound data source. To do this, you need to set up the <jdbc-connection-descriptor> element to use the jndi-datasource-name attribute. For example, we can rewrite the above <jdbc-connection-descriptor> to use a JNDI data source, bound to the JBoss application server running the JavaEdge, as follows:

```
<jdbc-connection-descriptor
        platform="MySql"
        jdbc-level="2.0"
        jndi-datasource-name="java:/MySqlDS"
/>
```

It is important to note that when a JNDI data source is used in the `<jdbc-connection-descriptor>` tag, no `driver`, `protocol`, or `dbalias` is needed. All of this information is going to be defined via the application server's JNDI configuration. In our above example, the `username` and `password` attributes are not specified for the same reason.

Now, let's discuss how to map the JavaEdge classes to the database tables stored in our database.

Setting up a Simple Java Class-to-Table Mapping

Let's start with a simple mapping, the `MemberVO` class. The `MemberVO` class does not have any relationships with any of the classes in the JavaEdge application. The source code for the `MemberVO` is shown below:

```java
package com.wrox.javaedge.member;

import com.wrox.javaedge.common.*;

public class MemberVO extends ValueObject implements java.io.Serializable {

  private Long memberId;
  private String firstName;
  private String lastName;
  private String userId;
  private String password;
  private String email;

  public MemberVO() {}

  public MemberVO(String email, String firstName, String lastName,
                  Long memberId, String password, String userId) {
    this.email = email;
    this.firstName = firstName;
    this.lastName  = lastName;
    this.memberId  = memberId;
    this.password  = password;
    this.userId    = userId;
  }

  // access methods for attributes
  public String getFirstName() {
    return firstName;
  }

  public void setFirstName(String firstName) {
    this.firstName = firstName;
  }

  public String getLastName() {
    return lastName;
  }
```

```java
  public void setLastName(String lastName) {
    this.lastName = lastName;
  }

  public String getUserId() {
    return userId;
  }

  public void setUserId(String userId) {
    this.userId = userId;
  }

  public String getPassword() {
    return password;
  }

  public void setPassword(String password) {
    this.password = password;
  }

  public String getEmail() {
    return email;
  }

  public void setEmail(String email) {
    this.email = email;
  }

  public Long getMemberId() {
    return memberId;
  }

  public void setMemberId(Long memberId) {
    this.memberId = memberId;
  }
} // end MemberVO
```

As you can see the MemberVO class consists of nothing more than get()/set() methods for member attributes. To begin the mapping, we need to set up a <class-descriptor> tag:

```xml
<class-descriptor class="com.wrox.javaedge.member.MemberVO"
                  table="member">
...
</class-descriptor>
```

The above <class-descriptor> has two attributes in it: class and table. The class attribute gives the fully qualified Java class name that is going to be mapped. The table attribute defines the name of the database table to which the class is mapped.

A <class-descriptor> tag contains one or more <field-descriptor> tags. These tags are used to map the individual class attributes to their corresponding database columns. The column mappings for the MemberVO are as shown overleaf:

```
<field-descriptor id="1" name="memberId" column="member_id"
                  jdbc-type="BIGINT" primarykey="true"
                  autoincrement="true"/>
<field-descriptor id="2" name="firstName" column="first_name"
                  jdbc-type="VARCHAR"/>
<field-descriptor id="3" name="lastName" column="last_name"
                  jdbc-type="VARCHAR"/>
<field-descriptor id="4" name="userId" column="userid"
                  jdbc-type="VARCHAR"/>
<field-descriptor id="5" name="password" column="password"
                  jdbc-type="VARCHAR"/>
<field-descriptor id="6" name="email" column="email"
                  jdbc-type="VARCHAR"/>
```

Let's take the `<field-descriptor>` tag for the `memberId` and look at its components. This `<field-descriptor>` tag has six attributes. The first is the `id` attribute. This attribute contains a unique number that identifies the `<field-descriptor>`. This number must match the order in which the columns exist in the database. In other words, do not mix the order of the columns being mapped in the above field descriptors.

The `name` attribute defines the name of the Java attribute that is going to be mapped. The `column` attribute defines the name of the database column. By default, OJB directly sets the private attributes of the class using Java reflection. By using reflection, you do not need `get()` or `set()` methods for each attribute. By having OJB set the mapped attributes directly via reflection, you do not need to make the mapped attributes `public` or `protected`.

It is a good programming practice to have all attributes accessed in an object have a `get()`/`set()` method. However, while performing O/R mappings via OJB, there are two advantages of setting the private mapped attributes of a class directly. First, you can implement read-only data attributes by having OJB directly setting private attributes of a class and then providing a `get()` method to access the data. If you have OJB for mapping data using `get()` and `set()` methods, you cannot have only a `get()` method for an attribute, you must also have a `set()` method because OJB requires it.

The second advantage is that you can hide the underlying details of how the data is stored in the database. For example, all stories in the JavaEdge database are stored as BLOBs (Binary Large Objects). Their Java data type representation is an array of byte. Rather than forcing the clients using the mapped Java class to convert the `byte[]` array to a String object, we can tell OJB to map directly to the private attribute (of type `byte[]`) of the `Story` class. Then, we provide `get()`/`set()` methods for converting that array of bytes to a String object. The application need not to know that its data is actually being saved to the JavaEdge database as a BLOB.

If we were to tell OJB to map the data from the `story` table to the `StoryVO` object using the `get()`/`set()` methods of `StoryVO`, we would need to have a pair of `get()` and `set()` that would return an array of bytes as a return type and accept one as a parameter. This would unnecessarily expose the implementation details.

However, it is often desirable to have OJB go through `get()`/`set()` methods of the class. For example, in cases where there is a lightweight data transformation logic present in the `get()`/`set()` methods of the class that ensures the data is always properly formatted, sidestepping the `get()`/`set()` method would be undesirable. Fortunately, OJB's field manipulation behavior can be customized. The `OJB.properties` file contains a property called `PersistentFieldClass`. This property can be set with three different values, to change the way in which OJB sets properties for a class. These values are:

Property Value	Description
`org.apache.ojb.broker.metadata` `PeristentFieldDefaultImpl`	Default behavior. Directly sets a class attribute by using Java reflection.
`org.apache.ojb.broker.metadata` `PeristentFieldPropertyImpl`	Sets a class attribute by using the attribute's `get()`/`set()` method. The attribute defined in the `<field-descriptor>` tag must have a JavaBean-compliant `get()`/`set()` method. For example, if the attribute name is `memberId`, there must be a corresponding `getMemberId()` and `setMemberId()` method in the class.
`org.apache.ojb.broker.metadata` `PeristentFieldMaxPerformanceImpl`	This property value uses a class that bypasses several OJB internal field-management mechanisms and sets the fields directly. It is significantly faster than setting the attributes via other methods of access.

The `jdbc-type` attribute in the `<field-descriptor>` tag defines the OJB data type to which the `<field-descriptor>` maps. OJB supports a rich number of data types, including all the JDBC 2.0+ mapping types. However, you will still be dependent on the JDBC driver implementation for any idiosyncrasies centering on the JDBC 2.0+ data types.

The table below is a partial list of the JBDC mappings and their corresponding Java types supported by OJB:

JDBC Type	Java Type
TINYINT	byte
SMALLINT	short
INTEGER	int
BIGINT	long
REAL	float
FLOAT	double
DOUBLE	double
NUMERIC	java.math.BigDecimal
DECIMAL	Java.math.BigDecimal
BIT	byte
DATE	java.sql.Date
TIME	java.sql.Time
TIMESTAMP	Java.sql.Timestamp
CHAR	String
VARCHAR	String

Table continued on following page

JDBC Type	Java Type
LONGVARCHAR	String
CLOB	Clob
BLOB	Blob
BINARY	byte[]
VARBINARY	byte[]
LONGVARBINARY	byte[]

The above table is based on the OJB documentation. For a full explanation of OJB data type support, please refer to the HTML documentation supplied with the OJB distribution.

OJB allows you to define your own field conversions so that if there is a mismatch between an existing Java class (that is, domain model) and your database schema (that is, data model), you can implement your own FieldConversions class. The discussion of the FieldConversions class is outside the scope of this book. However, there is an excellent tutorial provided with the OJB documentation that comes with the OJB distribution (*ojb distribution*/doc/jdbc-types.html).

The fifth attribute in the memberId tag is the primarykey attribute. When set to true, this attribute indicates that the field being mapped is a primary key field. OJB supports the concept of a composite primary key. Having more than one <field-descriptor> element with a primarykey attribute set to true, tells OJB that a composite primary key is present.

The last attribute is autoincrement, which tells OJB to automatically generate a sequence value, whenever a database insert occurs for database record that has been mapped into the class. If the autoincrement flag is set to false or is not present in the tag, it is the responsibility of the developer to set the primary key.

Let's see how to set up **OJB Auto-Increment Features**. To use this feature, you need to install the OJB core tables. To install the OJB core tables, you need to perform the following steps:

1. Edit the ojb-distribution/build.properties file. At the top of the file you will see several different database profiles. Uncomment the mysql profile option (since that is the database being used for the JavaEdge application) and put any other database already uncommented in a comment.

2. Edit the ojb-distribution/profile/mysql.profile file. In this file, supply the connection information for the mysql database. For the JavaEdge application, these properties will look as follows:

```
dbmsName = MySql
jdbcLevel = 2.0
urlProtocol = jdbc
urlSubprotocol = mysql
urlDbalias = //localhost:3306/javaedge
createDatabaseUrl = ${urlProtocol}:${urlSubprotocol}:${urlDbalias}
buildDatabaseUrl = ${urlProtocol}:${urlSubprotocol}:${urlDbalias}
databaseUrl = ${urlProtocol}:${urlSubprotocol}:${urlDbalias}
databaseDriver = org.gjt.mm.mysql.Driver
databaseUser = jcarnell
databasePassword = netchange
databaseHost = 127.0.0.1
```

3. Run the `prepare-testdb` target in the `build.xml` file. This can be invoked by calling the following command at the command line:

`ant prepare-testdb`

4. This will generate the SQL scripts needed for the core tables and execute them against the JavaEdge database.

5. The OJB distribution comes with a number of unit tests and database tables. Running the `prepare-testdb` target will generate these additional unit test tables. In a production environment, the only tables needed by OJB are:

- ❑ OJB_HL_SEQ
- ❑ OJB_LOCKENTRY
- ❑ OJB_NRM
- ❑ OJB_DLIST
- ❑ OJB_DLIST_ENTRIES
- ❑ OJB_DSET
- ❑ OJB_DSET_ENTRIES
- ❑ OJB_DMAP
- ❑ OJB_DMAP_ENTRIES

In addition to the attributes described in the above `MemberVO` example, there are a number of additional attributes that can be defined in the `<field-descriptor>` tag. These attributes include:

- ❑ `nullable`
  If set to `true`, OJB will allow `null` values to be inserted into the database. If set to `false`, OJB will not allow a `null` value to be inserted. This attribute is set to `true` by default.

- ❑ `conversion`
  The fully qualified class name for any `FieldConversions` classes used to handle the custom data conversion.

- ❑ `length`
  Specifies the length of the field. This must match the length imposed on the database column in the actual database scheme.

- ❑ `precision/scale`
  Used to define the precision and scale for the float numbers being mapped to the database column.

In this section, we described how to implement a simple table mapping using OJB. However, the real power and flexibility related to OJB come into play while using OJB to cleanly capture the data relationships between entities in a database. The next several sections will demonstrate how to map common database relationships using OJB.

Mapping One-to-One

The first data relationship we are going to map is a one-to-one relationship. In the JavaEdge application, the StoryVO class has a one-to-one relationship with the MemberVO object (that is, one story can have one author that is a MemberVO).

We are not going to show the full code for the StoryVO class. Instead, we are going to show an abbreviated version of the class as shown below:

```
package com.wrox.javaedge.story;

import java.util.Vector;

import com.wrox.javaedge.common.ValueObject;
import com.wrox.javaedge.member.MemberVO;

public class StoryVO extends ValueObject {

  private Long storyId;
  private String storyTitle;
  private String storyIntro;
  private byte[] storyBody;
  private java.sql.Date submissionDate;
  private Long memberId;
  private MemberVO storyAuthor;
  public Vector comments = new Vector(); // of type StoryCommentVO
  //Remove a large hunk of the get()/set() methods to save space
  public Vector getComments() {
    return comments;
  }

  public void setComments(Vector comments) {
    this.comments=comments;
  }

  public MemberVO getStoryAuthor() {
    return storyAuthor;
  }

  public void setStoryAuthor(MemberVO storyAuthor) {
    this.storyAuthor = storyAuthor;
  }

} // end StoryVO
```

The StoryVO class has a single attribute called storyAuthor. The storyAuthor attribute holds a single reference to a MemberVO object. This MemberVO object holds all the information for the JavaEdge member who authored the story.

The following code is the <class-descriptor> tag that maps the StoryVO object to the story table and captures the data relationship between the story and member table.

```xml
<class-descriptor class="com.wrox.javaedge.story.StoryVO"
                  table="story">
  <field-descriptor id="1" name="storyId" column="story_id"
                    jdbc-type="BIGINT"  primarykey="true"
                    autoincrement="true"/>
  <field-descriptor id="2" name="memberId" column="member_id"
                    jdbc-type="BIGINT"/>
  <field-descriptor id="3" name="storyTitle" column="story_title"
                    jdbc-type="VARCHAR"/>
  <field-descriptor id="4" name="storyIntro"  column="story_intro"
                    jdbc-type="VARCHAR"/>
  <field-descriptor id="5" name="storyBody" column="story_body"
                    jdbc-type="LONGVARBINARY"/>
  <field-descriptor id="6" name="submissionDate"
                    column="submission_date" jdbc-type="DATE"/>

  <collection-descriptor name ="comments"
                    element-class-ref=
                            "com.wrox.javaedge.story.StoryCommentVO"
                    auto-retrieve="true" auto-update="true"
                    auto-delete="true">
    <inverse-foreignkey field-id-ref="2"/>
  </collection-descriptor>

  <reference-descriptor name="storyAuthor"
                    class-ref="com.wrox.javaedge.member.MemberVO"
                    auto-retrieve="true">
    <foreignkey field-id-ref="2"/>
  </reference-descriptor>

</class-descriptor>
```

The above <reference-descriptor> tag maps a record, retrieved from the member table, to the MemberVO object reference called storyAuthor. The <reference-descriptor>, has four attributes associated with it: name, class-ref, auto-retrieve, and auto-update.

The name attribute is used to specify the name of the attribute in the parent object, to which the retrieved data is mapped. In the above example, the member data retrieved for the story is going to be mapped to the storyAuthor attribute.

The class-ref attribute tells OJB the type of class that is going to be used to hold the mapped data. This attribute must define a fully qualified class name for a Java class. This class must be defined in the <class-descriptor> element in the repository.xml file.

The remaining two attributes, auto-retrieve and auto-update, control how OJB handles the child relationships, when a data operation is performed on the parent object. When set to true, the auto-retrieve tells OJB to automatically retrieve the member data for the story. If it is set to false, OJB will not perform a lookup and it will be the responsibility of the developer to ensure that child data is loaded.

> If OJB cannot find a child record associated with a parent or if the auto-retrieve attribute is set to false, it will leave the attribute that is going to be mapped in the state that it was, before the lookup was performed. For instance, in the StoryVO object, the storyAuthor property is initialized with a call to the default constructor of MemberVO class. If OJB is asked to look up a particular story and no member information is found in the member table, OJB will leave the storyAuthor attribute in the state that it was before the call was made. It is extremely important to remember this, if you leave child attributes with a null value.

You need to be careful about the depth of your object graph while using the `auto-retrieve` attribute. The indiscriminate use of the `auto-retrieve` attribute can retrieve a significant number of objects, because the child objects can contain other mapped objects, which might also be configured to automatically retrieve any other child objects.

The `auto-update` attribute controls whether OJB will update any changes made to set of child objects, after the parent object has been persisted. In other words, if the `auto-update` method is set to `true`, OJB will automatically update any of the changes made to the child objects mapped in `<class-descriptor>` for that parent. If this attribute is set to `false` or is not present in `<reference-descriptor>` tag, OJB will not update any mapped child objects.

OJB also provides an additional attribute, called `auto-delete`, that is not used in the `StoryVO` mapping. When set to `true`, the `auto-delete` method will delete any mapped child records when the parent object is deleted. This is a functional equivalent of a cascading delete in a relational database. You need to be careful while using this attribute, as you can accidentally delete records that you did not intend to delete, or end up cluttering your database with "orphaned" records, which have no context outside the deleted parent records.

> Note that the `auto-update` and `auto-delete` attributes function only while using the low-level Persistence Broker API (which we use for our code examples). The JDO and ODMG APIs do not support these attributes.

One or more `<foreignkey>` tags are embedded in the `<reference-descriptor>` tag. The `<foreignkey>` tag is used to tell OJB the id attribute of the `<field-descriptor>` attribute that the parent object is going to use to perform the join. The `<field-descriptor>`, contained inside the `<foreignkey>` tag, points back to the `<field-descriptor>` in the `<class-descriptor>` that is going to be used to join the class, defined in the `class-ref` attribute.

Consider the following snippet of our code:

```
<reference-descriptor name="storyAuthor"
                      class-ref="com.wrox.javaedge.member.MemberVO"
                      auto-retrieve="true" auto-update="true">
  <foreignkey field-id-ref="2"/>
</reference-descriptor>
```

The above code maps to the `<field-descriptor>` memberId. OJB will then use the memberId to map to the memberId attribute defined in the MemberVO `<class-descriptor>`. It is important to note that, while `<reference-descriptor>` tag above is mapping to the storyAuthor attribute in the StoryVO class, the name of the attribute being mapped in the `<foreignkey>` element must match the name of a `<field-descriptor>` defined in another class.

Thus, in the above example, the `<foreignkey>` maps to the memberId attribute of the StoryVO class descriptor. This means that there must be a corresponding `<field-descriptor>` for memberId in the `<class-descriptor>` element, which maps to the MemberVO object.

Mapping One-to-Many

Mapping a one-to-many relationship is as straightforward as mapping a one-to-one relationship. The story table has a one-to-many relationship with the story_comment table. This relationship is mapped in the StoryVO mappings via the `<collection-descriptor>` tag.

The `<collection-descriptor>` tag for the `StoryVO` mapping is shown below:

```
<collection-descriptor name ="comments"
      element-class-ref="com.wrox.javaedge.story.StoryCommentVO"
      auto-retrieve="true" auto-delete="true">
  <inverse-foreignkey field-id-ref="2"/>
</collection-descriptor>
```

The `name` attribute for the tag holds the name of the attribute in the mapped class, which is going to hold the child data retrieved from the database. In the case of the `StoryVO` mapping, this attribute will be the `comments` attribute. The `comments` attribute in the `StoryVO` code, shown in earlier section, is a Java `Vector` class.

OJB can use a number of data types to map the child data in a one-to-many relationship. These data types include:

- ❏ `Vector`
- ❏ `Collection`
- ❏ `Arrays`
- ❏ `List`

OJB also supports user-defined collections, but this subject is outside the scope of this book. For further information, please refer to the OJB documentation.

The `element-class-ref` attribute defines the fully-qualified Java class that is going to hold each of the records retrieved into the collection. Again, the Java class defined in this attribute must be mapped as a `<class-descriptor>` in the `repository.xml` file.

The `<collection-descriptor>` also has attributes for automatically retrieving, updating, and deleting the child records. These attributes have the same name and follow the same rules as the ones discussed in the section called *Mapping One-to-One*. There are a number of additional attributes in the `<collection-descriptor>` tag. These attributes deal with using proxy classes to help improve the performance and tags for performing the sorts. We will not be covering these attributes in greater detail.

A `<collection-descriptor>` tag can contain one or more `<inverse-foreignkey>` elements. The `<inverse-foreignkey>` element maps to a `<field-descriptor>` defined in the `<class-descriptor>` of the object that is being "joined".

> It is very important to understand the difference between an `<inverse-foreignkey>` and `<foreign-key>` element. An `<inverse-foreignkey>` element, used for mapping one-to-many and many-to-many relationship, points to a `<field-descriptor>` that is located outside the `<class-descriptor>`, where the `<inverse-foreignkey>` is defined. A `<foreign-key>` element, which is used for one-to-one mapping, points to a `<field-descriptor>` defined inside the `<class-descriptor>`, where the `<foreign-key>` element is located.
>
> This small and subtle difference can cause major headaches if the developer doing the O/R mapping does not understand the difference. OJB will not throw an error and will try to map the data.

Mapping Many-to-Many

The JavaEdge database does not contain any tables that have a many-to-many relationship. However, OJB does support many-to-many relationships in its table mappings. Let's refactor the one-to-many relationship between `story` and `story_comment` to a many-to-many relationship. To refactor this relationship, we need to create a join table called `story_story_comments`. This table will contain two columns: `story_id` and `comment_id`. We need to make only a small adjustment to the `StoryVO` mappings to map the data retrieved, via the `story_story_comment` table, to the `comments` vector in the `StoryVO`.

The revised mappings are as shown below:

```
<class-descriptor class="com.wrox.javaedge.story.StoryVO"
                  table="story">
  <field-descriptor id="1" name="storyId" column="story_id"
                    jdbc-type="BIGINT"  primarykey="true"
                    autoincrement="true"/>
  <field-descriptor id="2" name="memberId" column="member_id"
                    jdbc-type="BIGINT"/>
  <field-descriptor id="3" name="storyTitle" column="story_title"
                    jdbc-type="VARCHAR"/>
  <field-descriptor id="4" name="storyIntro"  column="story_intro"
                    jdbc-type="VARCHAR"/>
  <field-descriptor id="5" name="storyBody" column="story_body"
                    jdbc-type="LONGVARBINARY"/>
  <field-descriptor id="6" name="submissionDate"
                    column="submission_date" jdbc-type="DATE"/>

  <reference-descriptor name="storyAuthor"
                        class-ref="com.wrox.javaedge.member.MemberVO"
                        auto-retrieve="true">
    <foreignkey field-id-ref="2"/>
  </reference-descriptor>

  <collection-descriptor name ="comments"
                         element-class-ref=
                                "com.wrox.javaedge.story.StoryCommentVO"
                         auto-retrieve="true" auto-delete="true"
                         indirection_table="STORY_STORY_COMMENTS">

    <fk-pointing-to-this-class column="STORY_ID"/>
    <fk-pointing-to-this-class column="COMMENT_ID"/>
  </collection-descriptor>

</class-descriptor>
```

There are two differences between this and one-to-many mapping. The first is the use of the `indirection_table` attribute in the `<collection-descriptor>` tag. This attribute holds the name of join table used to join the `story` and `story_comment` table. The other difference is that the `<collection-descriptor>` tag does not contain an `<inverse-foreignkey>` tag. Instead, there are two `<fk-pointing-to-this-class>` tags. The `column` attribute, in both these tags, points to the database columns, which will be used to perform the join between the `story` and `story_comment` tables.

You will notice that even though the mapping for the StoryVO has changed, the actual class code has not. As far as applications using the StoryVO are concerned, there has been no change in the data relationships. This gives the database developer a flexibility to refactor a database relationship, while minimizing the risk that the change will break the existing application code.

Now, we will see how OJB is actually used to retrieve and manipulate the data.

OJB in Action

OJB was used to build all the DAOs used in the JavaEdge application. Using an O/R mapping tool like OJB allowed the JavaEdge development team to significantly reduce the amount of time and effort needed to build our data-access tier. The following code is used to build the StoryDAO. All the DAOs were implemented using OJB Persistence Broker API. The code for other DAOs is available for download at http://wrox.com/books/1861007817.htm.

```java
package com.wrox.javaedge.story.dao;

import java.util.Collection;

import org.apache.ojb.broker.PersistenceBroker;
import org.apache.ojb.broker.PersistenceBrokerException;
import org.apache.ojb.broker.query.Criteria;
import org.apache.ojb.broker.query.Query;
import org.apache.ojb.broker.query.QueryByCriteria;
import org.apache.ojb.broker.query.QueryFactory;

import com.wrox.javaedge.common.DataAccessException;
import com.wrox.javaedge.common.DataAccessObject;
import com.wrox.javaedge.common.ServiceLocator;
import com.wrox.javaedge.common.ServiceLocatorException;
import com.wrox.javaedge.common.ValueObject;
import com.wrox.javaedge.story.StoryVO;

public class StoryDAO implements DataAccessObject {

  public static final int MAXIMUM_TOPSTORIES = 11;

  // Create Log4j category instance for logging
  static private org.apache.log4j.Category log =
              org.apache.log4j.Category.getInstance(StoryDAO.class.getName());

  public ValueObject findByPK(String primaryKey) throws DataAccessException {
    PersistenceBroker broker = null;
    StoryVO storyVO = null;

    try {
      broker = ServiceLocator.getInstance().findBroker();
      storyVO = new StoryVO();
      storyVO.setStoryId(new Long(primaryKey));

      Query query = new QueryByCriteria(storyVO);
      storyVO = (StoryVO) broker.getObjectByQuery(query);
```

```
      } catch (ServiceLocatorException e) {
        log.error("PersistenceBrokerException thrown in StoryDAO.findByPK(): "
                + e.toString());
        throw new DataAccessException("Error in StoryDAO.findByPK(): "
                                      + e.toString(),e);
    } finally {
      if (broker != null) {
        broker.close();
      }
    }

    return storyVO;
  }

  public Collection findTopStory() throws DataAccessException {
    PersistenceBroker broker = null;
    Collection results = null;

    Criteria criteria = new Criteria();
    criteria.addOrderByDescending("storyId");

    Query query = QueryFactory.newQuery(StoryVO.class, criteria);

    query.setStartAtIndex(1);
    query.setEndAtIndex(MAXIMUM_TOPSTORIES - 1);

    try {
      broker = ServiceLocator.getInstance().findBroker();
      results = (Collection) broker.getCollectionByQuery(query);

    } catch (ServiceLocatorException e) {
      log.error("PersistenceBrokerException thrown in
                StoryDAO.findTopStory(): " + e.toString());
      throw new DataAccessException("Error in StoryDAO.findTopStory(): " +
                                    e.toString(),e);
    } finally {
      if (broker != null) broker.close();
    }

    return results;
  }

  public void insert(ValueObject insertRecord) throws DataAccessException {
    PersistenceBroker broker = null;
    try {
      StoryVO storyVO = (StoryVO) insertRecord;

      broker = ServiceLocator.getInstance().findBroker();
      broker.beginTransaction();
      broker.store(storyVO);
      broker.commitTransaction();

    } catch (PersistenceBrokerException e) {
// if something went wrong: rollback
```

```
            broker.abortTransaction();
            log.error("PersistenceBrokerException thrown in StoryDAO.insert(): "
                    + e.toString());
            e.printStackTrace();

            throw new DataAccessException("Error in StoryDAO.insert(): "
                                    + e.toString(),e);

        } catch (ServiceLocatorException e) {
            log.error("ServiceLocatorException thrown in StoryDAO.insert(): "
                    + e.toString());
            throw new DataAccessException("ServiceLocatorException thrown in
                                    StoryDAO.insert()",e);
        } finally {
          if (broker != null) {
                    broker.close();
          }
        }
    }

public void delete(ValueObject deleteRecord) throws DataAccessException {
    PersistenceBroker broker = null;

    try {
        broker = ServiceLocator.getInstance().findBroker();
        StoryVO storyVO = (StoryVO) deleteRecord;

        //Begin the transaction.
        broker.beginTransaction();
        broker.delete(storyVO);
        broker.commitTransaction();

    } catch (PersistenceBrokerException e) {
        // if something went wrong: rollback
        broker.abortTransaction();
        log.error("PersistenceBrokerException thrown in StoryDAO.delete(): "
                + e.toString());
        e.printStackTrace();

        throw new DataAccessException("Error in StoryDAO.delete()", e);

    } catch (ServiceLocatorException e) {
        throw new DataAccessException("ServiceLocator exception in " +
                                "StoryDAO.delete()", e);
    } finally {
        if (broker != null) broker.close();
    }
}

public void update(ValueObject updateRecord) throws DataAccessException {
    PersistenceBroker broker = null;

    try {
        StoryVO storyVO = (StoryVO) updateRecord;
```

```
      broker = ServiceLocator.getInstance().findBroker();
      broker.beginTransaction();
      broker.store(storyVO);
      broker.commitTransaction();

  } catch (PersistenceBrokerException e) {
      // if something went wrong: rollback
      broker.abortTransaction();
      log.error("PersistenceBrokerException thrown in StoryDAO.update(): "
                + e.toString());
      e.printStackTrace();

      throw new DataAccessException("Error in StoryDAO.update()", e);

  } catch (ServiceLocatorException e) {
      log.error("ServiceLocatorException thrown in StoryDAO.delete(): "
                + e.toString());
      throw new DataAccessException("ServiceLocatorException error in "
                                    + "StoryDAO.delete()", e);
  } finally {
      if (broker != null) broker.close();
  }

}

public Collection findAllStories() throws DataAccessException {
  PersistenceBroker broker = null;
  Collection results = null;

  try {
    Criteria criteria = new Criteria();
    criteria.addOrderByDescending("storyId");

    Query query = QueryFactory.newQuery(StoryVO.class, criteria);

    query.setStartAtIndex(1);

    broker = ServiceLocator.getInstance().findBroker();
    results = (Collection) broker.getCollectionByQuery(query);

  } catch (ServiceLocatorException e) {
      log.error("ServiceLocatorException thrown in StoryDAO.findAllStories(): "
                + e.toString());
      throw new DataAccessException("ServiceLocatorException error in "
                                    + "StoryDAO.findAllStories()", e);
} finally {
      if (broker != null) broker.close();
  }

  return results;
  }
}
```

Now, we will examine the above code and discuss how OJB can be used to:

❑   Perform queries to retrieve data

❑   Insert and update data in the JavaEdge database

❑   Delete data from the JavaEdge database

Retrieving Data: A Simple Example

The first piece of code that we are going to look at shows how to retrieve a single record from the JavaEdge database. We will look at the findByPK() method from the StoryDAO:

```
public ValueObject findByPK(String primaryKey) throws DataAccessException {
  PersistenceBroker broker = null;
  StoryVO storyVO = null;

  try {
    broker = ServiceLocator.getInstance().findBroker();
    storyVO = new StoryVO();
    storyVO.setStoryId(new Long(primaryKey));

    Query query = new QueryByCriteria(storyVO);
    storyVO = (StoryVO) broker.getObjectByQuery(query);

  } catch (ServiceLocatorException e) {
    log.error("PersistenceBrokerException thrown in StoryDAO.findByPK(): "
            + e.toString());
    throw new DataAccessException("Error in StoryDAO.findByPK(): "
                                  + e.toString(),e);
  } finally {
    if (broker != null) broker.close();
  }

  return storyVO;
}
```

The first step in the code is to get an instance of a PersistenceBroker object:

```
broker = ServiceLocator.getInstance().findBroker();
```

A PersistenceBroker is used to carry out all the data actions against the JavaEdge database. We have written the code for retrieving a PersistenceBroker in the findBroker() method of the ServiceLocator class (discussed in Chapter 4. The method, shown below, will use the PersistenceBrokerFactory class to retrieve a PersistenceBroker and return it to the method caller:

```
public PersistenceBroker findBroker() throws ServiceLocatorException{
  PersistenceBroker broker = null;
  try {
    broker = PersistenceBrokerFactory.createPersistenceBroker();
```

```
  } catch(PBFactoryException e) {
    e.printStackTrace();
    throw new ServiceLocatorException("PBFactoryException error " +
            "occurred while parsing the repository.xml file in " +
            "ServiceLocator constructor", e);
  }
  return broker;
}
```

In the above method, the application is going to create a `PersistenceBroker` by calling the `createPersistenceBroker()` method in the `PersistenceBrokerFactory` without passing in a value. When no value is passed into the method, the `PersistenceBrokerFactory` will look at the root of the JavaEdge's `classes` directory for a `repository.xml` file (`/WEB-INF/classes`). If it cannot find the `repository.xml` file in this location, it will throw a `PBFactoryException` exception.

After a `broker` has been retrieved in the `findByPK()` method, an empty `StoryVO` instance, called `storyVO` is created. Since the `findByPK()` method is used to look up the record by its primary key, we call the `setStoryId()`, in which the `primaryKey` variable is passed:

```
storyVO = new StoryVO();
storyVO.setStoryId(new Long(primaryKey));
```

Once the `storyVO` instance has been created, it is going to be passed to a constructor in a `QueryByCritieria` object:

```
Query query = new QueryByCriteria(storyVO);
```

A `QueryByCriteria` class is used to build the search criteria for a query. When a "mapped" object, being mapped in the `repository.xml` file, is passed in as a parameter in the `QueryByCriteria` constructor, the constructor will look at each of the non-null attributes in the object and create a `where` clause that maps to these values.

Since the code in the `findByPK()` method is performing a lookup based on the primary key of the `story` table (that is, `story_id`), the WHERE clause generated by the `QueryByCriteria` constructor would look like:

```
WHERE story_id=?    /*Where the question mark would be the value set in the
                setStoryId() method*/
```

If you want to perform a lookup for an object by the story title, you would call `setStoryTitle()` method instead of the `setStoryID()`. This would generate the following `where` clause:

```
WHERE story_title=?
```

The `QueryByCriteria` object implements a `Query` interface. This interface is a generic interface for different mechanisms for querying OJB. Some of the other mechanisms for retrieving data, via the **OJB PB** API, include:

❏   `QueryBySQL`: Lets you issue SQL calls to retrieve data

❏   `QueryByMtoNCriteria`: Lets you issue queries against the tables that have a many-to-many data relationship

We will not be covering these objects in any greater detail. Instead, we are going to focus on building the criteria using the `QueryByCriteria` object.

Once a `query` instance is created, we are going to pass it to the `getObjectByQuery()` method in `broker`. This method will retrieve a single instance of an object based on the criteria defined in `Query` object passed into the method:

```
storyVO = (StoryVO) broker.getObjectByQuery(query);
```

If the `getObjectByQuery()` method does not find the object by the presented criteria, a value of `null` is returned. If more than one record is found by the above call, `PersistenceBrokerException` is thrown. It is important to remember that you need to cast the value returned by the `getObjectByQuery()` method to the type you are retrieving.

If we are using a `broker` to carry out the data actions, we need to make sure the `broker` is closed. A `broker` instance is a functional equivalent of a JDBC database connection. Failure to close the `broker` can result in connection leaks. To ensure that the `broker` connection is closed, we put the following code in a `finally` block:

```
finally{
   if (broker != null) broker.close();
}
```

Retrieving Data: A More Complicated Example

In the previous section, we looked at a very simple example of retrieving data using OJB. OJB can be used to build some very sophisticated queries by using its `Criteria` class. This class contains a number of methods that represent common components of a WHERE clause. Some of these methods are listed below:

Method Name	Description
`addEqualTo(String attribute, Object value)`	Generates an equal to clause, where `attribute = value`
`addGreaterThan(String attribute, Object value)`	Generates a greater than clause, where `attribute > value`
`addGreaterOrEqualThan(String attribute, Object value)`	Generates a greater than or equals to clause, where `attribute >= value`
`addLessThan(String attribute, Object value)`	Generates a less than clause, where `attribute < value`
`addLessOrEqualThan(String attribute, Object value)`	Generates a less than or equals to clause, where `attribute <= value`

Table continued on following page

Method Name	Description
addIsNull(String attribute)	Generates an IS NULL clause
addNotNull(String attribute)	Generates a NOT NULL clause
addIsLike(String attribute, Object value)	Generates a LIKE clause
addOrderByAscending(String fieldName)	Generates an Order By Ascending clause
addOrderByDescending(String fieldName)	Generates an Order By Descending clauses
addAndCriteria(Criteria criteria)	Uses And to ensure that both the criteria objects are applied
addOrCriteria(Criteria criteria)	Uses Or to ensure that one of the two criteria objects is applied
AddSql(String sqlStatement)	Adds a piece of a raw SQL to the criteria. This is extremely useful, if you want to use a vendor-specific SQL extension.

The above table is by no means exhaustive and it is highly recommended that you read the JavaDocs for the Criteria objects, to see the full list of methods available in the class.

Based on the methods above, let's build a more complex query. Let's say we want to write an OJB query that would retrieve a Collection of JavaEdge member records whose last name is "Smith" and whose first name starts with a "J". In addition, we want all of these records to be in ascending order of the first name. To do this we would write the following code fragment:

```
Criteria criteriaEquals = new Criteria ();  //Criteria for the equals
Criteria criteriaLike = new Criteria ();    //Criteria for the like

criteriaEquals.addEqualTo("last_name", "Smith");
criteriaLike.addIsLike("first_name", "J%");

criteriaEquals.addAndCriteria(criteriaLike);   //Anding the two pieces
criteriaEquals.addOrderByAscending("first_name"); //Adding an order by
Query query = new QueryByCritieria(MemberVO.class, criteriaEquals);

Collection results = broker.getCollectionByQuery (Query);
```

In the above code fragment, we first need to create Criteria objects for our query. We then need to set the behavior of each of the Criteria objects. The criteriaEquals instance sets the query clause to have the last name equal to "Smith". It does this by calling the addEqualTo() method and passing the database column (last_name) and the value ("Smith") as parameters into the method call:

```
criteriaEquals.addEqualTo ("last_name", "Smith");
```

> Note that while building your database queries, you need to use the name of the database column and not the attribute in the Java class.

The second condition is implemented by calling the addIsLike() method in the criteriaLike object and passing the parameter values of "first_name" and "J%":

```
criteriaLike.addIsLike ("first_name","J%");
```

To ensure that both the conditions are applied, the addAndCriteria() method of the criteriaEquals object is called and the criteriaLike object is passed as parameter:

```
criteriaEquals.addAndCriteria (criteriaLike);   //Anding the two pieces
```

The last step is to add the OrderBy clause to our where statement. This is done by calling the addOrderByAscending() method and passing in the name of the database column:

```
criteriaEquals.addOrderByAscending ("first_name"); //Adding an order by
```

The where clause generated by the building of the above criteriaEquals object would look as shown below:

```
WHERE last_name="Smith" and first_name like "J%" ORDER BY first_name ASCENDING
```

> To see the SQL code generated by OJB, you need to set org.apache.ojb.broker.accesslayer.sql.SqlGeneratorDefaultImpl.LogLevel to DEBUG. All the SQL code, generated by OJB, will be written to System.out. Also, there are a number of other logging options available that can be set in the OJB.properties file.

Once the criteria have been built out, it can be passed as a parameter to the QueryCriteria constructor:

```
Query query = new QueryByCritieria (MemberVO.class, criteriaEquals);
```

Note that this time we are passing in the MemberVO class and the criteriaEquals object that is built. Since we are retrieving more than one record, we are going to call the getCollectionByQuery() method in the broker instance:

```
Collection results = broker.getCollectionByQuery (Query);
```

The getCollectionByQuery() method will return a Collection of all of the records. The data type in the collection will be of the type Class, passed in the QueryCriteria constructor.

Storing Data Using OJB

Inserting and updating data with OJB is very easy. Both of these data operations require the use of the store() method in a PersistenceBroker instance. The following code is the insert() method for the StoryDAO method:

```
public void insert(ValueObject insertRecord) throws DataAccessException {
  PersistenceBroker broker = null;
  try {
    StoryVO storyVO = (StoryVO) insertRecord;

    broker = ServiceLocator.getInstance().findBroker();
    broker.beginTransaction();
    broker.store(storyVO);
    broker.commitTransaction();

  } catch (PersistenceBrokerException e) {
    // if something went wrong: rollback
    broker.abortTransaction();
    System.out.println(e.getMessage());
    e.printStackTrace();

    throw new DataAccessException("Error in StoryDAO.insert(): "
                                  + e.toString(),e);
  } catch(ServiceLocatorException e) {
    System.out.println("ServiceLocatorException thrown in StoryDAO.insert():
                        " + e.toString());
    throw new DataAccessException("ServiceLocatorException thrown in " +
                                  "StoryDAO.insert()",e);
  } finally {
    if (broker != null) broker.close();
  }
}
```

The first step for saving the data is to retrieve a `broker` instance. Once a `broker` instance is retrieved via the `ServiceLocator.getInstance().findBroker()` method, we need to set the transactional boundary for our transaction. This is accomplished by calling the `beginTransaction()` method on the `broker` instance:

```
broker.beginTransaction();
```

Now, we can actually insert or update the data into the database via a call to the `store()` method of the `broker` instance and pass the object that is to be stored in the database:

```
broker.store(storyVO);
```

The OJB runtime engine will determine whether the data contained within the `StoryVO` object needs to be inserted or updated. Depending on how the `repository.xml` mappings are done, the `store()` method call will also persist any of the child objects associated with the `StoryVO` instance.

The last step in the process is to commit the transaction via the `broker.commitTransaction()` method call:

```
broker.commitTransaction();
```

If any exceptions are thrown while processing the user request, such as a `PersistenceBrokerException`, a call to the `broker.abortTransaction` will roll back any changes currently made within that transactional context.

```
   } catch (PersistenceBrokerException e){
     // if something went wrong: rollback
     broker.abortTransaction();
     System.out.println(e.getMessage());
     e.printStackTrace();

     throw new DataAccessException("Error in StoryDAO.insert(): "
                                  + e.toString(),e);
   }
```

If any exception is caught, the transaction is aborted and the exception is rethrown as a
DataAccessException.

Deleting Data with OJB

The following code shows the delete() method from the StoryDAO:

```
public void delete(ValueObject deleteRecord) throws DataAccessException {
  PersistenceBroker broker = null;

  try {
    broker = ServiceLocator.getInstance().findBroker();
    StoryVO storyVO = (StoryVO) deleteRecord;

    //Begin the transaction.
    broker.beginTransaction();
    broker.delete(storyVO);
    broker.commitTransaction();
  } //Rest of the code has been omitted
```

The delete() method in a broker instance will remove a record from the database, based on the object
passed into the method. If you want to isolate the transaction, you must use the beginTransaction() and
commitTransaction() or abortTransaction() methods shown in the previous section.

Bringing It All Together

So far, we have demonstrated how to use the OJB to perform common data transactions. However, the
business logic should never be exposed to data access code, whether implemented via JDBC or OJB.
Therefore, we should wrap all the code using a Data Access Object pattern.

The following code is the implementation of the addStory() method of the StoryManagerBD class. It is
being shown to demonstrate how a DAO is actually used:

```
public void addStory(StoryVO storyVO) throws ApplicationException {
  try {
StoryDAO storyDAO = new StoryDAO();
    storyDAO.insert(storyVO);
  } catch (DataAccessException e) {
    throw new ApplicationException("DataAccessException Error in
        StoryManagerBean.addStory(): " + e.toString(), e);
  }
}
```

The preceding code is for inserting a `StoryVO` into the database. Note that, in the entire code, we have not tied our business logic to a particular data access technology or database. We can easily rewrite the above `StoryDAO` to use JDBC or entity beans and the application code would never know the difference. This small piece of abstraction can make a huge difference in terms of long-term maintainability and extensibility of the application.

For instance, we could easily write a different `StoryDAO` implementation using different data access technologies. The following object diagram illustrates this:

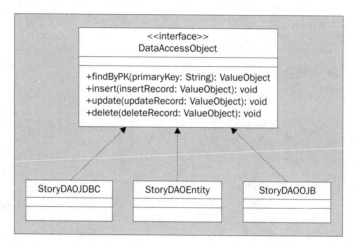

In the above model, there could be three different implementations of the `StoryDAO`. The application using the DAO would never be allowed to directly create one of the three classes above. Instead, we could introduce a `DAOFactory`, which would be responsible for creating the appropriate `StoryDAO` instance on behalf of the application. An example of the `DAOFactory` is shown below:

```
package com.wrox.javaedge.common;

import java.util.*;
import java.io.*;

public class DAOFactory {
  private static Properties classInfo = new Properties();
  private static DAOFactory daoFactory = null;

  public static final String MEMBERDAO = "dao.member.impl";
  public static final String STORYDAO  = "dao.story.impl";

  private DAOFactory() {
    try {
      String daoFileName = System.getProperty("datatier.properties", "");
      classInfo.load(new FileInputStream(daoFileName));
    } catch(IOException e) {
      System.out.println(e.toString());
    }
  }

  // Instantiate a new instance of the class
```

```
static {
  daoFactory = new DAOFactory();
}

// Returns a single instance of DAOFactory
public static DAOFactory getInstance() {
  return daoFactory;
}

// The getDAO() method will retrieve a DAO requested by the user.
public DataAccessObject getDAO(String desiredDAO) throws
    DataAccessException {
  Object dao = null;

  // If the classInfo properties object contains the key requested by the user.
  if (classInfo.containsKey(desiredDAO)) {

    try {
      // Get the fully qualified class name
      String className = (String) classInfo.get(desiredDAO);

      // Retrieve a Class object for the requested className
      Class desiredClass = Class.forName(className);

      // Retrieve a new instance of the requested DAO
      dao = desiredClass.newInstance();

    } catch(InstantiationException e) {
      throw new DataAccessException("InstantiationException " +
                          "in DAOFactory.getDAO(): " + desiredDAO, e);

    } catch(IllegalAccessException e) {
      throw new DataAccessException("IllegalAccessException " +
                          "in DAOFactory.getDAO(): " + desiredDAO, e);

    } catch(ClassNotFoundException e) {
      throw new DataAccessException("DataAccessException " +
                          "in DAOFactory.getDAO(): " + desiredDAO,e);
    }

    return (DataAccessObject) dao;

  } else {
    throw new DataAccessException("Unable to locate the DAO requested " +
                          "in DAOFactory.getDAO(): " + desiredDAO);
  }
}
```

We are not going to walk through the above code in great detail because we did not use a DAO Factory pattern in our JavaEdge implementation. Since this is a simple application and all of our data access code was going to be written in OJB, using the above DAOFactory implementation would be too heavy. However, the above DAOFactory implementation does allow us to declare DAO implementations that are going to be used for the application without directly hardcoding the creation of that object in the application source. The addStory() method, shown earlier, rewritten to use the above DAOFactory implementation would be as shown overleaf:

```
public void addStory(StoryVO storyVO) throws ApplicationException{
  try {
    DAOFactory daoFactory.getInstance()
    StoryDAO storyDAO = (StoryDAO) daoFactory.getDAO(DAOFactory.STORYDAO);
    storyDAO.insert(storyVO);

  } catch (DataAccessException e) {
    throw new ApplicationException("DataAccessException Error in " +
                                  "StoryManagerBean.addStory(): " +
                                  e.toString(), e);
  }
}
```

The actual Java class that implements the StoryDAO is defined in a Java properties file. The name and location of this properties file is determined by a user-defined Java system property called datatier.properties. A user can define this property by setting the CATALINA_OPTS environment variable to be equal to:

-Ddatatier.properties=**full name and path of the Java file containing the DAO class information.**

The following example shows this properties file:

```
dao.member.impl=com.wrox.javaedge.member.dao.MemberDAO
dao.story.impl=com.wrox.javaedge.story.dao.StoryDAO
```

Summary

Building a data access tier is more than picking a particular data access or database technology. It needs basic design patterns, which will allow the development team to abstract away the data access implementation details. In this chapter, we discussed the following two J2EE design patterns that help us accomplish these goals:

❑   The Data Access Object (DAO) pattern

❑   The Value Object (VO) pattern

The DAO pattern allows us to abstract away the CRUD (Create, Replace, Update, and Delete) logic associated with the data store interactions. We need to remember the following key points about the DAO pattern:

❑   DAOs should completely abstract away the details of how data is retrieved and manipulated.

❑   Watch the granularity of your DAOs. You need to understand how your data is used and make sure you do not model your DAOs solely based on your physical data model.

❑   DAOs afford the opportunity to combine the data from multiple data sources behind a single logical view. Do not write your DAOs to mirror the physical location of different pieces of the same customer data.

The VO pattern is used to wrap data retrieved from the database. It is an object-based representation of relational-oriented data. Key points of the Value Object pattern are:

❑ Watch the number of Value Objects returned by a DAO. Returning a large number of VOs results in a large amount of memory being consumed.

❑ Watch the level of your object graphs. If you make the object graphs too deep, it will result in multiple levels of data for a single record.

❑ Value Objects merely represent a particular view of the data. It is not necessary to have one Value Object return all of the data associated with a particular business entity. Understand how your data is being used and build your Value Objects accordingly.

We also discussed how O/R mapping tools could save a significant amount of the developers' time for writing the data access tier. One of these tools, OJB, is an easy-to-use open source tool that offers almost all the features found in the similar commercial products. In this chapter, we discussed how OJB can be used to:

❑ Perform mappings between Java classes and database tables. The mappings demonstrated in the chapter include:

  ❑ Simple table mappings

  ❑ One-to-One mappings

  ❑ One-to-Many mappings

  ❑ Many-to-Many mappings

❑ Perform data-related tasks including:

  ❑ Retrieving data using OJB

  ❑ Inserting and updating data using OJB

  ❑ Deleting data with OJB

The following chapters are going to focus on building the repeatable software development processes using open source development tools. Chapter 6 will focus on using Velocity to further separate your application logic using a templating language. Chapter 7 will use the Lucene search engine to allow us to add indexing and search capabilities to our application. Chapter 8 will demonstrate how to use the Jakarta Group's Ant tool to build a repeatable and automated build process.

6

Templates and Velocity

So far we've seen how the use of development frameworks and judicious use of design patterns can help to separate the concerns of our web applications. For the most part with concentrated on the main core of our application, and how to separate our application logic. Although not necessarily as important as the business logic, we can take this process one step further and separate our application's Java code from our presentation through the use of templates. So in this chapter, we will describe the problems that template engines can solve, and how to use one such template engine, Velocity.

We'll be covering:

❑   The syntax and directives for the Velocity Templating Language

❑   Using Velocity with Java

❑   Using Velocity in web applications

We are going to design and implement an RSS (Really Simple Syndication, or RDF Syndication Source) content feed for JavaEdge that works with Struts using Velocity, and demonstrate the use of the Velocity tag library for JSP.

Separating Presentation from Java Code

The Concern Slush antipattern occurs in applications when the business logic, application content, data access, look-and-feel, and navigation are all put together in a hard-to-maintain slush. An example of this would be a giant servlet that contains methods that make JDBC calls, intermingle the results with HTML markup, and then create JavaScript validation routines. It becomes even worse when many of these servlets for different parts of the application (search, shopping cart, order verification, etc.) are written by different developers.

> **One of the problems is that servlets and JSP make it easy for developers to mix anything they want into the presentation layer because it's just Java code.**

One of the solutions to avoid this antipattern is to investigate alternative presentation layer technologies that let Java developers restrict the objects available in the user interface code. This can lead to a productive working relationship between an HTML designer, who knows some template language concepts, and a Java developer who doesn't have to worry about look-and-feel or client-side scripting.

One of the possible solutions is the Jakarta Apache Group's **Velocity**. Velocity is a combination of a template processing engine and a template language that is designed to work with other web application frameworks in place of JSP. You can also use Velocity for general-purpose template tasks, such as generating e-mail, static HTML files, or legacy data-integration files. Using Velocity to generate HTML or XML from an application is very easy. Velocity can be used inside a JSP page with the Velocity tag library, which we will discuss in the section on *JSP and Velocity*.

Using Velocity to create templates for your application is similar to using XML as a data transfer format. In either case, you don't need to write your own parser. It provides a well-defined template language and a clean Java API for working with these templates.

Velocity cleanly separates presentation and Java code, as it is impossible to write Java code directly into a Velocity template. There isn't a Velocity equivalent of a JSP scriptlet. Velocity supports a limited number of **Velocity Template Language (VTL)** constructs that are needed for layout purposes. Java objects from your application can be merged with a Velocity template to produce HTML, XML, Java code, or any other text.

The Java developer can create new objects, such as a User, and pass them to the template. The HTML designer can use the properties on the User object inside a Velocity template, by putting variable references into the HTML. Velocity will replace these references with the properties in the specific User object that is passed into the template. This object and any other data or helper objects are passed to the template inside a container, known as a **context** in Velocity.

Another problem that frequently occurs is the desire to use a template to create text, HTML, or XML content by merging data with a file that contains all of the necessary mark-up and layout. This could be used to generate static content for a web site from tables in a database, or to generate e-mails with personalized content. It's easy to start off writing a simple Java application that reads in a text file, substitutes data for a few special tags provided to the application, and then writes its output to another file or set of files. Unfortunately, these applications have a tendency to grow, and eventually the special tags become a language of their own. Rather than trying to re-implement the if statement or a collection iterator inside your code, it's better to look for a third-party solution to solve the pain.

One solution would be to use XSLT, if your input data is XML and your output is XML or well-structured HTML. XSLT has a steep learning curve and it's much easier to teach Velocity to web designers. Some of your developers also may not be familiar with declarative programming, especially if they worked with HTML and JavaScript as user interface developers.

We'll demonstrate using Velocity as a template language. We're going to create a **Really Simple Syndication (RSS) 2.0** feed for our JavaEdge application. This is going to allow other web sites to pick up our headlines and display them. This is a standard for news sites, bloggers, and web communities. We're going to emphasize on how to use Velocity as a templating tool, rather than focusing on the details of content syndication.

For more details on content syndication and RSS 2.0, visit Dave Winer's Userland site:
http://backend.userland.com/rss

Velocity

In this section, we're going to discuss how to use Velocity and primarily the Velocity language and API.

We're going to cover:

❑   What Velocity does, and how the engine works

❑   Using Velocity's context

❑   Using the Velocity GUI to run Velocity code outside the servlet container for debugging

❑   The syntax and keywords of the Velocity Template Language (VTL)

❑   Using Velocity from JSP, with the Velocity tag library.

❑   Creating an RSS 2.0 feed with Velocity for the JavaEdge application

The Velocity web site can be found at http://jakarta.apache.org/velocity.

How Velocity Works

Velocity is a processing engine that is fed a **context**, which contains name-value pairs of variable names and Java objects, and a **template** that usually contains HTML or XML interspersed with Velocity markup. The context is merged with the template to create output, which is then displayed to the end user or written to a file. The template contains variable references and Velocity Template Language (VTL) directives. The context contains a map of variable names to Java objects.

When the template is evaluated, each Java object represented by a Velocity variable is pulled out of the context. The VTL directives in the template are processed in order. We will discuss the directives in the section called *The Velocity Templating Language.*

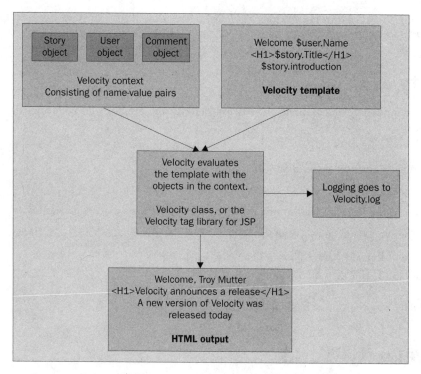

Variables can be put into the context by our Java application, just like a Map. Variables can also be put into the context when the template is evaluated with the #set() VTL directive. We'll discuss how to use the context in more detail in the next section.

Since variables in Velocity reference Java objects, it's possible to access properties or methods on these objects. Velocity uses reflection to determine which methods are available in the objects in the context. If the variable is just a reference to the object itself, the Velocity engine will call the toString() method in the object and render it to the output. This all happens behind the scenes, and you don't need to do anything special if the variable is not an instance of a String object. The names for the Java objects in the context are assigned when the Java application adds the object to the context, and are referenced in the Velocity template with a prefix of a dollar sign ($).

Here is an example of a Velocity template:

```
<a href="$link.create("ViewProfile.vm")">View Profile</a>
<p>
<a href="$link.create("AddUser.vm")">Add User</a>
<p>
<a href="$link.create("Login.vm")">Login</a>
<p>
Hello $user.FirstName
```

As you can see, the HTML contains additional markup that Velocity parses out. In this example, there are Java objects identified as $link and $user in the context. The template designer can call the public methods in these classes to get dynamic data back.

Running the Velocity Examples

To run the examples that we have used here to demonstrate Velocity, you may use an easy-to-use GUI tool called **VeloGUI**.

VeloGUI was written by Franck Arnulfo, and is available at:
http://www.pipoware.com/velogui/

The Velocity GUI can run as a Java Web Start application, or it can be downloaded to your local file system as a standalone application. It is perfect for checking Velocity syntax.

Downloading and installing VeloGUI using Sun's Java Web Start:

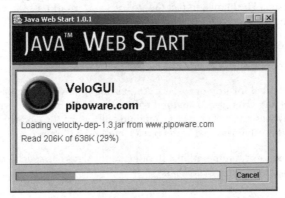

Here is a screenshot of the VeloGUI application in action:

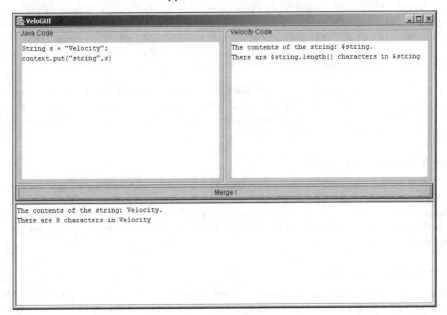

If you put your Java code in the first pane, your Velocity template in the second pane, and click the Merge! Button, the lower pane will display the results.

Velocity Context and Templates

The context is used as a container for objects from your Java application code that are used by Velocity templates. When Velocity evaluates a template, it will try to resolve the variable references in the template with objects in the context. Your application is responsible for putting these objects into the context. Only Java objects can be put into the context. Primitives need to be wrapped in an object (such as `Integer` or `Long`) before being placed into the context.

Context is the interface and `VelocityContext` is the concrete implementation of the interface. The Context can be used like a Hashtable, in fact the `VelocityContext` uses a `HashMap` object internally for storage. The two key methods are:

❑   `public Object put(String key, Object value)`

❑   `public Object get(String key)`

Null values are not accepted for `key` or `value`. An existing item will be replaced if the `put()` method is called with the same key. The `get()` method will return `null` if an item with the specified key was not found, or if the key was `null`. The `put()` method will return the `Object` that was placed into the context. If the key or the value was `null`, the `put()` method will return `null`.

Velocity handles Collections, Enumerations, Iterators, and Arrays as special cases – these are discussed in more detail in the section called *Collections*.

Using VelocityContext Objects

Instances of the `VelocityContext` class can be created by using the default constructor with no arguments. Alternatively, constructors exist for using an existing collection object that implements the `Map` interface or an existing context object or both. Using an existing context object is called **context chaining**. Use context chaining when you want to associate a context from code that you didn't write; it can be easier than extending a class and modifying the internals of its methods.

Context chaining can also be useful for creating a thread-safe context. For this, create a new `VelocityContext` object by passing the shared context into the constructor. Don't share `VelocityContext` objects between threads because the context may get modified by the Velocity engine as it executes macros or loops.

Creating Velocity Templates

The standard file extension for Velocity templates is `.vm`. Numerous add-ons exist for editing Velocity templates inside text editors. One of the authors of this book has contributed a Velocity syntax highlighting definition for the Windows shareware editor TextPad (http://www.textpad.com/). As of the writing of this book, no support exists for WYSIWYG creation of Velocity templates that goes above and beyond HTML.

Using Template Objects

The `Template` object represents a Velocity template. Use the `getTemplate()` method in the `Velocity` class to get an instance of the `Template` class:

```
public static Template getTemplate(String fileName)
```

There is another signature of getTemplate() that sets the character encoding of the template to one of the standard Java character sets. This works just like any other use of Java encodings:

```
public static Template getTemplate(String fileName, String encoding)
```

Some of the possible encodings are:

- ❑ UTF-8
- ❑ UTF-16
- ❑ US-ASCII
- ❑ ISO-8859-1

The default encoding is ISO-8859-1.

Using Methods on Objects in the Context

Any public method on an object in the reference (which is in the context) can be called. Any objects returned by those methods can have their public methods accessed. Velocity will render any objects to strings to display them. For example, consider the following Java code:

```
String s = "Velocity";
context.put("string", s);
```

If we have the following Velocity template:

```
The contents of the string: $string.
There are $string.length() characters in $string
```

It will result in this output:

The contents of the string: Velocity.
There are 8 characters in Velocity

If the method returns a primitive instead of an object, it is wrapped in the corresponding object by the Velocity engine.

Consider the following Java code:

```
Vector v = new Vector();
context.put("vector", v);
```

The Velocity template only contains one line:

```
What class is this? $vector.size().class
```

Calling the `size()` method in a `Vector` will return an `int`. Velocity doesn't know how to use primitives, so it's wrapped in an `Integer` object.

What class is this? class java.lang.Integer

Using get(), set(), and is() Method Shortcuts for Properties

Velocity uses shortcuts for accessing properties in objects in the context. JavaBeans use getter and setter methods for reading and modifying internal fields in the object. These fields usually have either private or protected scope and are inaccessible to outside objects without using the provided methods. Velocity provides a quick syntax for accessing these fields if the available getter method doesn't take any arguments. In Velocity, the following two lines are equivalent to each other:

```
$user.getEmail()
```

```
$user.Email
```

Velocity also supports the use of names that are not case-sensitive for properties. Velocity will first try to use the `$user.getEmail()` method, if it exists. If it doesn't exist, the runtime engine will attempt to run the `$user.getemail()` method. If neither of the above methods exist, Velocity treats the `$user` object as an implementation of the `Map` interface. The `get()` method is called with the property name as the key. Both of the following lines are equivalent, if there are no `getEmail()` or `getemail()` methods:

```
$user.get("Email")
```

```
$user.Email
```

One important point to remember is that the Velocity engine is smart enough to figure out that if a key doesn't exist in the object, nothing will be rendered, and the statement will be rendered as text. An example of this would be to create a `HashMap` object that contains a single key-value pair and then place it into the context. Here is a snippet of Java code that creates a `HashMap`:

```
Map capitals = new HashMap();
capitals.put("France", "Paris");
context.put("capitals", capitals);
```

The Velocity template would look as shown below:

```
The capital of France is $capitals.get("France")

The capital of France is $capitals.France

The capital of France is $capitals.france
```

The result is:

```
The capital of France is Paris

The capital of France is Paris

The capital of France is $capitals.france
```

When Velocity treats a property as a key in a `Map`, it is case-sensitive.

The last method to be tried by Velocity, when it sees a property, is the `isXXX()` method. Velocity treats the property as a `boolean`. A simple example of this is an empty `Vector` class and the `isEmpty()` method:

```
Vector vector = new Vector();
context.put("vector", vector);
```

The Velocity template would be as shown below:

```
Is the vector empty? $vector.isEmpty()

Is the vector still empty? $vector.Empty

Is the vector really empty? $vector.empty
```

and the output will be:

Is the vector empty? true

Is the vector still empty? true

Is the vector really empty? true

Velocity can also use a shortcut to set the value of a property in an object or the value of a key in a collection; this is very similar to how Velocity handles getter methods. We'll demonstrate this using a `HashMap`:

```
Map movies = new HashMap();
movies.put("Favorite", "Thomas Crown Affair");
context.put("movies", movies);
```

Velocity template:

```
My favorite movie is: $movies.Favorite

Now I changed my mind
#set ($movies.Favorite = "Vertigo")

I've got to go get the $movies.Favorite DVD.
```

Results:

My favorite movie is: Thomas Crown Affair

Now I changed my mind

I've got to go get the Vertigo DVD.

The Velocity Templating Language (VTL)

As we've already seen, Velocity uses its own syntax in templates so that the template content is completely separated from any additional code. In this section, we are going to go through the main syntax of the Velocity Templating Language (VTL).

Variables and the #set Directive

The Velocity Templating Language has very simple rules for variables. Velocity will replace a variable reference in a template with the String representation of an object. If the object referenced by a variable is not a String object, Velocity calls its toString() method to render output. This is the default behavior; however, you can override the toString() method in the way that you want to show the output.

Variable naming is similar to other programming languages. Names must start with a letter (upper case or lower case), but the following characters can be letters, numeric digits, underscores ("_"), or hyphens ("-"). The variable is then referenced by prefixing a dollar sign ($) to the name.

To assign a value to a variable, we need to use one of Velocity's directives. Every directive is prefixed with the hash symbol (#). Several directives are defined inside Velocity and others can be defined using macros, as we'll see in the section called *Velocity Macros*. The directive that we're going to use is #set. The #set directive works in the same way as a Java variable assignment.

Here is an extremely simple Velocity template:

```
#set ($dog = "Gossamer")

The dog is named $dog.
```

and the results of this Velocity template are:

```
The dog is named Gossamer.
```

Quiet Reference Notation

Normally, Velocity will display a variable reference in the results, even if the variable doesn't exist in the context. This is because the reference could just be included in the original text. Here is a quick demonstration of this:

Velocity template:

```
$pizza will not do anything special
```

Result:

```
$pizza will not do anything special
```

If we use Velocity's quiet reference notation, the template engine will not display the reference if it doesn't exist. Add an exclamation point (!) between the dollar sign and the beginning of the variable name to enable this feature.

Velocity template:

```
$!pizza will hide itself
```

Result:

will hide itself

String Concatenation

Velocity can be easily used to add two or more strings to create a new string in a Velocity variable. The references to the variables should just be placed inside the quotes on the right-hand side of the equals sign, as shown in the following example:

```
#set ($city = "Austin")
#set ($state = "Texas")

#set ($address = "$city, $state")
This is the address: $address
```

This is the resulting output:

This is the address: Austin, Texas

Velocity can use a slightly more complicated notation, known as the **formal reference**. This is useful for avoiding ambiguity in variable names. For example, if we had $tunafish, the variable referenced could actually be $tuna with fish attached on the end but Velocity would only look for a variable called $tunafish. For the formal reference, variables are described with this syntax: ${variable_name}. We'll have to use a somewhat unlikely example to demonstrate this:

```
#set ($city = "Austin")
#set ($state = "Texas")

#set ($myAddress = "${city}isin$state")

This is the weird address: $myAddress
```

This results in:

This is the weird address: AustinisinTexas

Without the {} around city the result would have been as follows:

This is the weird address: $cityisinTexas

One of the most common mistakes made by new Velocity users, is to use Java-style string concatenation inside a Velocity template, such as this:

```
##Incorrect use of string concatentation with Velocity
#set ($name = $firstName + $lastName)
```

The only use of the + operator is for Velocity arithmetic operations.

To concatenate **Strings** in Velocity, use this syntax: **#set ($something = "$string1$string2")**

Comments

Velocity uses a double hash (##) for line comments and the #* ... *# pair for the block of multi-line comments. Here is a quick example demonstrating their use:

Velocity template:

```
## A line comment
Some text in the template
#* A two-line
block comment *#
```

Results:

Some text in the template

Escaping Rules

The backslash (\) is used to escape special Velocity characters inside templates, such as $, #, and \. For variable references, this is needed only when the variable is already defined. Keep in mind that Velocity escaping behaves differently when variables are defined and when they aren't. Here is an example that prints out the text $string, instead of the declared variable reference $string:

```
#set ($string = "something")
$string
\$string
```

The results:

something
$string

If $string wasn't declared as a variable reference, the results would look like this:

$string
\$string

One interesting quirk is involved in printing the comment tag (##) in a template. Velocity appears incapable of using escapes to print out this combination, so the author came up with a solution:

Velocity template:

```
#set ($hash = "#")
$hash$hash
```

Results:

```
##
```

Collections

Velocity can handle several different types of collections:

❑   `Collection`

❑   `Map`

❑   `Iterator`

❑   `Enumeration`

❑   Arrays of objects

In each case, Velocity uses an instance of `Iterator` internally with the #foreach directive discussed in the section called *#foreach...#end*. For collections and maps, Velocity gets the iterator directly from the object. For arrays and enumerations, Velocity internally wraps the array or enumeration in an object that implements the `Iterator` interface. If an object that implements the `Iterator` or `Enumeration` interfaces is placed in the context directly, it is used and is not capable of being reset to the first element when it reaches the end. Velocity will only be able to use that object once per template with the #foreach directive. This problem does not arise with `Collection`, `Map`, or arrays. Velocity will just retrieve a new iterator if needed. Velocity will place a warning into the log file when it finds an `Iterator` or `Enumeration` used in a #foreach statement. It's the best practice to use a `Collection`, `Map`, or array instead, if possible.

Control Flow Directives

Velocity contains only two flow directives: #if...#else...#elseif...#end and #foreach...#end. This makes Velocity a very simple programming language.

#if...#else...#elseif...#end

The #if directive is similar to the if statement in any other language. The #if directive may be followed with #elseif or #else to create a list of conditions that could be true. The #end directive must be used to close the #if directive. The #if directives can be nested inside other #if directives. Velocity also supports the logical (or Boolean) operators – AND (&&), OR (||), and NOT (!).

To evaluate the conditions on an #if or #elseif directive, Velocity uses three rules:

❑ The value must be true for a Boolean object (boolean primitives are automatically converted because Velocity only deals with objects, not primitives)

❑ If the referenced variable doesn't exist in the context at all, Velocity evaluates the condition as false. If the object referenced by the variable isn't null, the condition is true. Remember that variables in the context can't be null.

❑ The strings true and false are evaluated as-is. This is useful for passing arguments into macros, which we'll discuss in the section called *Velocity Macros.*

Here is an example demonstrating this functionality:

```
#set ($pages = 5)

#if ($pages == 0)
  There are no pages to display.
#elseif ($pages = 1)
  This the only page.
#else
  There are $pages pages that can be shown.
#end
```

and here is the output of this Velocity template:

There are 5 pages that can be shown.

Here is a more advanced example, to demonstrate the use of #if...#else to determine if an object is in the context. We check if the variable $novalue is in the context, but it's not. We add the variable $something to the context and check if it exists. It does exist, so we will see its value in the output. We also evaluate the word true as a condition:

```
#if ($novalue)
  No value - we won't see this
#else
  The novalue variable doesn't exist
#end

#set ($something = "something")
#if ($something)
  $something
#end

#if (true)
  This statement is true.
#else
  This statement is false.
#end
```

The results from evaluating this template:

The novalue variable doesn't exist

something

This statement is true.

Here is an example demonstrating the logical operators. The $notavariable variable doesn't exist in the context, and will be evaluated as false:

```
#if (!true)
   This statement is true.
#else
   This statement is false.
#end

#if (true && $notavariable)
   This statement is true.
#else
   This statement is false.
#end

#if (true || $notavariable)
   This statement is true.
#else
   This statement is false.
#end
```

The output for our Boolean operator example template:

This statement is false.

This statement is false.

This statement is true.

#foreach...#end

The Velocity #foreach directive is used for looping the contents of a Collection, Iterator, Array, or Enumeration. It's used for grabbing each object in the list and doing some changes to it. If you need to know where you are in the list, Velocity provides a built-in variable that gives the loop counter. This variable is named $velocityCount by default, although the identifier can be configured in Velocity's velocity.properties file. It's really recommended not to change this because other people who use your template will not know what your counter variable is. The other configurable option is to determine whether Velocity's loop counter starts at zero or one. The counter defaults to one. An example that uses the #foreach directive and the $velocityCount variable is pretty straightforward:

```
Vector numbers = new Vector();
numbers.add("one");
numbers.add("two");
numbers.add("three");
numbers.add("four");
context.put("numbers", numbers)
```

The Velocity template:

```
#foreach ($number in $numbers)
   The number is $number
   The velocity count is $velocityCount
#end
```

Results:

```
The number is one
The velocity count is 1
The number is two
The velocity count is 2
The number is three
The velocity count is 3
The number is four
The velocity count is 4
```

It's also very easy to loop the contents of a Hashtable or HashMap. Get the set of keys from the hash table's keyset() method, loop it, and output each value as it appears by calling the get() method in the Hashtable with the key.

Velocity Macros

Velocity's macros are known as **Velocimacros** and they are essential for both maintainability and good UI design. Pieces of the UI can be broken out into reusable chunks that can take parameters. These macros can then be stored in a global library template file. This allows UI elements to be shared between templates, across the application. Here's an example of a UI element macro, inline in a Velocity template:

```
#macro (button src url alt)
<a href="$url"><img src="/images/$src" ALT="$alt"></a>

#end
#set ($image = "shoppingcart.jpg")
#button($image "/cart.vm" "Our shopping cart")
```

The results:

```
<a href="/cart.vm"><img src="/images/shoppingcart.jpg" alt="Our shopping cart"></a>
```

Suppose that you had used this macro to build buttons all over your templates and then your web designers, your customers, or your business analysts, came back to you and told you that all images had to be served up from another server in another department, or all links needed to have JavaScript messages in the status bar. It's easy to change something like this by using macros.

We defined the macro by using the #macro directive, which takes at least one argument. The first argument is the name of the macro, which is button in this case. The following arguments become the parameters to the Velocimacro. You can have zero parameters to a Velocimacro. When you call a Velocimacro, you have to use all of its parameters; there can't be any optional parameters. Arrays, Booleans, boolean literals (true or false), Strings, and Objects can all be passed in as arguments. For more on the boolean arguments, refer the section called *#if...#end*.

We could also move our button macro out to a library, where it could be used across templates. Velocity's macro template libraries are defined in the Velocity properties file:

```
velocimacro.library = GlobalMacros.vm
```

We could either add our `button` macro to that file, or we could create our own macro template file. The `GlobalMacros.vm` file doesn't exist, so we'd have to create it. The `velocimacro.library` property can contain a whole list of macro template files, separated by commas:

```
velocimacro.library = MacroLibrary1.vm,MacroLibrary2.vm
```

There are several other macro properties that can be set and they are defined in the excellent Velocity user guide that is available on the web site and also with the distribution. They concern scope, allowing inline macros, allowing inline macros to have the same name as global macros, and whether or not to reload the macro library when it changes.

> One catch of the global macro library is that if the property `velocimacro.library.autoreload` is not set to `true`, you will have to restart your application server when you change a global library to see the changes. You may need to have different values for this setting for production servers and developer's machines.

External Templates or Files

Velocity templates can load external templates or files, just like most page-oriented languages you may already be familiar with. The files or templates are found using the Velocity resource loader. To use them, there are two directives:

- ❑ `#parse`: for Velocity templates
- ❑ `#include`: for everything else, including plain text, HTML, and XML

The `#parse` directive takes a single argument, which is the template to be loaded. Like other Velocity directives, this can be a string literal or a Velocity variable:

```
#set($fileName = "page.vm")
#parse($fileName)
```

The `#include` directive is useful for loading pieces of HTML or text into another template. These are relative to the resource loader paths specified in the Velocity configuration file. If you aren't using a configuration file, it's relative to the working directory for the application. The directive also takes either a string literal or a variable. Velocity doesn't process the content it loads with the `#include` directive in its engine:

```
#set($htmlScrap = "sidebar.html")
#include($htmlScrap)
```

If the file that you are loading with the `#include` directive doesn't exist, Velocity will throw a `ResourceNotFoundException` when the template is evaluated.

Arithmetic

Velocity contains the standard arithmetic operators: +, -, *, /, and %. But the engine can only make use of integers for arithmetic operations. Any floating-point calculations will have to be done in your Java code, for example, calculating the sales tax on items in a shopping cart (which anyway belongs to the business logic). Velocity will throw an error when trying to parse a floating-point number assigned to a variable. When Velocity tries to divide two integers, it will only return the integer portion of the result. Here are some examples of Velocity's arithmetic code:

```
#set ($two = 2)
#set ($three = 3)
#set ($five = $two + $three)
3 + 2 = $five

#set ($answer = 8 - 4)
$answer

#set ($four = 17 / 4)
17/4 is $four in Velocity because it only uses integers

#set ($remainder = 17 % 4)
The remainder is $remainder
```

Results:

3 + 2 = 5

4

17/4 is 4 in Velocity because it only uses integers

The remainder is 1

Velocity isn't designed for heavy math, so be careful of the calculations that you put into a template. It can be too easy to break the Model-View-Controller paradigm. Getting back to our above sales tax example, it sounds relatively easy to just calculate the tax in the presentation layer – get the total, multiply by the sales tax percentage, and display the tax as a line item. But what happens when your simple algorithm needs to be expanded? For example, in the state of Pennsylvania, sales tax isn't charged on clothes. The original neat code grows into a manifestation of the Concern Slush antipattern.

We would recommend using Velocity's arithmetic for very simple calculations – we have used it in two places:

❑ Modifying adjacent HTML elements with JavaScript and DHTML. If you use a dynamic effect like a rollover, you may need to change neighboring HTML elements to set a color or a background image. This is a simple addition or subtraction.

❑ Modifying the backgrounds of every other table row. By using the Velocity counter, $velocityCount, and the modulus operator (%) to determine whether the counter is odd or even, you can alternate the backgrounds of table rows. This makes the list easier to read.

Here's a Velocity template that demonstrates the different-colored alternating rows:

```
#set( $countries = ["Australia", "Canada", "France", "Bhutan", "Belize"] )

<table cellspacing="0" cellpadding="2" width="400">
#foreach ($country in $countries)

  #if (($velocityCount % 2) > 0)
    <tr bgcolor="#FFFFFF">
  #else
    <tr bgcolor="#CFCFCF">
  #end

  <td>$velocityCount</TD><TD>$country</td>
  </tr>

#end
</table>
```

Here is the HTML output:

```
<table cellspacing="0" cellpadding="2" width="400">

<tr bgcolor="#FFFFFF">

<td>1</td><td>Australia</td>
</tr>

<tr bgcolor="#CFCFCF">

<td>2</td><td>Canada</td>
</tr>

<tr bgcolor="#FFFFFF">

<td>3</td><td>France</td>
</tr>

<tr bgcolor="#CFCFCF">

<td>4</td><td>Bhutan</td>
</tr>

<tr bgcolor="#FFFFFF">

<td>5</td><td>Belize</td>
</tr>

</table>
```

and here is how it looks in a browser:

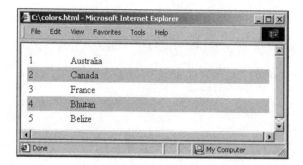

Using the Velocity Engine from Java

We are going to discuss how to evaluate Velocity templates from inside a Java application. There are several different ways of doing this. We will start with the most general case, applicable to all Java applications. It uses the `org.apache.velocity.app.Velocity` class to evaluate a Velocity template.

Web applications can use Velocity as a presentation layer. We'll using the Velocity tag library for JSP to evaluate Velocity Template Language (VTL) embedded in a JSP page. The tag library handles all of the template processing and evaluation.

Processing the Template

The Velocity Java API makes it extremely simple to process a template. Here is the template we are going to use:

```
The shape is $shape
```

If the template is dynamically generated, the template can either be a `String` or be accessible with a `Reader`. Velocity supplies two `evaluate()` methods in the `Velocity` class with different signatures to process dynamic templates:

❑ `boolean evaluate (Context context, Writer writer, String logTag, Reader reader)`

❑ `boolean evaluate (Context context, Writer writer, String logTag, String instring)`

The `logTag` is what Velocity uses to mark entries in the log with the module that the entries came from.

Here is an example log entry that uses the same log tag as the example below: `SimpleVelocity`:

```
2003-01-27 04:11:48,858 - #parse(): cannot find template '../simple.txt', called
from template SimpleVelocity at (1, 21)
```

Both methods return `true` if they succeed, `false` if there was an error. Errors will go to the Velocity log, which will be in the current working directory. The logger can be configured to output to another location using one of the built-in logging subsystems. For more information on logging with Velocity, refer the Velocity Developer's Guide that comes with the Velocity distribution.

The simple Velocity evaluation class:

```
//Java imports
import java.io.*;

//Velocity imports
import org.apache.velocity.VelocityContext;
import org.apache.velocity.app.Velocity;
import org.apache.velocity.context.Context;
import org.apache.velocity.exception.MethodInvocationException;
import org.apache.velocity.exception.ParseErrorException;

public class SimpleVelocityEvaluate {

  public static void main(String args[]) {
    //create a writer that goes to the console.
    StringWriter writer = new StringWriter();

    try {
      //Initialize Velocity
      Velocity.init();

    } catch (Exception e) {
      System.out.println("Error initializing Velocity");
      e.printStackTrace();
      return;
    }

    //Our velocity context
    Context context = new VelocityContext();

    //Put something in the context
    context.put("shape", "circle");

    //Define our template
    String template = "The shape is $shape";

    try {
      Velocity.evaluate(context, writer, "SimpleVelocity", template);
      System.out.println("success: " + writer.toString());

    } catch (IOException ioe) {
      System.out.println("IO error with Velocity");
      ioe.printStackTrace();

    } catch (MethodInvocationException mie) {
      System.out.println("Method Invoke error with Velocity");
      mie.printStackTrace();

    } catch (ParseErrorException pe) {
      System.out.println("Parsing error with Velocity");
      pe.printStackTrace();
    }
  }
}
```

After our simple example is executed from the command line, we will get a single line of output:

```
success: The shape is circle
```

This example demonstrated how to use Velocity at a very basic level, by merging a context with a very simple template created out of a `String` object. Next, we're going to discuss how Velocity is configured for loading templates from a file system or a classpath.

Resource Loaders

Velocity uses resource loaders to find templates to process. More than one resource loader can be configured in the `Velocity.properties` configuration file to be used with Velocity, and Velocity will search through them in order.

Here are two example resource loaders:

```
resource.loader = file
file.resource.loader.description = Velocity File Resource Loader
file.resource.loader.class =
   org.apache.velocity.runtime.resource.loader.FileResourceLoader
file.resource.loader.path = /templates/
file.resource.loader.cache = false
file.resource.loader.modificationCheckInterval = 2

resource.loader = classpath
classpath.resource.loader.description = Velocity Classpath Resource Loader
classpath.resource.loader.class =
   org.apache.velocity.runtime.resource.loader.ClasspathResourceLoader
```

The first resource loader is a file resource loader. It's also named `file`. The `description` is just that, a description for developers who are interested. The `class` should be set to one of Velocity's built-in loader classes, or to a class that subclasses `org.apache.velocity.runtime.resource.loader.ResourceLoader`.

Available loaders that come with Velocity are:

❑ `ClasspathResourceLoader`: for loading resources from a classpath

❑ `DataSourceResourceLoader`: for templates in a data source such as MySQL or Oracle

❑ `FileResourceLoader`: for templates on the local file system

❑ `JarResourceLoader`: for templates in a JAR file

❑ `URLResourceLoader`: for templates which are available from a URL.

The second resource loader is a classpath loader. It doesn't require any configuration beyond its name and class. Put your templates into a directory, a JAR file, or a ZIP file and make sure that it is in the classpath for your application. Velocity will read the resources right out of the classpath.

The two more useful resource loaders are the ones listed in the example, `file` and `classpath`. The JAR resource loader can be used if your templates are trapped in a JAR file and the data source resource loader will load templates out of a database that has `id`, `template`, and `timestamp` columns. Use your application server to define the data source. You'll have to rebuild Velocity to use this loader, so refer to the Velocity Developer's Guide for more details. There is also a URL loader for a more universal approach to retrieve resources.

The file loader needs a `path` to look for templates in. This is relative to the web app's root directory. The file loader can be set to `cache` templates. We recommend that you set this to `false` during development. Velocity will then read the templates off the disk every time you ask for them, which means no waiting time or restarts to debug templates. Set the cache to `true` when your application goes into production or testing. The `modificationCheckInterval` tells Velocity how often to check for a new template (in seconds).

Using Velocity in a Web Application

Velocity makes a great web presentation layer. There are several different options for using Velocity as a part of a web application.

❑ Embedding Velocity inside a JSP page with the Velocity tag library

❑ Extending `VelocityServlet` to create a web application based on servlets

❑ Use Velocity as an alternative presentation layer for Struts with the Velocity Struts package

❑ Use Velocity with another application framework such as Jakarta Apache Turbine

We're going to embed Velocity in our JSP page for our RSS example. The Velocity tag library will create a template out of the contents of the JSP page, between the closing and ending Velocity tags, in the JSP. The Velocity context will be created from the objects in the page, request, session, and application scopes. The Velocity tag will then evaluate the template against the context and the output of the template will be put into the JSP page as normal HTML.

Another solution would be to extend an abstract servlet class named `VelocityServlet` that comes with the Velocity distribution. This would be outside Struts, and would be very useful if you were building a simple application that didn't need any of the services, utility classes, or structure from an application framework. This servlet comes with one method that must be overridden, called `handleRequest()`, which returns an instance of the `Template` object. Inside this method, any data from your application should be put into the context. Based on the request, you will have to determine which Velocity template to retrieve from the resource loaders. The base servlet handles the entire template processing, and returns the result in the servlet response. The `web.xml` configuration file should be set up to forward all requests for files with the extension `.vm` to your servlet.

The Velocity Struts project has a promising future. The goal of this project is to allow Velocity templates to be a replacement for JSP pages inside Struts. No changes are needed for the Struts library. The Velocity Struts code is in the Velocity toolbox, which contains several other pre-release projects that supplement the Velocity core. The core of this project is the `VelocityViewServlet`, which allows access to **tools**, which are objects that are always put into the context. These tools are defined in a file called `toolbox.xml`. The tools that come with the Velocity Struts package allow access to Struts message resources, forms, links, and errors.

With this servlet, the template also gets automatic access to the parameters in the servlet request and session.

JSP and Velocity

JSP can be used with Velocity through the **Velocity tag library**. If Velocity syntax matches your project needs better than JSP scriptlets or the expression language, it's a simple task to integrate Velocity with your existing JSP-based application. The Velocity tag library doesn't depend on Struts or any other MVC frameworks to work.

There is only one tag for Velocity – the contents of the tag are parsed as a Velocity template. The Velocity context contains the beans in the page, request, session, and application scopes. Velocity provides two different methods for accessing beans from the scope. The default method is to allow access to any bean in each scope. You should try to avoid namespace conflict with the names of beans. But if you do have the same name for beans in different scopes, Velocity searches the scopes in the following order:

1. Page

2. Request

3. Session

4. Application

This presents a problem if you have a bean named `user` in the request scope, but you actually want to access the `user` bean in the application scope. The tag library provides a built-in Velocity object in the context called the `$scopeTool`, which can retrieve objects out of a given scope. If you would like to keep access to your beans restricted by scope, you can set the `strictaccess` attribute on the `velocity` tag to `true`, which disables the default access to any bean in any scope. All bean access will have to go through the scope tool.

There currently isn't a way to use JSP tags directly inside a Velocity template. The best practice for using JSP tags with Velocity is to factor out the logic code from the tag into a simple bean that can be added to Velocity's context for use. Another solution would be to write an object that wraps the existing Java methods of your tag into a cleaner API for use with Velocity.

Creating the JavaEdge RSS Feed with Velocity

We have several requirements for this piece of the JavaEdge application:

❑ Create an RSS feed that reflects the last stories to be added to JavaEdge

❑ Include all of the stories on the JavaEdge home page

❑ Use Velocity to create the solution, so we can demonstrate this clever tool

❑ Follow the RSS 2.0 specification

The first piece of the design puzzle is to determine how we are going to create the RSS feed. Other web sites will need a permanent URL on our JavaEdge application that we can give them to pull our content headlines from.

Here are some possible designs for this problem:

- ❏ Create a static file on the file system and update it every time a story is added by a user.

- ❏ Create a static file on the file system and update it at fixed intervals by a scheduler.

- ❏ Use a Struts action on URLs that contain the path /news.rss, and dynamically generate the RSS file every time the web site is hit.

- ❏ Use the same design as above, except the RSS file will be cached for a fixed interval, such as 10 minutes.

- ❏ Create another servlet and make it solely responsible for handling RSS requests. This servlet could handle any requests for a path with /news.rss.

The first design seems like the easiest solution, but we could end up with a jumbled application architecture if we add code to create an RSS file into the post story Struts actions. In addition, if we create an interface for editing or deleting posted stories we will have to include code in these new actions to handle the RSS file creation. Also, we could run into a thread safety problem if we aren't careful when more than one person posts a story to JavaEdge.

The second design could hook into the Struts plug-in system to run as a scheduled process. We use this approach in the chapter on Lucene to run the search engine indexer. It would be nice to have "late-breaking" news immediately show up on our RSS feed, so we won't use this solution. This design would be more appropriate for a high-traffic site like Slashdot because the RSS creation process wouldn't run on every RSS request.

The third design is the one that we will use for our web site. By building everything into Struts, we keep the application architecture simple. At the same time, we can create actions and templates specifically for RSS. We'll need to choose a URL for the RSS file. Generally, this URL is simple because it will have to be copied into other applications. We will use the following URL: http://localhost:8080/JavaEdge/execute/news.rss.

The fourth design is too complicated for our site; it is similar to the second design, in that it is more appropriate for a high-traffic web application.

The last design, the independent servlet, is worth looking into. This would free us from any Struts requirements we might have on making our functionality into an action. We could generate the RSS from a template directly inside the servlet. We'd like to leave the option open to leverage Struts better in the future, so we'll stick with our Struts-based design.

The next part of the puzzle is to decide which parts of the RSS specification to implement. There are many optional elements and attributes we could include in our RSS file. We'll create an example RSS file that will demonstrate the elements and attributes we intend to use. By referencing the RSS specification, you can determine which fields should be added to our solution to fit your requirements.

The root element of the RSS file is going to be the `<rss version="2.0">` element. The `<rss>` element has a `<channel>` element. The `<channel>` element contains all of the metadata for our JavaEdge content feed, along with all of the news items we are publishing:

```
<?xml version="1.0"?>
<rss version="2.0">
  <channel>
```

The `title` will be used by the web site that consumes the RSS file. The link should point back to our JavaEdge installation:

```
<title>JavaEdge: Late Breaking Headlines</title>
<link>http://localhost:8080/JavaEdge/execute/</link>
```

Our `description` element could end up being used – we picked one that will stand out in the crowd. The `language` element is optional; refer the RSS 2.0 documentation for more information. The next element, `docs`, points to the RSS specification from Dave Winer at Userland. The generator should be the name of our application, and it's an optional element:

```
<description>The hard-hitting Java journalism you demand.</description>
<language>en-us</language>
<docs>http://backend.userland.com/rss</docs>
<generator>
      Wrox JavaEdge Application (Struts and Velocity)
</generator>
```

After the above metadata, we get to the news headlines that we syndicate out. Each headline is wrapped in an `item` element. The `title` is used to generate a link from the consuming link, and we provide a URL to our site that will point to the story. We will need to generate the `storyId`, but we'll leave the rest of the URL in the template, so we can use whatever URL we want the external world to know. The description will be the story introduction from the JavaEdge database. We'll need to expose a publication date so others can determine how new our content is:

```
<item>
  <title>JSTL tutorial available</title>

  <link>http://localhost:8080/JavaEdge/execute
        /storyDetailSetup?storyId=17</link>
  <description>We are pleased to announce that our editors have created
              a JSTL tutorial and made it available for everyone to
              use.</description>
  <pubDate>Wed, 1 Jan 2003 12:04:31 GMT</pubDate>
</item>

<item>
  <title>Latest release of Turbine</title>

  <link>http://localhost:8080/JavaEdge/execute
        /storyDetailSetup?storyId=18</link>
  <description>The Turbine developers have released another great
        version of their Turbine framework, and it is now up for download
        on Jakarta Apache</description>

  <pubDate>Wed, 8 Jan 2003 12:04:31 GMT</pubDate>
</item>
  </channel>
</rss>
```

That's all that is required for the sample RSS file.

The last design decision is how to make sure the RSS file only contains valid XML. Velocity ships with a tool called **Anakia**, which is used for transforming XML into other formats using Velocity. It was originally conceived of as a documentation-generation tool. Anakia comes with a simple class called `org.apache.velocity.anakia.Escape`, which only has one method, `getText(String st)`. This method escapes character data for safe use in XML or HTML, by replacing four special characters (<, >, ", &) with their XML entities.

Installing Velocity and the Tag Library

The Velocity distribution can be downloaded from its home page at http://jakarta.apache.org/velocity. Download the binary archive for the latest released version (currently Velocity-1.3.1-rc2), and unzip it to a handy directory. Velocity comes with two pre-built JAR files for easy deployment. The smaller JAR file only contains classes in the `org.apache.velocity` package and sub-packages. The larger file contains all of the classes that Velocity depends on. These are from the Jakarta Apache ORO, Commons, and Avalon LogKit projects. If you don't already have these libraries in your project, you can use the JAR that contains the dependencies for simplicity. If you want to keep the use of Java libraries granular, the needed JAR files are all contained in the `build/lib` subdirectory of the Velocity installation.

The Velocity tag library can be downloaded from the Wrox web site: http://wrox.com/books/1861007817.htm. The Velocity home page also points to the tag library. If you get the tag library source code out of CVS and build it yourself, be sure that you are using a compatible version of Velocity, as the source code is always being updated.

Implementing the RSS Feed

There are three steps that we need to take to implement the RSS feed:

- ❑ Add our action to `struts-config.xml`
- ❑ Create a setup action for RSS
- ❑ Create a JSP that uses Velocity to generate the XML for the RSS

The template is contained inside the opening and closing tags of the Velocity tag. When the JSP page is executed, the Velocity tag creates a context out of the objects in the page, request, session, and applications scopes and then evaluates the template with the context. The output of the merge is displayed in the JSP page.

Configure struts-config.xml

We need to add an action to `struts-config.xml`. As the URL for our RSS file is going to be http://localhost:8080/JavaEdge/execute/news.rss, the action is mapped to the `/news.rss` path. This action is simple; it only calls an `Action` class (`RSSSetupAction`) that puts the necessary data into the request scope. If that is successful, it calls a JSP page (`rss.jsp`):

```
<?xml version="1.0" encoding="ISO-8859-1"?>
<!DOCTYPE struts-config PUBLIC "-//Apache Software Foundation//DTD Struts
        Configuration 1.0//EN"
        "http://jakarta.apache.org/struts/dtds/struts-config_1_0.dtd">
```

```
<struts-config>
  ...

  <action path="/news.rss"
          type="com.wrox.javaedge.struts.rss.RSSSetupAction">
    <forward name="rss.success" path="/WEB-INF/jsp/rss.jsp"/>
  </action>

  ...

</struts-config>
```

RSSSetupAction.java

This Action class puts all of the needed data and utility classes into the request scope. These objects are going into the request scope so they can be used to build up the RSS page. Any objects in the page, request, session, or application scopes become accessible to our Velocity template through the context. We need the collection of story objects from the home page in the request scope, so we borrowed some code from the home page setup action to do this. All the heavy lifting is done by the story DAO, which we discussed in Chapter 5. We also move the description into the action, to be put into the context and pulled out by the template. We did this just to demonstrate how we could change the description or any of the other fields on the fly.

We also add an object to the request scope to handle escaping XML entities, so that our RSS file is always valid XML. This is a utility object, and we can just use the methods from it in the Velocity template.

We decided to match the date format used in the RSS 2.0 documentation, which required a date format class. We used the SimpleDateFormat class to set up a formatter object that would give us the output we needed. The date format object we created was also put into the request scope:

```
package com.wrox.javaedge.struts.rss;

import org.apache.struts.action.Action;
import org.apache.struts.action.ActionMapping;
import org.apache.struts.action.ActionForm;
import org.apache.struts.action.ActionForward;
import org.apache.log4j.Logger;
import org.apache.velocity.anakia.Escape;

import javax.servlet.http.HttpServletRequest;
import javax.servlet.http.HttpServletResponse;

import com.wrox.javaedge.story.dao.*;
import com.wrox.javaedge.common.*;
import java.util.*;
import java.text.SimpleDateFormat;
```

We are going to extend the Action class and override the perform() method to add several objects to the request scope. The Velocity tag will pull these objects out of the request scope and put them into the Velocity context for the template we will discuss in the section called *rss.jsp*:

```
/*
 * Retrieves the top stories from JavaEdge and puts them in the session for
 * the RSS to use.
 */
public class RSSSetupAction extends Action {

    private static Logger logger = Logger.getLogger(RSSSetupAction.class);

    /*
     * The perform() method comes from the base Struts Action class. We
     * override this method and put the logic to carry out the user's
     * request in the overridden method
     * @param mapping An ActionMapping class that will be used by the
     * Action class to tell the ActionServlet where to send the end-user.
     *
     * @param form The ActionForm class that will contain any data submitted
     * by the end-user via a form.
     * @param request A standard Servlet HttpServletRequest class.
     * @param response A standard Servlet HttpServletResponse class.
     * @return An ActionForward class that will be returned to the
     * ActionServlet indicating where the user is to go next.
     */
    public ActionForward perform(ActionMapping mapping,
                                 ActionForm      form,
                                 HttpServletRequest request,
                                 HttpServletResponse response) {

        try {
```

We are going to get the `Story` Data Access Object. Our RSS feed will use the same stories we show on the home page, and we can reuse the `findTopStory()` method that we already built for the home page in Chapter 3:

```
/*
 * Creating a Story Data Access Object and using it to retrieve
 * the top stories.
 */
StoryDAO storyDAO = new StoryDAO();
Collection topStories = storyDAO.findTopStory();
```

The top stories from the DAO are going to go into the request, so we can access them from the Velocity template in the page we are going to show the user:

```
/*
 * Putting the collection containing all of the stories into
 * the request.
 */
request.setAttribute("topStories", topStories);
```

We'll also put a hard-coded description into the request scope. This is here to demonstrate how easy it is to get a string into a Velocity template from a Struts action:

```
/*
 * Put the description into the request.
 */
request.setAttribute("description",
         "The hard-hitting Java journalism you demand.");
```

We're going to use an XML entity escaping object, called `Escape`, from Velocity to ensure that we have valid XML inside the RSS feed. This helper object can go right into the request scope:

```
/**
 * Put the escape object into the context
 * to escape XML entities.
 */
request.setAttribute("escape", new Escape());
```

We will include a date formatter in the request scope for the RSS 2.0 feed. Much like the above XML escaper, it is a helper object:

```
/**
 * Create a date format to match the RSS 2.0 dates
 * Ex. Sun, 19 May 2002 15:21:36 GMT
 * http://backend.userland.com/rss
 */
String pattern = "EEE, dd MMM yyyy HH:mm:ss z";
SimpleDateFormat dateFormat = new SimpleDateFormat(pattern);

/**
 * Stick the date format into the request
 */
request.setAttribute("dateFormat",dateFormat);
```

If we had a problem retrieving the top stories out of the Story data access object, we catch the exception, log it as an error, and then return a forward for the main application error page. Otherwise, we return a forward that will take us to the `rss.jsp` file. These mappings were set up in the `struts-config.xml` configuration file:

```
} catch(DataAccessException e) {
    logger.error("Data access exception",e);
    return (mapping.findForward("system.error"));
}

return (mapping.findForward("rss.success"));
    }
}
```

rss.jsp

We'll walk through the JSP page we need to make the RSS file. This is the declaration for the Velocity tag library:

```
<%@ taglib uri="/WEB-INF/veltag.tld" prefix="vel" %>
```

We're going to enclose our entire Velocity template in between the Velocity JSP tag. The Velocity context will contain all of the beans in the page, request, session, and application scopes. The template will be merged with the context, and the output will be put into the JSP page just like any other JSP tag. We could have set the `strictaccess` attribute to `true`, and then any objects we needed out of the JSP scopes would have to be retrieved with the Velocity scope tool first. There are different methods for each scope, so there won't be a naming clash problem:

```
<vel:velocity>
```

This is the declaration for RSS version 2.0:

```
<?xml version="1.0"?>
<rss version="2.0">
```

There is only one channel for each RSS file:

```
<channel>
```

This is the title and link others are going to use when they create links to JavaEdge:

```
<title>JavaEdge: Late Breaking Headlines</title>
<link>http://localhost:8080/JavaEdge/execute/</link>
```

We'll use Velocity's `#if...#end` directive to only add a description element if one exists. We are checking to make sure the description has been placed into the context:

```
#if ($description)
```

Here, we're building an RSS `<description>` element. We're using the `Escape` utility class to make sure the description text is valid XML. If either the escape or the description objects don't exist in the context, we won't display the Velocity code. We accomplish this by using `$!` for our Velocity references:

```
<description>$!escape.getText($!description)</description>
```

End the `#if` directive, and put in elements for the language (English), and the location of the RSS documentation (Userland):

```
#end
<language>en-us</language>
<docs>http://backend.userland.com/rss</docs>
```

We're showing off our JavaEdge application here, so that when people use our RSS, they can see that it was generated using our application:

```
<generator>
     Wrox JavaEdge Application (Struts and Velocity)
</generator>
```

The `#foreach...#end` directive is useful for getting each single value out of a collection or array, and then doing some work with it. The collection is `$topStories`, and the single value is `$story`:

```
#foreach ($story in $topStories)
```

The `<item>` element corresponds to a content piece, or a news story:

```
<item>
```

For the title, we're going to use the same escape tool as for the description above. We're going to access the `storyTitle` property on the `$story` reference, which is actually a `StoryVO` object. Velocity has shortcuts for getters and setters on beans, so we can access it with just the property name:

```
<title>$!escape.getText($!story.storyTitle)</title>
```

The `<link>` element contains a URL that points back to the story. We set the story ID dynamically from the story object:

```
<link>http://localhost:8080/JavaEdge/execute
        /storyDetailSetup?storyId=$!story.storyId</link>
```

The story introduction becomes the RSS description. The code is similar to the above `<title>` element.

```
#if ($story.storyIntro)
    <description>$!escape.getText($!story.storyIntro)</description>
#end
```

Here we add the publication date for RSS. The story submission dates don't have times, only dates, so this will always read 12:00 for the time. The date formatter we built in the object is used to format the submission date, if the date exists on the story object:

```
#if ($story.submissionDate)
    <pubDate>$!dateFormat.format($!story.submissionDate)</pubDate>
#end
```

Close out all the XML tags and the `#foreach...#end` directive:

```
        </item>
        #end
    </channel>
  </rss>
</vel:velocity>
```

Output: News.rss

We can test our RSS functionality by opening the URL http://localhost:8080/JavaEdge/execute/news.rss in our web browser. Here is the news.rss file that is generated by our project:

```xml
<?xml version="1.0"?>
<rss version="2.0">
  <channel>
    <title>JavaEdge: Late Breaking Headlines</title>
    <link>http://localhost:8080/JavaEdge/execute/</link>
    <description>The hard-hitting Java journalism you demand.</description>
    <language>en-us</language>
    <docs>http://backend.userland.com/rss</docs>
    <generator>
          Wrox JavaEdge Application (Struts and Velocity)
    </generator>
    <item>
      <title>This is a story title jcc</title>
      <link>http://localhost:8080/JavaEdge/execute
            /storyDetailSetup?storyId=17</link>
      <description>This is a unit test story intro.</description>
    </item>
    <item>
      <title>This is a story title jcc</title>
      <link>http://localhost:8080/JavaEdge/execute
            /storyDetailSetup?storyId=16</link>
      <description>This is a unit test story intro.</description>
    </item>
    <item>
      <title>This is a story title jcc</title>
      <link>http://localhost:8080/JavaEdge/execute
            /storyDetailSetup?storyId=15</link>
      <description>This is a unit test story intro.</description>
    </item>
    <item>
      <title>This is a story title jcc</title>
      <link>http://localhost:8080/JavaEdge/execute
         /storyDetailSetup?storyId=14</link>
      <description>This is a unit test story intro.</description>
    </item>
    <item>
      <title>storyTitle</title>
      <link>http://localhost:8080/JavaEdge/execute
            /storyDetailSetup?storyId=4</link>
      <description>storyIntro</description>
      <pubDate>Thu, 16 Jan 2003 00:00:00 CST</pubDate>
    </item>
    <item>
      <title>J2EE vrs. .NET</title>
      <link>http://localhost:8080/JavaEdge/execute
         /storyDetailSetup?storyId=3</link>
      <description>Found an interesting article comparing J2EE vrs.
            Microsofts .NET</description>
      <pubDate>Thu, 16 Jan 2003 00:00:00 CST</pubDate>
    </item>
    <item>
      <title>New Book Released:  Open Source for Beginners</title>
      <link>http://localhost:8080/JavaEdge/execute
            /storyDetailSetup?storyId=2</link>
```

```
    <description>New book available on Open Source Development.
        A must have for beginners.</description>
    <pubDate>Thu, 16 Jan 2003 00:00:00 CST</pubDate>
  </item>
  <item>
    <title>Knoppix Linux Rocks</title>
    <link>http://localhost:8080/JavaEdge/execute
        /storyDetailSetup?storyId=1</link>
    <description>I ran across a great linux distribution. It's called
        Knoppix. Completely boots off a CD. Check it out at:
        http://www.knoppix.org/</description>
    <pubDate>Thu, 16 Jan 2003 00:00:00 CST</pubDate>
  </item>
</channel>
</rss>
```

Summary

In this chapter, we've discussed how to use Velocity inside a Struts web application as a presentation layer. We've also shown how to use Velocity from any Java application as a template processing engine. We discussed the Velocity Template Language (VTL) in detail and gave examples for most VTL directives. We also covered Velocity macros, iterators, and logical operators along with the VTL syntax.

We discussed Velocity contexts, and how to get data in and out of the context. We showed how to use the Velocity object to merge a template with the context. Resource loaders are used to find templates and text or HTML that is included in a template.

We've demonstrated using the Velocity tag library with JSP inside our JavaEdge application to create an RSS 2.0 feed. We built a Struts action to populate the request scope with objects and data. We used those objects in the Velocity template that was embedded between opening and closing Velocity tags in the JSP.

7

Creating a Search Engine with Lucene

Every web site that has more than a few pages requires some attention to be given to information architecture, including navigation, a site map, and a search engine. The JavaEdge application needs a search engine that can be plugged into our existing web infrastructure. To avoid maintaining two different technology stacks on our servers, any search engine that we decide to use should be deployable into Tomcat, WebLogic, WebSphere, or another J2EE application server or servlet container. Also, we need something that can be easily customized to match the look and feel of our site.

In this chapter, we will discuss some of the issues with search engines and present the design needed for an effective search tool. We'll use **Lucene**, which is the open source search engine from the Jakarta Apache Group, as our solution and show how to configure Lucene to work with the JavaEdge application.

Search Requirements for the JavaEdge Application

To make full use of the JavaEdge application, it's crucial that users can simply search for the content in which they are interested and view previously published stories and comments. We want to incorporate the logical design of our content into the new search facility. Users should be able to use our search engine like any other web search engine they may be familiar with (for example, Google, Lycos, MSN Search, etc.). The user interface should be similar to these popular sites and, therefore, intuitive for the end user.

Our search engine must remain relevant and provide high quality results. This means that when content is added or updated, our search engine should reflect those changes as soon as possible. Furthermore, we have to minimize the amount of time any stale content appears in the search results. It is very frustrating to click on a search link to find out that the content doesn't have anything to do with the search results. Most users select results only from the first page or at the most first few pages into the site. Hence, we have to find a search engine that can reliably rank and score results.

Another consideration for the user interface is that it needs to be consistent with the rest of the JavaEdge site. A link to the search engine should be available from every page. While displaying the results, a summary or description of each link should be given, so the users can figure out what they're likely to get when they select a particular result.

We need a solution that fits in with our existing architecture. If we used a product that isn't J2EE-compatible, we would have a tougher integration problem. It's certainly possible to use a search engine that is written only in Perl, C, or Python with our JavaEdge application, but it would be much harder to integrate with Struts. We would prefer the solution to be ready to go with our Struts framework. But if this isn't the case, we will need to create an integration code between our application and the search engine.

Another requirement is that the search engine should be open source, so we can modify its behavior. Some Java open source web search engines are Lucene, Egothor, and HouseSpider. HouseSpider uses a Java applet to search the items and display the results. This approach is a little different from the search interface that most commercial web search engines use, such as Google. We're looking for an application that can be customized to look like the rest of the JavaEdge site. Egothor and Lucene are both server-side Java search engines. Both projects could be used to fill our search engine needs. Neither contains a web crawler as a part of the core package and each includes similar parsing, stemming, and indexing functionality.

Lucene gets a preference for the JavaEdge application because it is part of the Jakarta Apache Group and has higher visibility than Egothor. You can find more information on Lucene at: http://jakarta.apache.org/lucene/.

Search Engine Fundamentals

We need to discuss how a web search engine works before we can start our Lucene discussion. You may already be familiar with how search engines such as Google are designed. Google uses web crawlers (also known as spiders), which are fed with many starting points. These starting points are usually the URLs that webmasters submit to Google so that they can be indexed. The web crawlers then download the contents of each URL, and follow the links in the HTML to download more web pages. There are usually a lot of web crawlers distributed across a large number of machines. Crawlers are also used to update the existing content in search engine indexes, to ensure that the search engine results are fresh. Search engines can determine how fast the content changes and by measuring this velocity, they can determine when the existing content should be re-indexed.

The content that the crawlers find is fed into an indexer, which processes HTML (and in case of Google, PDF files) into text content that can be searched across. The indexer also processes the words inside the HTML. Each word that is stored in the index is converted to lower case. Many common words, such as the, a, an, I, and so on, are usually not indexed in a way in which they can be directly searched on. For example, if you search Google for just the word "the", you wouldn't get very useful results. These words are known as **stop words**. Another common processing technique is to use a **stemmer**. Stemmers are designed for a specific language and they process words into their root stems. For example, the word "dogs" would be stored as the word "dog" in the index, and a search for either would return the results that have both the words.

When a user decides to ask the search engine for hits matching a query, the search engine will need to get the query (typically from a web form), and then parse the query into a data structure that it understands. The details of processing this query vary for different search engines. This parsed query will then be fed to a searcher. The searcher will take the query and process the query words in the same way as the content was processed into the index. The results matching this processed query are then sorted using internal algorithms. This sorting takes into account the size of the content, number of matches, how close the matched terms are, and many other factors that depend on the search engine implementation. The results are then passed back to the application code for display to the end user.

Functionality Provided by Lucene

Lucene implements the indexing and querying capabilities, described in the above search engine architecture. Lucene does not include a web crawler or spider, although there is a project called LARM that is currently in its early stages and will provide a web crawler. LARM is not a part of the core Lucene distribution. If you are planning to write a web crawler, it will be much easier to start with LARM.

Lucene provides a set of English language analyzers to process content for stop words and acronyms, and to convert to lower case. There are also German and Chinese language analyzers available. There are implementations for the Porter stemming algorithm and the Snowball stemmer. An HTML parser that uses WebGain's JavaCC comes with Lucene as part of the Lucene demo. It's also possible to use other HTML parsers, such as NekoHTML or JTidy, which aren't bundled with Lucene.

Several different query objects are available, including a Boolean query, a phrase matching query (that can look for exact phrases or words that are near each other), a prefix matching query, a wildcard query, and a fuzzy search query object.

Lucene can also score each hit in the query results. This means that the most likely hits for the given search terms will be given the highest score. It's up to the developers to determine how to display the scores in the search results. It's also possible to assign added weight (known as a boost) to certain terms in the query, which affects the score given to the search results.

Lucene includes some highlighting features, as an add-on to the core API, for marking the search terms in the results. This is a complicated task because the searcher relies on matching the processed words in the query (terms) against the terms stored in the index and neither may match the original words in the content, displayed to the user as a summary in the search results.

Lucene doesn't include any summarization technology. It's possible to cache documents, but there isn't any functionality provided with Lucene. Instead, it's handled in the application that uses Lucene.

Lucene's Architecture

Lucene is a component with a well-defined API that can be driven from another application. Here we're going to discuss some of Lucene's architecture:

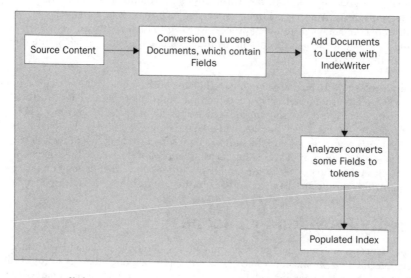

The indexer requires all the source contents to be converted into Lucene documents. Each document is a collection of fields. Each field has a name and a value. The developers can decide the field names. This document is then added to the index with an `IndexWriter` object. This object is responsible for updating the Lucene index with the new entries. The index is stored on the file system. The field values are fed through an analyzer. The analyzer converts the content into tokens. Tokens can be delimited in the source content by whitespace, punctuation, or anything else that the analyzer can determine. The tokens are stored as a document entry in the index.

Searching through Lucene is done using queries:

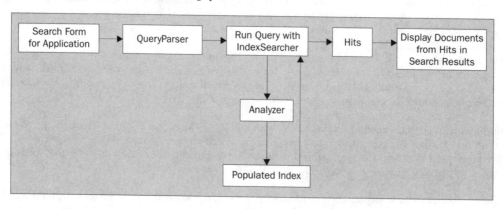

Each query from the form on a web page needs to be translated, with the QueryParser, into a query object that Lucene can understand. That query is then passed on to the IndexSearcher class. The query is run through an analyzer to translate the query terms into tokens that can be matched against results in the index. The index searcher gets back a Hits object, which contains the number of hits, the Document object for each hit, and the score for each hit. Our application then takes the Hits object and displays the search results to the user.

Index

The indexer is responsible for adding new content to our search engine. Lucene works with org.apache.lucene.document.Document objects to build its index. Our existing content will have to be processed into Document objects that Lucene can understand. These objects are composed of Field objects. These Field objects are name-value pairs that Lucene uses as keywords in its index. In addition, we require our indexer to get a list of all the content in the JavaEdge application, so that it can crawl through the content and update or refresh the search engine index.

We need to design the indexer so that it can:

❏   Get content from the JavaEdge application

❏   Determine what content needs to be refreshed in the index

❏   Ensure that the index gets updated on a frequent basis

Let's discuss each of these issues in more detail.

Get Content from the JavaEdge Application

The first design decision is how to get content out of the JavaEdge application. Lucene can be used with any kind of data source, for which an indexer can be written, including web sites, database tables, or free-form text. We could create an indexer that used the JavaEdge application web pages to generate Document objects for Lucene. This would be the most general case for a web search engine; it need not know anything about how the web site was built internally, since it would only communicate via HTTP.

In addition, the search engine is loosely coupled with our web site, that is, if we change some of our classes, we won't have to rewrite the entire search engine. This approach usually requires a general-purpose web spider for the indexing. We could create a list of every URL with content in our system and feed it to the spider. The disadvantage of this method is that our data would be less structured. We couldn't separate pieces of information into fields for Lucene unless we wrote a screen scraper tool to pick the pieces of information from the web page. This approach can be fragile unless metadata is embedded in the web page to highlight information for the indexer.

Another approach would be to create an indexer, which could use JavaEdge's data-access layer to get a list of all stories and comments in the application and use that to build Lucene's index for the application. This would have the advantage of being able to use our internal Story and Comment value objects to directly access data. The code that transforms our content into Lucene documents would be a relatively straightforward tool. As more properties are added to stories and comments, we could add them as fields for the search engine. For this approach, we won't have to do any HTML parsing. We will use this approach for the JavaEdge application.

The last approach would be to ignore the data-access layer and write an indexer that would directly access the database using JDBC. It shares many advantages with the above approach, but it is better to abstract away the database access behind the data-access layer that we have already created.

Keeping the Search Index Fresh

The search engine should be able to determine when content has been changed. It is not desirable to have stale content in the search engine index. This will result in incorrect results being generated, leading to a frustrating user experience.

There are two solutions to solve this problem:

- ❑ Always completely rebuild the index when content has been added or changed
- ❑ Check each piece of content to determine whether it has been updated or deleted since the last index.

A combination of these solutions can be used. For example, you might want to perform an incremental index update every hour and perform a full rebuild only when the server is less loaded during the night. These sorts of decisions can only be made with lots of performance, load, and stress testing. You will discover the optimal strategy after the first few weeks when an application is in a production environment.

If we always rebuild the index when we generate the site, we solve the problem of having stale content, which would only be around for the time between application updates. With Lucene, controlling when to rebuild the index is a simple Boolean flag passed to the IndexWriter class. For this solution, the best approach is to create the index in a separate directory, make sure the index is created without any errors, and then point Lucene's reader to the new index. However, we won't use this method for the JavaEdge application.

To check whether each piece of content is fresh, we can compare each story to the entry stored in the search index. We could create a Lucene document out of each story and then compare the content field in the index with the content field in the document. If the fields aren't identical, we can delete the item out of the index and then add the updated document to the index. If the story isn't found in the index, we can add it to the index. This is how we implemented incremental indexing in JavaEdge.

If we delete a story feature in JavaEdge, we would also need to go through each document in Lucene's index and determine if it still exists as a story in JavaEdge. If it does, we'll need to delete it from the index.

Updating the Index

The Lucene index is contained in a directory on the file system. The developers can choose any location for this directory, but your application will have to keep track of where the index is located. If the index doesn't exist, we will have to create a new index in the chosen directory. When the index already exists, we will need to make sure we don't destroy the index when we open up a file writer. The index creation behavior is controlled with a single Boolean flag in the constructor of the IndexWriter class. Our application will use Lucene's IndexReader class to determine whether an index already exists.

Our next design decision is to determine when to update the index. There are three ways of doing this:

- ❑ Administrator updates the index on a manual basis
- ❑ Index is updated on a fixed time interval (such as 10 minutes or an hour)
- ❑ The index is updated every time a piece of content is changed in the JavaEdge application

The first solution is not very effective. The application administrator would have to be responsible for doing an action that can easily be automated. We can add a feature to the JavaEdge application to trigger an index rebuild any time the administrator wants. This could be added in the second version, in an administrator's interface.

The next approach is attractive. Timer functionality was added to the Java Developer's Kit in version 1.3, which allows us to easily write code that is invoked at a regular interval by a scheduler thread. We could load the timer class into Struts by implementing the `org.apache.struts.action.PlugIn` interface. Struts plug-ins have `init()` and `destroy()` methods that are respectively called by Struts whenever it is loaded or shut down. Using `init()`, we could invoke the scheduler, which would then run our indexer for a time period that can be configured by the administrator. For example, we could update every ten minutes. If this period loads the server heavily, we can increase it. We are going to use the above approach with JavaEdge, by creating a Struts plug-in. The time interval can be modified in the `struts-config.xml` file.

To implement the final approach, we need to create an object that could take a `storyID` and add or update the corresponding story in the index. From the `PostStory` action in Struts, we would add that story to the Lucene index. (Refer to Chapter 3 for the discussion on the `PostStory` action). In the `Postcomment` action, we would update the story in the Lucene index by calling a class that we would write to abstract the process of adding a story to the search index. However, this method can become problematic. If the site gets a large number of comments and stories posted every hour, the search engine will be adding or updating content all of the time. If an error occurs during the indexing process, the index may be out of synchronization with the content in the JavaEdge application.

Analyzers

Search engines need to process data to be used in the index to ensure consistent search results. This processing is called **tokenizing**, which consists of splitting up the data. Lucene tokenizes data in fields to be used in the search engine index. It uses analyzers to perform all of the processing for tokenization. Lucene also uses analyzers for querying the index. The user's query is also tokenized and the searcher looks for results in the index that match the tokens for the query. Each analyzer does tokenization differently; we are going to discuss these differences here.

Each token consists of four different fields:

- ❑ The text
- ❑ The beginning position in the original text
- ❑ The end position in the original text
- ❑ The type of token

Most of this goes on behind the scenes. We're just going to use one of Lucene's built-in analyzers.

If these analyzers aren't giving you the results that you want, you may have to subclass an existing analyzer and use it for your own search engine. You may want to refer to the Lucene web site in the contributions and sand box section for more analyzers. Also check the mailing list archives for the Lucene users and developers mailing lists. If you use a language other than English, German, or Chinese, you will have to write your own analyzer. You may search the Lucene user mailing list archives to determine if someone else has written an analyzer for your language. The Lucene mailing list directions and archives can be found at: http://jakarta.apache.org/site/mail.html.

Lucene has several built-in analyzers. The three that are most interesting are:

- ❑   SimpleAnalyzer
- ❑   StopAnalyzer
- ❑   StandardAnalyzer

The SimpleAnalyzer is the most basic of the built-in analyzers. It creates a stream of tokens by splitting words into tokens, whenever it reaches a character that isn't a letter. For English, it strips out punctuation and converts individual words into tokens. It also converts all letters in the tokens to a lower case.

The StopAnalyzer does everything that the SimpleAnalyzer does, but in addition, it removes some common English words, known as stop words. Most search engines remove these words from the list of tokens to make the search more effective. In Lucene, the stop words are defined as an array in the source code for the StopAnalyzer class. They are also independently defined in the StandardAnalyzer class. If you need to change them, you will have to extend the standard analyzer. Here is the list of English stop words in Lucene 1.2:

a	and	are	as
at	be	but	by
for	if	in	into
is	it	no	not
of	on	or	s
such	t	that	the
their	then	there	these
they	this	to	was
will	with		

We are going to use the StandardAnalyzer for our search engine. It does everything that the SimpleAnalyzer and StopAnalyzer do. The StandardAnalyzer also uses the StandardFilter class to do processing. This filter removes the ending apostrophe s ('s) from words, such as it's, Sun's, Judy's, etc. The StandardAnalyzer would create a token with "it", instead of "it's". Hence, a search for either of those terms would match the other. If the word is an acronym (IBM, N.I.H., NBA), the StandardAnalyzer also strips any dots (.) from it. The tokens for N.F.L. and NFL would be the same.

Stemming

Lucene comes with a filter class called PorterStemFilter, which allows you to create stems for the words in your index. The filter uses a class called PorterStemmer, which is a Java implementation of an algorithm for removing suffixes from words (leaving the root) by Martin Porter. You will have to create your own analyzer class to use this filter, and directions are given in the source code for PorterStemFilter. We're not going to use this stemming functionality in our application.

Here are several examples of words that have been stemmed with the Porter stemming algorithm: (taken from Martin Porter's web site: http://snowball.tartarus.org/porter/stemmer.html):

Word	Stemmed as
happy	happi
happiness	happi
happier	happier
drive	drive
driven	driven
drives	drive
driving	drive

Indexing HTML

We can use the NekoHTML parser, written by Andy Clark, to index any reasonably well-formed HTML files. NekoHTML can be found at http://www.apache.org/~andyc/neko/doc/index.html. One of the most difficult parts of writing a search engine is parsing HTML that isn't correct, but is still on the web because it works in the leading browsers. NekoHTML can strip the HTML tags out of our HTML files. It can be configured with filters to let certain tags through to the output and also retrieve the attributes or contents of any tags we want. We could get the contents of <META> tags or <TITLE> tags and use them as fields in our Lucene documents. NekoHTML has to be used with the Xerces XML parser for parsing our HTML. We have used the Xerces 2.0.0 JAR files.

Here is a short example demonstrating the use of NekoHTML to strip all HTML tags from an HTML file. We used the Xerces DOM serializer for output, but you can use the one of your choice. However, you'll have to tell the serializer to write to a different output:

```java
package com.wrox.javaedge.search;

import org.cyberneko.html.parsers.DOMParser;
import org.cyberneko.html.filters.ElementRemover;

import org.apache.xerces.xni.parser.XMLDocumentFilter;
import org.apache.xerces.util.DOMUtil;
import org.apache.xml.serialize.OutputFormat;
import org.apache.xml.serialize.XMLSerializer;

import org.xml.sax.SAXNotRecognizedException;
import org.xml.sax.SAXException;
import org.w3c.dom.Document;

import java.io.IOException;

public class HTMLParser {

    public static void main(String[] args)
        throws SAXException, SAXNotRecognizedException, IOException {
```

```
        DOMParser parser = new DOMParser();

        ElementRemover remover = new ElementRemover();

        //keep the link element
        remover.acceptElement("A",null);

        XMLDocumentFilter[] f = {remover};

        parser.setProperty("http://cyberneko.org/html/properties/filters", f);
        parser.parse("test.html");

        Document xmlDoc = parser.getDocument();

        OutputFormat outputFormat = new OutputFormat(xmlDoc);
        outputFormat.setPreserveSpace(true);
        outputFormat.setOmitXMLDeclaration(true);
        outputFormat.setOmitDocumentType(true);
        XMLSerializer serializer = new XMLSerializer(System.out, outputFormat);
        serializer.serialize(xmlDoc);
    }
}
```

Here is the sample HTML file (test.html) that we used:

```
<html>
  <head>
    <title>HTML test</title>
  </head>
  <body>
    Here is some sample <b>text</b>.
    <p>
    And a link <a href="http://www.cnn.com/" alt="cnn">CNN</a>.<br>

  </body>
</html>
```

The Lucene distribution comes with a simple demo application. The demo includes an HTML parser that was built with WebGain's JavaCC. If you are interested in using JavaCC as part of your application, you may want to take a look at the source code in the demo directory.

Implementing the Index

In this section, we'll examine in detail the classes used to implement the index. This consists of the IndexContent class, which adds stories into the index, the DocumentConversionTool class, which translates those stories into Lucene documents, and the scheduler classes. The scheduler classes implement a Struts plug-in and a TimerTask. We also update struts-config.xml with the settings for our scheduler plug-in. (Refer to Chapter 2 for the discussion on the struts-config.xml file)

Building the Scheduler

In this section, we'll be looking at the `IndexScheduler` class, which schedules the content indexing process. It is really just a wrapper around a JDK `Timer` class that runs a complete index of the site on schedule. The `IndexScheduler` class uses a class called `IndexTask`, which extends `TimerTask` from the JDK. The only method creates an index by using the `IndexContent` utility class. The scheduler will run the indexing process every hour. We will make this time period configurable in the `struts-config.xml` file.

Struts 1.1 has a built-in mechanism for running code when the Struts application is launched. Struts calls these application-lifecycle objects as **plug-ins**. Plug-ins are an alternative to creating a servlet, which is loaded when the servlet container initializes. Any code that needs to be initialized at the startup may be implemented as a plug-in.

We need to write a plug-in class to implement the `org.apache.struts.action.PlugIn` interface. This interface has only two methods:

❑   `init(ActionServlet servlet, ApplicationConfig config)`:
    We're going to use this method to invoke a timer to schedule our indexer.

❑   `destroy()`:
    Used when the Struts application is shutting down. We are not going to use this.

Our plug-in will be configured in the `struts-config.xml` file. We already have one plug-in configured in the file. The `validator` plug-in configuration uses the `<set-property>` element to call a JavaBeans setter in the `org.apache.struts.validator.ValidatorPlugIn` class. (Refer to Chapter 3 for the discussion on the `validator` plug-in). Our indexer plug-in is simple and takes only a timeout value for the scheduler as a property.

Here is the code for both plug-ins in `struts-config.xml`:

```xml
<?xml version="1.0" encoding="ISO-8859-1"?>
<!DOCTYPE struts-config PUBLIC "-//Apache Software Foundation//DTD Struts
Configuration 1.1//EN"
"http://jakarta.apache.org/struts/dtds/struts-config_1_1.dtd">

<struts-config>
  ...
  <plug-in className="org.apache.struts.validator.ValidatorPlugIn">
    <set-property property="pathnames" value="/WEB-INF/validator-rules.xml,
                                              /WEB-INF/validation.xml"/>

  </plug-in>

  <plug-in className="com.wrox.javaedge.struts.search.IndexerPlugIn">
    <set-property property="time" value="3600000"/>
  </plug-in>
  ...
</struts-config>
```

The plug-in class calls the scheduler from the `init()` method. The `setTime()` method is called by Struts before the `init()` method is executed. We supply a default, in case the time property isn't configured properly for the plug-in.

Here is the code for `IndexerPlugIn.java`:

```java
package com.wrox.javaedge.struts.search;

import org.apache.struts.action.ActionServlet;
import org.apache.struts.action.PlugIn;
import org.apache.struts.config.ApplicationConfig;

import com.wrox.javaedge.search.IndexScheduler;

public class IndexerPlugIn implements PlugIn {

  protected IndexScheduler scheduler;

  // default is one hour
  protected long time = 60*60*1000;

  // Doesn't do anything in this implementation
  public void destroy() {
  }

  public void init(ActionServlet servlet, ApplicationConfig config) {
    scheduler = new IndexScheduler(time);
  }

  public void setTime(long time) {
    this.time = time;
  }
}
```

The scheduler uses the JDK 1.3 `Timer` class to run a timer task that starts the indexer. We use an initial delay of one minute before the indexer is first started.

The following code shows `IndexScheduler.java`, which schedules a content indexing process. The constructor takes the number of milliseconds of delay before the execution of the timer task from the search configuration:

```java
package com.wrox.javaedge.search;

import java.util.Timer;

public class IndexScheduler {

  // jdk 1.3 and above timer class
  Timer timer;

  public IndexScheduler(long time) {
    timer = new Timer();
    timer.schedule(new IndexTask(), 1000, time);
  }
}
```

Finally, we have the task that runs the search engine indexer by calling the `createIndex()` method in our `IndexContent` utility class:

```
package com.wrox.javaedge.search;

import java.util.TimerTask;

public class IndexTask extends TimerTask {

  public void run() {
     IndexContent indexer = new IndexContent indexer.createIndex();
  }
}
```

The IndexContent Class

The `IndexContent` class takes our stories and comments from JavaEdge and gives them to Lucene for indexing. We use Lucene's `IndexWriter` class to access a Lucene index stored on disk. We tell the writer to create an index if one doesn't exist, and to use the old one if it already exists when we call the constructor on the index writer.

All of the stories are pulled out of JavaEdge using the `Story` data-access object. (Refer to Chapter 5 for the discussion on the data-access tier). Each of the stories in turn is run through the document conversion tool and the resulting document is indexed by Lucene. Most of the details are hidden, but you can see the code, as Lucene is an open source tool.

The methods implemented in this class are summarized in the table below:

Method	Description
GetWriter()	Gets a copy of the index writer that we use to add entries to the index. Uses the standard analyzer.
CreateIndex()	Creates an index from all the stories. Stories are retrieved using the getAllStories() and are converted to a Lucene Document before being added to the index, using the index writer obtained in getWriter().
GetAllStories()	Makes a call out to storyDAO to get all the stories.
CloseWriter()	Closes down the writer, after running the index optimizer.

Here is the full code for the `IndexContent` class:

```
package com.wrox.javaedge.search;

import java.io.IOException;
import java.util.*;

import org.apache.lucene.analysis.Analyzer;
import org.apache.lucene.analysis.standard.StandardAnalyzer;
import org.apache.lucene.document.Document;
```

```
import org.apache.lucene.index.IndexWriter;
import org.apache.lucene.index.IndexReader;
import org.apache.lucene.index.Term;
import org.apache.lucene.search.Searcher;
import org.apache.lucene.search.IndexSearcher;
import org.apache.lucene.search.Query;
import org.apache.lucene.search.Hits;
import org.apache.lucene.queryParser.QueryParser;
import org.apache.lucene.queryParser.ParseException;
import org.apache.log4j.Category;

import com.wrox.javaedge.common.DataAccessException;
import com.wrox.javaedge.story.StoryVO;
import com.wrox.javaedge.story.dao.StoryDAO;

public class IndexContent {

  // Create Log4j category instance for logging
  static private Category log =
    Category.getInstance(IndexContent.class.getName());

  public IndexWriter getWriter() throws IOException {

    Analyzer analyzer = new StandardAnalyzer();
    IndexWriter writer;

   // check to see if an index already exists
    if (IndexReader.indexExists(SearchConfiguration.getIndexPath())) {
      writer = new IndexWriter(SearchConfiguration.getIndexPath(),
                               analyzer, false);
    } else {
      writer = new IndexWriter(SearchConfiguration.getIndexPath(),
                               analyzer, true);
    }
    return writer;
  }

  public IndexReader getReader() throws IOException {

    IndexReader reader =
                IndexReader.open(SearchConfiguration.getIndexPath());
    return reader;
  }

  public void createIndex() {
    try {
      // Lucene's index generator
      IndexWriter writer = getWriter();

      // Lucene's index reader
      IndexReader reader = getReader();

      // set up our analyzer
      Analyzer analyzer = new StandardAnalyzer();
```

```
// set up our searcher
String indexPath = SearchConfiguration.getIndexPath();
Searcher searcher = new IndexSearcher(indexPath);

// from the DAO
Collection stories = getAllStories();
if (stories == null) {
  return;
}

// Easier to use an iterator for retrieving the stories
Iterator iter = stories.iterator();
while (iter.hasNext()) {
  // this could throw a class cast exception
  StoryVO story = (StoryVO) iter.next();

  // we wrote the Document Conversion Tool specifically for the
  // story value objects
  Document doc = DocumentConversionTool.createDocument(story);

  // get out the content field
  String content =
        doc.getField(DocumentConversionTool.CONTENT_FIELD).stringValue();

  // get the search entry for this story id
  // create a query that looks up items by our searchId
  Query query = QueryParser.parse(story.getStoryId().toString(),
              "storyId", analyzer);

  // get all of the hits for the query term out of the index
  Hits hits = searcher.search(query);

  // should only have one or zero entries for each story id,
  // otherwise log a warning
  if (hits.length() == 0) {
    // this story is brand new
    // add the converted document to the Lucene index
    writer.addDocument(doc);
    log.info("new story added: " + story.getStoryId());
  } else if (hits.length() == 1) {
    log.info("story is old: " + story.getStoryId());
    // get the entry out of the search engine
    Document oldDoc = hits.doc(0);

    // get the old content
    String oldContent =
          oldDoc.getField(DocumentConversionTool.CONTENT_FIELD).
                                              stringValue();

    // if it has been updated, delete it from the index, then re-add it.
    if (!content.equals(oldContent)) {
      log.info("story is being updated: " + story.getStoryId());
      reader.delete(new Term("storyId",story.getStoryId().toString()));
      writer.addDocument(doc);
```

```
            } else {
              log.warn("Wrong number of entries for story id: " +
                    story.getStoryId() + ": " + hits.length() + " found." );
            }
          }
        }
        closeWriter(writer);

      } catch (IOException ie) {
        log.error ("Error creating Lucene index: " + ie.getMessage(), ie);

      } catch (ClassCastException cce) {
        log.error ("Error casting object to StoryVO: " + cce.getMessage(), cce);

      } catch (ParseException pe) {
        log.error ("Error parsing Lucene query for storyId: " +
              pe.getMessage(), pe);
      }
    }

    public Collection getAllStories() {
      try {
        StoryDAO storyDAO = new StoryDAO();
        return storyDAO.findAllStories();

      } catch (DataAccessException dae) {
        log.error("Error retrieving all stories from DAO: " + dae.getMessage(),
              dae);
      }
      return null;
    }

    public void closeWriter(IndexWriter writer) throws IOException {
      if (writer == null) {
        return;
      }
      writer.optimize();
      writer.close();
    }
  }
}
```

The DocumentConversionTool Class

From the above code listing of the IndexContent class, you can see that the createIndex() method
uses a DocumentConversionTool class to convert the index content from a StoryVO class to a
Lucene Document. The DocumentConversionTool class contains methods that read content out of
the Lucene story and comment value objects and transform them:

Method	Description
createDocument()	This method is the core of the class. It takes a populated JavaEdge StoryVO object as a parameter, creates a new Lucene Document object and then populates it with Lucene fields. Responsible for creating content, title, introduction, date, and storyId fields.
addContent()	Adds content from the story and comment value objects to the content field. Uses the title, introduction, story body, and comment bodies to generate the content.

Our Lucene Document object is going to contain a set of fields that are specific to our JavaEdge application. Specifically, the body of each comment will be appended to the introduction, title, and body of the story, so that we can search through the entire text of the story.

All of our fields will use String objects for the values. Lucene is also capable of using Reader objects for the values if the field is to be tokenized and indexed, but not stored in the index as a copy. The table below summarizes the Document Fields:

Field	Meaning
content	The introduction of each story will be appended to the body of each story, and then the body of each comment will be appended to this
title	The title of the story
date	The date the story was submitted
introduction	The introduction for the story
storyId	The ID for the story, so we can retrieve it from the data-access object layer in the future

Here is the code listing for DocumentConversionTool:

```java
package com.wrox.javaedge.search;
import org.apache.lucene.document.DateField;
import org.apache.lucene.document.Document;
import org.apache.lucene.document.Field;

import com.wrox.javaedge.story.StoryVO;
import com.wrox.javaedge.story.StoryCommentVO;

import java.util.Iterator;

public class DocumentConversionTool {
    public static Document createDocument(StoryVO story) {

    // create a Document object
    Document document = new Document();

    // create a field that is only stored in the index
```

```
      Long storyId = story.getStoryId();
      if (storyId != null) {
        document.add(Field.UnIndexed("storyId", storyId.toString()));
      }
    }
```

We are going to use the `storyId` field to create links from the search results to the actual story. We intend to allow it to be searched on for the incremental indexing feature, so we will use the `Keyword()` method in the `Field` object to add our `storyId` to the `document`. The `Keyword()` method creates a field that is stored in the index for access later, and can be used for querying.

Most of our Lucene fields are going to be created by calling the `Text()` method on the `Field` class:

```
      // create a field that is tokenized, indexed, and stored in the index
      String title = story.getStoryTitle();
      document.add(Field.Text("title", title));

      // create a field that is tokenized, indexed, and stored in the index
      String introduction = story.getStoryIntro();
      document.add(Field.Text("introduction", introduction));
```

The `Field.Text()` method creates fields that are indexed, tokenized, and stored in the index. If a field is tokenized, that means it is broken up into individual elements by a Lucene analyzer (refer to the section called *Analyzers*). You should use this method when you need to retrieve the contents of the field during the query results. For the JavaEdge application, we need the `title` and `introduction` to display the search results:

The `date` is created with the help of a special class called `DateField`:

```
      //create a field that is indexed and stored in the index
      java.util.Date date = story.getSubmissionDate();
      document.add(Field.Keyword("date", DateField.dateToString(date)));

      addContent(story, document, title, introduction);

      return document;
    }
```

The `DateField` class contains methods for converting between Java date and time objects and Lucene's internal string representation of dates. Here, we've used the `dateToString()` method to store our dates as strings in Lucene's format.

Finally, we've got the `addContent()` method, which adds the story title, the introduction, body content, and comment bodies to the `content` field of the `Document` object. This field is our all-purpose content field that we will use for querying. Our title, introduction, story body, and comment bodies are all appended together to create one large content value:

```
      protected static void addContent(StoryVO story,
                                       Document document,
                                       String title,
                                       String introduction) {
        // create the content for the search query
        // and then store it in the index, tokenized and indexed
```

```
        String content = title + " " + introduction +
                    " " + story.getStoryBody();

        Iterator iter = story.getComments().iterator();
        while (iter.hasNext()) {
            StoryCommentVO comment = (StoryCommentVO) iter.next();
            if (comment != null) {
                content = content + " " + comment.getCommentBody();
            }
        }

        document.add(Field.UnStored("content",content));
    }
}
```

Note that we use the `Field.Text()` method to create this field, so we can retrieve our content later to compare it with existing versions for the incremental indexer.

Querying the Index

Our search form layer has to be integrated with the presentation layer. We will need to create a search form using Struts and then make it accessible from the JavaEdge navigation. We'll need a link to the search form in the JSP header file, which will require an addition to the `ApplicationResources.properties` resource bundle. While we're modifying the resource bundle, we will need to add some messages for the JSP page that come out of the properties file.

After submitting a query from the JSP page that we are going to build, our request will go to an `Action` class called `Search`, which will perform some error checking and exception handling, but won't contain any logic. Instead, it will delegate most of its work to a utility class we are going to build, called `SearchIndex`.

We're also going to use our own class to transport the results between Lucene and the JSP, called `SearchResults`. This class will hold the hits from Lucene, along with the original search terms. More properties could be added to this class in the future to support new Lucene functionality.

For our query form, we will create a class that extends the Struts `ActionForm` class. The only property in this class will be called `query` and it will be a `String`.

The implementation of the search form can, therefore, be broken up into several pieces:

- ❑ The navigation links to the search form
- ❑ The JSP for the search form (this JSP will also display results if they exist)
- ❑ Modifying `struts-config.xml`
- ❑ The Struts `Action` for the query
- ❑ A class that interfaces with Lucene directly to retrieve search results from a query
- ❑ Navigation Links

The resources bundle of `ApplicationResources.properties` contains the navigation URLs. We had to add our path for the search engine form action to the bundle of header URLs. The relevant portion of this configuration is highlighted below:

```
# Sample ResourceBundle properties file
#URL For the Login Screen

#Header URLS

javaedge.header.search=<a href="/javaedge/execute/SearchSetup">Search</a>
...
#Search Form
javaedge.search.form.text.header=Search JavaEdge
javaedge.search.form.text.intro=Use the below form for searching JavaEdge
javaedge.search.form.querylabel=Search terms
```

In addition to creating the link in the `ApplicationResources.properties`, we needed to update the navigation bar JSP file to show our search link. The relevant code is highlighted in the code listing for `header.jsp` below:

```
<%@ page language="java" %>
    <td width="17%" bgcolor="#99CCFF" align="center">
        <bean:message key="javaedge.header.viewallstories"/>
     </td>


    <td width="17%" bgcolor="#99CCFF" align="center">
        <bean:message key="javaedge.header.search"/>
     </td>


    <logic:notPresent scope="session" name="memberVO">
      <td width="17%" bgcolor="#99CCFF" align="center">
        <bean:message key="javaedge.header.signup"/>
      </td>
    </logic:notPresent>

  </table>
  </html:form>
  </center>
</div>
```

JSP Pages

There are two JSP pages for the search functionality. The first, `searchForm.jsp`, is a simple wrapper page that includes a title, a header, content, and footer inside a template:

```
<%@ page language="java" %>

<%@ taglib uri="/WEB-INF/struts-bean.tld" prefix="bean" %>
<%@ taglib uri="/WEB-INF/struts-html.tld" prefix="html" %>
<%@ taglib uri="/WEB-INF/struts-logic.tld" prefix="logic" %>
<%@ taglib uri="/WEB-INF/struts-template.tld" prefix="template" %>
```

```
<template:insert template='/WEB-INF/jsp/template.jsp'>
  <template:put name='title' content='Search JavaEdge' direct='true'/>
  <template:put name='header' content='/WEB-INF/jsp/header.jsp'/>
  <template:put name='content' content='/WEB-
                     INF/jsp/searchFormContent.jsp'/>
  <template:put name='footer' content='footer.jsp'/>
</template:insert>
```

Our second page, `searchFormContent.jsp`, provides an HTML form for querying the search engine, and it also displays any query results. We're going to walk through this JSP page and explain it step-by-step.

The first part of the JSP page contains standard references to the language and tag libraries used:

```
<%@ page language="java" %>
<%@ taglib uri="/WEB-INF/struts-bean.tld" prefix="bean" %>
<%@ taglib uri="/WEB-INF/struts-html.tld" prefix="html" %>
```

The next tag library is Velocity. Velocity is a simple templating language we can use as a drop-in replacement for JSP syntax inside a JSP file. The Velocity tag library allows us to write Velocity code directly into our JSP page. We used Velocity for the search results to demonstrate how simple it can be. For the discussion on Velocity and installing the Velocity tag library, refer to Chapter 6.

```
<%@ taglib uri="/WEB-INF/veltag.tld" prefix="vel" %>
```

First, we display some header text at the top of the page. These messages are pulled out of the `ApplicationResources.properties` file in the `WEB-INF/classes` directory:

```
<br/><br/>
<h2><bean:message key="javaedge.search.form.text.header"/></h2>

<html:errors/>
```

We use the `Search` action we've configured with Struts after we submit the form:

```
<html:form action="Search">
<table>
  <tr>
    <td>
      <bean:message key="javaedge.search.form.text.intro"/>

    </td>
    <td>
      <br/><br/> 
    </td>
  </tr>
  <tr>
    <td>
      <bean:message key="javaedge.search.form.querylabel"/>
```

Struts can call the query setter on our form class (`SearchForm`):

```
      <html:text name="searchForm" property="query"/>
    </td>
  </tr>
  <tr>
    <td align="center">
      <html:submit property="submitButton" value="Submit"/>  
      <html:cancel value="Cancel"/>
    </td>
  </tr>
</table>
<p>
```

This is the beginning of the Velocity code for the search results. We use the tag library we declared above. First, we check for the existence of an object called searchResults. If it exists, we need to display those results. If it doesn't exist, we won't run any more code on this page.

```
<vel:velocity>
    #if ($searchResults)
```

We'll set up some short names for properties on the searchResults object. Velocity uses shortcut syntax to reference properties that are really accessed with getter and setter methods:

```
#set($length = $searchResults.length)
#set($hits = $searchResults.hits)
```

If we searched for something that wasn't in our index, we'll display a nice message telling the user we couldn't find anything for their terms:

```
#if ($length == 0)
    No Search results found for terms $searchResults.terms
#else
```

Otherwise, we'll tell the user how many results they have:

```
<B>$length Search Results present</B>
#set($docsLength = $length - 1)
```

We can iterate through our results. The hits object isn't an iterator, so we have to use a range ([0..$docsLength]) to move through our results. A future improvement would be to include paging for our results:

```
#foreach ($ctr in [0..$docsLength])
    #set($doc = $hits.doc($ctr))
    <TR bgcolor="#99CCFF">
        <TD>
```

Here, we're making calls to the Lucene Document object to get the title field, rendered as a string. We do the same for the introduction:

```
                    $doc.getField("title").stringValue()<BR/>
                </TD>
            </TR>
            <TR>
                <TD>
                    $doc.getField("introduction").stringValue()
                </TD>
            </TR>
            <TR>
```

The `storyId` is used to make a link to the full story:

```
                <TD align="right">
                    #set($storyId = $doc.getField("storyId").stringValue())
                    <a href='/JavaEdge/execute/storyDetailSetup?storyId=
                    $storyId'>Full Story</a><BR/><BR/>
                </TD>
            </TR>

        #end
      #end
   #end
</vel:velocity>

</html:form>
```

Configuring Struts for our Pages and Actions

For our search results page, we need to add entries to `struts-config.xml`. The relevant parts of the configuration file are highlighted below. The search form class had to be defined under the `<form-beans>` element so we could use it for the action mappings.

The action mappings are similar to other mappings we used for JavaEdge. One minor difference is that both of our actions use the same JSP page, which allows us to keep the search query code in one place.

```
<?xml version="1.0" encoding="ISO-8859-1"?>
<!DOCTYPE struts-config PUBLIC "-//Apache Software Foundation//DTD Struts
Configuration 1.1//EN"
                        "http://jakarta.apache.org/struts/dtds/struts-
config_1_1.dtd">

<struts-config>
    <form-beans>

    ...
        <form-bean name="searchForm"
                   type="com.wrox.javaedge.struts.search.SearchForm"/>
    </form-beans>

    <global-forwards type="org.apache.struts.action.ActionForward">
        <forward name="system.error" path="/WEB-INF/jsp/systemError.jsp"/>
        <forward name="default.action" path="/execute/homePageSetup"/>
    </global-forwards>
```

```
<action-mappings>

...

    <action path="/SearchSetup"
            type="com.wrox.javaedge.struts.search.SearchFormSetupAction"
            name="searchForm"
            scope="request"
            validate="false">
        <forward name="search.success" path="/WEB-INF/jsp/searchForm.jsp"/>
    </action>

    <action path="/Search"
            type="com.wrox.javaedge.struts.search.Search"
            input="/WEB-INF/jsp/searchForm.jsp"
            name="searchForm"
            scope="request"
            validate="false">
        <forward name="search.success" path="/WEB-INF/jsp/searchForm.jsp"/>
    </action>

</action-mappings>
<plug-in className="org.apache.struts.validator.ValidatorPlugIn">
    <set-property property="pathnames" value="/WEB-INF/validator-rules.xml,
                                              /WEB-INF/validation.xml"/>
</plug-in>
<plug-in className="com.wrox.javaedge.struts.search.IndexerPlugIn">
    <set-property property="time" value="360000"/>
</plug-in>
</struts-config>
```

Struts Forms and Actions

There are three classes associated with the search forms:

- ❑ SearchForm extends ActionForm and represents the form on the search page
- ❑ SearchFormSetupAction is used to set up the search form
- ❑ Search gets the search results from Lucene and puts them into the request

The Search action retrieves the query terms from the form bean, after checking to make sure the form is actually for the search engine. All of the work with Lucene is done by a utility class, called SearchIndex, so Search doesn't need to import any Lucene classes.

> **It's good practice to keep your actions away from any back-end integration code you have, in case you need to switch web frameworks in the future, or you need to support non-web clients.**

Most of the Search action concerns itself with error checking and exception handling. We try to catch every exception before it bubbles up to the servlet runner. Instead of showing a stack trace or exception to the end user, we will display the system-failure error page for the JavaEdge application.

```java
package com.wrox.javaedge.struts.search;

import java.io.IOException;
import javax.servlet.http.HttpServletRequest;
import javax.servlet.http.HttpServletResponse;

import org.apache.log4j.Logger;
import org.apache.lucene.queryParser.ParseException;
import org.apache.struts.action.Action;
import org.apache.struts.action.ActionForm;
import org.apache.struts.action.ActionForward;
import org.apache.struts.action.ActionMapping;

import com.wrox.javaedge.search.SearchIndex;
import com.wrox.javaedge.search.SearchResults;

public class Search extends Action {

    private static Logger logger = Logger.getLogger(Search.class);

    public ActionForward execute (ActionMapping mapping,
                                  ActionForm form,
                                  HttpServletRequest request,
                                  HttpServletResponse response){

        logger.info("***Entering Search***");

        if (!(form instanceof SearchForm)) {
            logger.warn("Form passed to Search not an instance of SearchForm");
            return (mapping.findForward("system.failure"));
        }

        // get the query from the form bean
        String query = ((SearchForm)form).getQuery();

        // get the search results
        SearchIndex searchIndex = new SearchIndex();

        SearchResults results = null;
        try {
            results = searchIndex.search(query);
            logger.info("Found " + results.getLength() + " hits.");

        } catch (IOException e) {
            logger.error("IOException with search index for: " + query,e);
            return (mapping.findForward("system.failure"));

        } catch (ParseException e) {
            logger.error("ParseException with search index for: " + query,e);
            return (mapping.findForward("system.failure"));
        }

        // put the search results into the request
        request.setAttribute("searchResults", results);
```

```
            logger.info("***Leaving Search***");

            return (mapping.findForward("search.success"));
        }
    }
```

The form we use for the search engine query isn't very complicated at all. It only has one property, `query`:

```java
package com.wrox.javaedge.struts.search;

import javax.servlet.http.HttpServletRequest;

import org.apache.struts.action.ActionErrors;
import org.apache.struts.action.ActionForm;
import org.apache.struts.action.ActionMapping;
import org.apache.struts.action.ActionServlet;
import org.apache.struts.util.MessageResources;

public class SearchForm extends ActionForm {

    protected String query = "";

    public ActionErrors validate(ActionMapping mapping,
                                 HttpServletRequest request) {
        ActionErrors errors = new ActionErrors();

        return errors;
    }

    public void reset(ActionMapping mapping,
                      HttpServletRequest request) {
        ActionServlet servlet = this.getServlet();
        MessageResources messageResources = servlet.getResources();

    }

    public String getQuery() {
        return query;
    }

    public void setQuery(String query) {
        this.query = query;
    }
}
```

The `SearchFormSetupAction` class for the search engine form doesn't do anything right now. It's possible that your form may need to change to support different uses. For now, we just have some skeleton code that can be used later for more advanced search form functionality:

```java
package com.wrox.javaedge.struts.search;

import org.apache.struts.action.Action;
import org.apache.struts.action.ActionMapping;
import org.apache.struts.action.ActionForm;
```

```
import org.apache.struts.action.ActionForward;
import javax.servlet.http.HttpServletRequest;
import javax.servlet.http.HttpServletResponse;
import javax.servlet.http.HttpSession;

import com.wrox.javaedge.member.*;
import com.wrox.javaedge.member.dao.*;
import com.wrox.javaedge.common.*;
import java.util.*;

public class SearchFormSetupAction extends Action {

  // Performs no work for the action
  public ActionForward perform(ActionMapping mapping,
                               ActionForm form,
                               HttpServletRequest request,
                               HttpServletResponse response){
    return (mapping.findForward("search.success"));
  }
}
```

Utility Class for Lucene integration

The integration code for querying with Lucene is contained in one utility class, `SearchIndex`. This class takes a query string, and returns a `SearchResults` object, but doesn't contain any references to Struts, just as the action that calls it knows nothing about Lucene. If we ever need to move to another software package for either, this should make the task that much simpler:

```
package com.wrox.javaedge.search;

import java.io.IOException;
import java.util.*;

import org.apache.log4j.Logger;
import org.apache.lucene.analysis.Analyzer;
import org.apache.lucene.analysis.standard.StandardAnalyzer;
import org.apache.lucene.queryParser.ParseException;
import org.apache.lucene.queryParser.QueryParser;
import org.apache.lucene.search.Hits;
import org.apache.lucene.search.IndexSearcher;
import org.apache.lucene.search.Query;
import org.apache.lucene.search.Searcher;

public class SearchIndex {

  protected static Logger logger = Logger.getLogger(SearchIndex.class);

  public SearchResults search(String terms)
      throws IOException, ParseException {
```

First, we create a `SearchResults` object (we'll cover this class in the next section):

```
    SearchResults results = new SearchResults();

    logger.info("Search terms are: " + terms);
```

It's possible that someone has passed us a bad query string, and if they did, we'll log it, and give them back empty results. It's up to the JSP search results page to handle any error messages:

```
if (terms == null) {
  logger.warn("Terms passed to SearchIndex are null");
  return results;
}
```

The `StandardAnalyzer` we use here is the same analyzer we used to build the index. It's necessary to use the same analyzer to search the index as we used to build the index. Each analyzer processes words in fields into terms differently, and Lucene creates terms from the query and retrieves documents with matching terms from the index:

```
// set up our analyzer
Analyzer analyzer = new StandardAnalyzer();
```

The searcher goes into the index that is stored on disk in segments and read it through. It then comes back with a set of hits:

```
// set up our searcher
String indexPath = SearchConfiguration.getIndexPath();
Searcher searcher = new IndexSearcher(indexPath);
```

The query parser takes our search terms, the name of the field we are searching, and our analyzer. We had created a field that contains the text out of the other fields for use in searching. We'll find the stories we're looking for, even if the search terms are in the title, introduction, or comments and not the body of the story:

```
// create a query object out of our query
Query query = QueryParser.parse(terms, DocumentConversionTool.CONTENT_FIELD,
                                analyzer);
```

The searcher will give us the hits returned from the index for our query. The `Hits` class from Lucene only contains three methods. The `length()` method gives the number of hits from the current search. The `doc()` method retrieves the Lucene document from the index (passed in as a parameter), by position. The `score()` method gives you the score Lucene assigned to each document, based on its position in the results. We then fill up the results object with our hits, length, and terms:

```
// get all of the hits for the query term out of the index
Hits hits = searcher.search(query);

results.setHits(hits);
results.setLength(hits.length());
results.setTerms(terms);

if (hits == null) {
  logger.info("Hits object is null for: " + terms);
```

```
    }

    // debugging
    logger.info("Number of hits found for: "
                + terms + " is " + hits.length());

    return results;
  }
}
```

SearchResults Class

This class is a simple wrapper class that contains:

❑   The `hits` object, which points to each document that was found in the index

❑   The `length` of the hits object, which is the number of documents found

❑   The original `terms` used in the search form

This class is passed around between the action, the utility class, and the JSP content page:

```
package com.wrox.javaedge.search;

import org.apache.lucene.search.Hits;

public class SearchResults {

  protected int length = 0;
  protected Hits hits = null;
  protected String terms = null;

  public Hits getHits() {
    return hits;
  }

  public int getLength() {
    return length;
  }

  public void setHits(Hits hits) {
    this.hits = hits;
  }

  public void setLength(int length) {
    this.length = length;
  }

  public String getTerms() {
    return terms;
  }

  public void setTerms(String terms) {
    this.terms = terms;
  }
}
```

Summary

In this chapter, we've discussed the issues of integrating Lucene into a Struts-based application. We've also used Velocity in our JSP page with the Velocity tag library. We've demonstrated keeping business logic or integration code out of our Struts action classes, and keeping Struts code out of our back-end integration classes.

Lucene is a well-built API for creating applications that use searches. We've shown that Lucene doesn't have to be used with HTML files over HTTP. On the contrary, it excels at integrating with existing content data stores.

For this integration, we created:

❏ A scheduler system that runs as a Struts plug-in to perform incremental indexing

❏ A conversion tool that translates JavaEdge stories and comments into native Lucene documents

❏ A utility class that takes a query string and returns Search Results

❏ JSP content and wrapper pages for the search form and results

❏ A simple demonstration of using Velocity inside JSP as a tag library

❏ A Struts action that sits between our JSP and our utility class and handles errors and exceptions

❏ An example that uses NekoHTML to parse text out of an HTML file.

In the final chapter, now that our JavaEdge application is complete, we'll look at how we can use the Ant build tool to coordinate all the various technologies we have covered in this book.

8

Building the JavaEdge Application with Ant and Anthill

Building an application is more than just compiling the source code. Ideally, building an application would comprise all the steps required to produce readily consumable artifacts. But we must notice that different audiences are going to require different consumable artifacts. For example, the development team may require Javadocs and last night's test results as artifacts, whereas the QA team may not care about the Javadocs as much as the revision log. The end user may not care about either of these and just want a URL in the case of an online application or an executable in the case of a traditional program. So building an application may need to produce a whole range of artifacts, each consumable by one or more of the target audiences of the build.

This chapter is going to introduce build practices that stand up to the rigors of real-world development. We will explore some of the problems that can arise as a result of poor build and configuration management practices and show you how to get around with the aid of two tools. Throughout the chapter we will develop build practices that can accommodate a multi-person, potentially geographically distributed, development team working with a separate QA team.

The Goals of a Build Process

We know that the build system for the JavaEdge application needs to produce readily consumable artifacts. Let's go through and identify what each of those artifacts should be.

Build Artifacts

We know that we will need to compile the Java source code and produce some artifacts that are executable. For a Java web-based application like JavaEdge that means that we will need to produce a WAR file. Once we have a WAR file we can deploy it in a servlet container such as Tomcat.

Also, we would like to have some indication of the quality of each build. This is especially important since we are working in a team of developers. We want to make sure that the last change made by one of the developers did not break a change that we made earlier today. One method used to measure the quality of builds is **unit tests**. While it is beyond the scope of this chapter to into detail about unit tests, let's just say that each unit test determines whether one particular piece of the application is working properly or not. If we have unit tests written for each piece of functionality in the application, and if we run such unit tests as part of every build, then we will know whether the last change made by one of the developers broke anything or not.

JavaEdge is a database-driven application, which presents several complications. For one, the only way to truly test whether the application works is to test it against a database. Another, perhaps bigger, problem is that we need to ensure that the latest version of the Java code is compatible with the latest version of the database. This may not sound like a big deal when we're working on a small application, but in a large development team where the DBAs are separate from the application developers, this really becomes an issue. It is not uncommon for a developer to add an attribute to a class meaning to have a corresponding column added to a table, only to forget and cause the application to fail. This problem is compounded by the fact that often the DBAs do not keep their database scripts under source control as the application developers do with their source code.

But that kind of practice is very dangerous and we are not going to follow it on the JavaEdge project. All the scripts required to create and initialize the database are part of the source code for the project, and we need to make sure that the Java source is compatible with the database scripts during every build. To do that, we will create a new database using the database scripts that are part of our project during every build and we will run a series of tests to ensure that the Java code still works with the latest database.

All these tests that we are going to run as part of every build are going to end up as consumable artifacts in the form of test results. Having test results for every build of the application will allow the developers to keep tabs on what problems need to be addressed.

On real-world applications that can grow well into hundreds of thousands of lines of code, having up-to-date Javadocs is very important. On large projects, developers typically work on the modules assigned to them and do not need to know the details about the rest of the application. As long as their modules obey the contracts expected by the other parts of the application (such contracts often being in the form of interfaces) everything is fine. But sometimes, developers need to browse the documentation for other parts of the system. In such cases, having up-to-date and easily accessible Javadocs is very important. For this reason our build system will produce Javadocs of the entire application on every build.

Another very useful artifact that we can easily produce during our builds is a to-do list. Very often developers will leave notes for themselves and other developers about what remains to be done on a module or class. Having these notes live in the source code is one thing, but generating project wide reports of all these notes allows the entire team to communicated more effectively. We will generate such project-wide to-do reports as part of every build.

Perhaps one of the basic artifacts of any build is the binary distribution of the project. Such a distribution includes all the binary artifacts (the WAR file in our case) and supporting libraries plus documentation. Our build system will produce a `tar.gz` file containing the binary distribution of the project.

Source code metrics are very useful for evaluating and reviewing the design of an application. As an application is being developed it evolves, and so does its design. It is not uncommon for a beautifully elegant design present at the inception of coding to gradually lose shape day after day, to the point that it is almost unrecognizable. It is very difficult to see this happen when you are close to the project. Keeping tabs on source code metrics is definitely not going to prevent the design decay, but it may allow you to stop it earlier than you would have otherwise. For this reason we are going to compute and report source code metrics for our project with every build.

The last artifact that we will produce during our builds is an HTML version of all the project's Java source code. Having all the source code for our application available for online browsing is very helpful when faced with a question about how a particular feature is implemented during a meeting. Rather than having to go back to your workstation and fire up your IDE to view the source, you can jump onto any computer equipped with a browser and reach the same conclusion.

That completes the list of artifacts that our build system is going to produce for the JavaEdge application. Let's take a look now at some of the other goals that our build system must attain in order to make it successful on a large real-world project.

Version Control

When working on production projects, one of the most important goals of any build system is the ability to generate reproducible builds. That means that the build that was produced this morning and sent to the QA team should be reproducible if we need to go to production with it in the afternoon. The ability to generate reproducible builds hinges on the use of a **Version Control System (VCS)** to manage the project's source code. Although a discussion of Version Control Systems falls under the area of configuration management and is outside the scope of this chapter, every real-world production-level project needs to use a VCS. The JavaEdge application was developed with the aid of a VCS and the practices presented in this chapter assume the use of a VCS as well.

Let's take a look at a scenario that could all too easily happen (and does happen too often in practice). A developer implements a feature in the project and commits what they think are all the changes. Then, the developer may build the software and hand it to the QA team for testing. There are already two problems with this scenario:

❑   The first is that the developer might have missed a file that has been modified and hence a file in the source code control system might be different from the one on the developer's environment.

❑   The second problem arises when the developers do not tag every build released to a QA team in the source code repository. Once the development and QA teams get into a code and test cycle, the QA team reports any issues to the development team and the development team fixes them and produces a build for testing. In the future, a decision might be made that one of the builds that the QA team received is the one that is going to go into the production. But, the developers might have continued to implement the fixes after they made that build and now there is no way to recover the exact contents of that build.

Our build system needs to prevent the above scenario. The most foolproof way to do that is to ensure that any build that is going to be handed off to another party (the QA team in the above scenario) goes through a **build management server**. The build management server must then ensure that only sources that exist in the VCS are included in the build, that every build is assigned a unique and traceable build number, and that the sources used to create the build are recoverable (this is accomplished by applying a label to the VCS). Only by incorporating a build management server into our build system can we ensure reproducible builds and avoid the problems illustrated in the scenario above.

The final goals that our build system must achieve are that it must provide for automated nightly builds and for a project intranet that can hold the latest artifacts produced by the build. Achieving these goals is crucial when working in a development team. Having a nightly build helps keep all the team members aware of the current status and progress of the project. A central project intranet that houses all the latest artifacts including unit test reports and to-do lists is an often-used resource during development.

Our Final Build System Goals

Let's recap the goals for our build system. Our build system will do the following:

- ❏ Compile and package the source code
- ❏ Run unit tests to indicate the quality of every build
- ❏ Create the database for our application and test the application against the database
- ❏ Generate Javadocs
- ❏ Generate a to-do lists based on notes left in the source code
- ❏ Create a binary distribution of our application
- ❏ Generate source code metrics
- ❏ Generate a browseable HTML version of our source code
- ❏ Use a build management server to:
    - ❏ Ensure that only source code that exists in the VCS is included in the build
    - ❏ Assign a unique and traceable build number to every build
    - ❏ Apply a label to the VCS ensuring that we can reproduce any build
    - ❏ Conduct an automated nightly build
    - ❏ Create a project intranet to hold all the build artefacts

The Tools

We are going to use a tool called **Ant** to produce all the artifacts that are required by our build. Later we will see how an open source build management server called **Anthill** can help us attain the remaining goals for our build system.

Jakarta Ant

In a nutshell, Ant is a build tool much like make, but Ant is Java-based and truly cross-platform. Also, one of the big advantages of Ant is that it is far easier to use and extend than make or any of its derivatives. Ant started because the author of Jakarta Tomcat needed a truly cross-platform way to build Tomcat and make introduced too many OS dependencies (it inherently relies on OS-specific commands). Ant is bundled with many IDEs and has become the standard tool for building Java projects. You can download Ant from http://jakarta.apache.org/ant/.

Ant build files (also referred to as Ant scripts or build scripts) are written in XML. Ant reads these build files and then performs the steps described in them to create a build of the software. There is a well-defined structure for XML build files that are considered valid by Ant. This structure consists of the following parts and XML tags:

- ❏ Project
- ❏ Target
- ❏ Task
- ❏ Properties
- ❏ Core Types
    - ❏ Pattern Sets
    - ❏ File Types
    - ❏ Directory Types
    - ❏ Path Types

Now, we will cover each of these parts in detail.

Project

Each Ant build file has exactly one `<project>` element. This element is defined as shown in the following code:

```
<project name="JavaEdge" basedir="../" default="all">
```

The `project` element has three possible attributes:

- ❏ `name`
  Provides the name of the project and is an optional attribute.

- ❏ `basedir`
  Specifies the directory that serves as the base directory for all relative paths used in the build script. This is also an optional attribute.

- ❏ `default`
  Specifies the default target within the build script. Whenever Ant is told to run the build script and a target to be run is not specified, Ant will run the default target. By convention, a default target called "all" is included in scripts to provide an easy way to run every target in the script. This is a required attribute.

Target

A target is a group of tasks. Targets can be dependent on other targets and can call other targets as well as other Ant build scripts. Each target accomplishes some specified functionality. For example, the `compile` target compiles all the source code, the `jar` target packages the source code into a JAR file, and so on. A project build script is made up of these individual targets that can be chained together via dependencies and explicit calls to other targets. You may find the examples shown below in a typical build script:

```
<target name="compile">
<target name="jars" depends="compile">
```

Note that the `jars` target depends on the `compile` target. That means that when we run the `jars` target, Ant will run the `compile` target first. This allows us to create a hierarchy of ordered and related tasks.

Task

An Ant project consists of tasks that actually know how to compile our software, how to package it into a JAR file, how to generate Javadocs, or how to do many other useful things. Tasks are just Java classes that implement the `Task` interface. This interface provides a contract between the task and Ant so that Ant can configure the task and then execute it. The following example will give you an idea of a task in our build script:

```
<copy todir="${build.classes.dir}">
  <fileset dir="${src.java.dir}">
    <include name="**/*.properties"/>
    <include name="**/*.version"/>
  </fileset>
</copy>
```

A task is represented via an XML element whose name typically corresponds to the task's class name. In the above example, the element name is `copy`, which corresponds to the `copy` task. The `copy` task is implemented by the class `org.apache.tools.ant.taskdefs.Copy`, which extends the class `org.apache.tools.ant.Task`.

The task element can have attributes and nested elements. The above `copy` task has one attribute (`todir`) and a nested element (`<fileset>`). When Ant parses our XML-based build script, it uses the values of the attributes in a task element to configure an instance of the corresponding Java `Task` class. When Ant reaches the `<copy>` element, it creates an instance of the `Copy` task class and then sets the value of the `todir` attribute in the `copy` task instance to the value in our build script.

Nested elements are treated very similarly except that their values typically correspond to another Java `Task` instance. In the above example, the `<fileset>` nested element corresponds to an instance of the `org.apache.tools.ant.types.FileSet` class. Ant creates an instance of the class corresponding to the nested element, configures its attributes and nested elements, and then passes a reference to it the object corresponding to the containing task (`copy` in this case).

Properties

Properties are basically name and value pairs. A project build script can have any number of properties. Properties can be defined in the build script using the `<property>` element, they can be imported from a properties file, or they can be set at the command line:

```
<property name="db.user" value="root"/>
<echo message="${db.user}"/>
```

The example above illustrates how a build property would be defined in an Ant build script. The property in our example has the name db.user and the value root. To access the value of a property, you would surround the property name with ${property.name}. In the example above, the echo task would print the value (root) of the (db.user) property.

It may be helpful to think of properties within the build script as constants (or static final variables in Java) in the application code. The benefits of properties in build scripts are very similar to constants in code. Rather than hard-coding values all throughout your code, you should use constants to establish a value that is used frequently in your code. This makes it much easier to change the values of your constants, since you have to make the change only at one place. And, using constants in a strongly typed language helps catch the typing errors. Unfortunately, Ant does not catch spelling errors in the names of properties, instead it uses the literal value of the flawed property reference ${misspelled.property.name}.

To put the values of the properties into a property file and have Ant load these values from a property file is a very useful feature. This feature allows the same Ant build script to be reused on many different environments as long as the environment specifics are handled via properties. For example, your build script needs to know the location of a project "A" on your machine. If you put the location of project "A" into a property file, you can run the same build script without any modifications on another computer, which has project "A" installed in a different location. We need to change only the property file referenced by the build script.

Core Types

Ant has a built-in understanding of how to work with files and directories in a cross-platform environment. There is a very powerful mechanism, based on patterns, for working with the groups of files or directories within Ant.

Pattern Sets

Many tasks can operate on a collection of files. For example, the copy task can copy multiple files at once rather than one file at a time. Likewise, the compile task can compile all the source code (java files) rather than compiling one file at a time. Ant allows us to define a group of files that match certain criteria with a <patternset> element. This element allows the definition of inclusion and exclusion rules. Files that match the inclusion rules, but not the exclusion rules, are included in the group of files pointed to by the patternset. The inclusion and exclusion rules are specified as nested elements. Consider the following example:

```
<patternset id="source">
  <include name="com/wrox/**/*.java"/>
  <include name="**/*.properties"/>
  <exclude name="**/*.java~"/>
</patternset>
```

A `patternset` can have multiple `<include>` and `<exclude>` elements. Patterns within `<include>` and `<exclude>` elements are specified using syntax, where `*` matches zero or more characters while `?` matches exactly one character. The pattern `*.java` will match files such as `MyClass.java` or `Story.java`. A pattern such as `*/*.java` would match any Java file in a subdirectory, for example, `story/Story.java` or `member/Member.java`. Ant introduces an additional variation, here, so that the `**` pattern matches zero or more subdirectories. A pattern such as `com/wrox/**/*.java` would match any Java files in any subdirectory (or deeper) of the `com/wrox` directory, for example, the file `com/wrox/MyClass.java`, or `com/wrox/javaedge/story/StoryVO.java`.

File Types

Ant has a special element called `<fileset>` to describe a group of files. It uses pattern sets to describe the files included in the group. A `<fileset>` element can have a nested `<patternset>` element. Also, it can act as a `patternset` and, therefore, can nest `<include>` and `<exclude>` elements directly. The `<fileset>` element has one required attribute called `dir`, which specifies the base directory for the inclusion and exclusion rules of the pattern set. The following example will give you an idea:

```
<fileset dir="${basedir}">
  <include name="conf/*.*"/>
  <include name="dist/*.?ar"/>
  <include name="lib/*.?ar"/>
</fileset>
```

This element can also be written as follows:

```
<fileset dir="${basedir}">
  <patternset>
    <include name="conf/*.*"/>
    <include name="dist/*.?ar"/>
    <include name="lib/*.?ar"/>
  </patternset>
</fileset>
```

Many tasks accept `<fileset>` elements as nested elements to describe the files on which the task acts. For example, the `javac` task, `jar` task, `copy` task, and so on. Also, some tasks extend `fileset` and add functionality. For example, the `tarfileset` used by the `tar` task, which we'll be discussing in the section called *Packaging for Distribution*.

Directory Types

The `<dirset>` element is similar to `<fileset>`. However, instead of describing a group of files, the `<dirset>` element describes a group of directories. Like `<fileset>`, a `<dirset>` can include a nested pattern set or it can act as a pattern set itself and contain nested `<include>` and `<exclude>` elements. Since the `<dirset>` is implemented with the help of a pattern set, it supports the same pattern matching rules as `<patternset>` and `<fileset>`. Let's take a look at the following example:

```
<dirset dir="${basedir}">
  <include name="com/wrox/**/dao"/>
</dirset>
```

In the above example, all subdirectories of `com/wrox` that are named `dao` are included in the `dirset`.

Path Types

The last built-in types that we are going to cover are paths and path-like structures. While building Java software, we must always remain aware of the classpath used to compile our software. Also while running Java applications such as Ant, we can sometimes specify to the classpath that certain tasks get loaded, as Ant includes its own classloader. Ant provides us with a convenient way to construct a classpath, which can be referenced throughout our build scripts. The `<classpath>` element is used to construct a classpath within Ant. A classpath is simply a list of locations that can hold Java classes and resources. These locations can identify directories or JAR files. The `<classpath>` element supports a number of nested elements including `<pathelement>`, `<dirset>`, and `<fileset>`. Take a look at the following example:

```
<classpath>
  <pathelement path="${classpath}"/>
  <fileset dir="lib">
    <include name="**/*.JAR"/>
  </fileset>
  <pathelement location="classes"/>
</classpath>
```

In this example, all the entries specified by the value of the `${classpath}` property, all JAR files in the `lib` directory and all its subdirectories, and the contents of the `classes` directory are included in the classpath.

Anthill

Anthill is a build management server. It can also be used for continuous integration. The Anthill home page can be found at http://www.urbancode.com/project/anthill/. Typically, Anthill runs on a server that has access to your Version Control System (VCS). The machine on which the Anthill runs should not be a development machine since it will verify that everything required for building your project is in the VCS. Anthill can be configured to build your project(s) on a schedule, such as every hour or every night at midnight. When the schedule fires, Anthill begins the build as illustrated in the following diagram and described in the steps that follow:

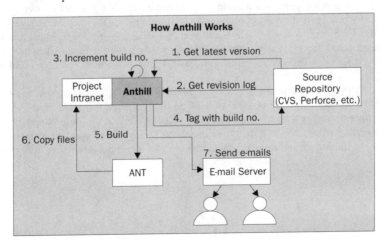

1. Anthill gets an up-to-date copy of the project from the VCS at the start of every build.

2. Anthill obtains a log of revisions since the last build. If this list of revisions is not empty, indicating that there has been development activity on the project since the last build, Anthill moves on to the next step. On the other hand, if the list is empty, there is no reason to continue with the build and Anthill cleans up the temporary files that it may have created.

3. Once Anthill makes the decision that a build is required, it increments the version number assigned to the project.

4. Depending on the project settings, Anthill may apply a label, with the current version number, to the project in the VCS. This is to ensure that this particular build can be recovered at any time in the future.

5. Anthill calls Ant to run the project build script. The project build script has been checked out along with the rest of the project from the VCS. As discussed in the section on *Setting up a New Project*, Anthill knows where that build script is, based on the information that we supply when we set up the project in Anthill.

6. When Anthill calls Ant to build the project in Step 5, it passes in two extra parameters to Ant. These parameters are the version and the deployment directory. The build script can use these parameters as a part of the build process. Any files that the build script copies over to the location pointed to by deployment directory location parameter are later visible via the project intranet site created by Anthill.

7. Once Ant has built the project, whether successfully or not, Anthill sends out e-mails with the build results to all interested parties. The e-mails contain the status of the build (success or failure), links to the project intranet site and the build log, and the revision log listing every revision included in the build.

Anthill ensures that only the code that is checked into the source code control system is included in our build, and that we can always recover a build. One could argue that you can do everything that Anthill does right from within Ant. Ant does contain tasks to interact with various VCSs, to checkout the latest sources from the VCS, and to apply a label, and you can schedule an Ant script to run at regular intervals using an operating system-specific scheduler (either Cron on Linux or Scheduled Tasks on Windows). But doing everything that Anthill does using only Ant would not be a good idea.

One problem that you'd encounter very quickly is the bootstrapping problem; how can you run a build script to checkout the latest source from the VCS when the build script itself is in the VCS? Even once you got past that problem, having a build script that runs on a schedule is not quite the same as having a web-based application that allows you to quickly see the status of any one of your projects, to browse the project artifacts, to initiate a build of any project outside of a schedule, and many other things.

Defining the Build Process for JavaEdge

In this section, we will develop the Ant build script that is used to produce all our build artifacts. Then we will demonstrate how the JavaEdge project is configured in Anthill so that all its builds are managed. Before we get to the Ant build script however, let's take a look at the directory structure that we used to organize the JavaEdge project.

The Project Directory Structure

Before we start building the application, we need to understand the structure of the project directories. Projects vary widely in their directory structure but having a consistent and, yet, a flexible directory structure is a key to a good build process.

The directory structure that we have used in the JavaEdge project has evolved over the past several years and has definitely been influenced by Ant. It is as shown in the following diagram:

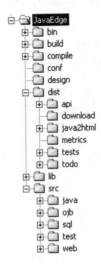

Directory	Description	Under Source Control?
bin	Holds any scripts, such as batch files required to start and run the project and/or any test harnesses. Not every project requires a bin directory. Only the projects that result in executable applications (as opposed to library type projects) will require this directory.	Yes (If present)
build	Is used for building the project. Any Ant build scripts and batch files should be placed here. If Ant creates subdirectories under this during a build, it should return the directory to the same state in which it was found, before the build.	Yes

Table continued on following page

Directory	Description	Under Source Control?
compile	Is used to hold the class files compiled during the development. Generally, the developers configure their IDE or compilation scripts so that the output points to this directory. This directory is used only locally for development purposes.	No
conf	Holds any configuration scripts used by the module; for example, Log4j configuration files should be located here. Also, any properties files used by the module should also be located in this directory. Our project does not require any configuration settings so this directory is not present.	Yes
design	Holds UML and any other design documents. The files created by a UML modeling tool should be placed in the UML subdirectory. We do not have any design documents or UML models for our project, thus this directory is not present.	Yes
dist	Holds the binary artifacts of the module. If the Ant build script creates any JAR, EJB JAR, WAR, or EAR files, they should be placed in this directory. The contents of this directory do not belong under source control, as they can be recreated by executing the Ant build script.	No
	The dist directory also contains a number of subdirectories for other types of artifact produced besides archives:	
	❑ The api subdirectory holds the Javadoc that is produced automatically by the Ant publish script.	
	❑ The download subdirectory holds the zipped distribution source files as .tar.gz files.	
	❑ The java2html subdirectory holds the HTML created automatically from the Java source by the Ant build script.	
	❑ The metrix subdirectory holds the source code metrics produced automatically by the Ant publish script.	
	❑ The tests subdirectory holds the results of running unit tests on the code files.	
	❑ The todo subdirectory holds the HTML created to represent the to-do tasks marked as Javadoc comments in the Java source.	

Directory	Description	Under Source Control?
lib	Holds any JAR files that are required to build this project. For example, if the project requires an XML parser, the parser JAR file should be included in this directory, the reason being that we want to ensure that we have the exact version of the libraries, on which the project is dependent and that were used while developing the project.	Yes
src	Holds all the source code for the project. It defines subdirectories to further help organize the source. The java subdirectory is used to hold Java source code. The web subdirectory is used to hold the (non-Java) contents of a WAR file, if the project needs one. (The contents of WEB-INF\lib and WEB-INF\classes would be filled in by the Ant build script, when the actual WAR file is constructed). Additional subdirectories may be created, as needed, to help keep code organized. For example, we also have sql, ojb, and test subdirectories for JavaEdge.	Yes

Now that we have our directory structure, and a project that fits into this structure, let's get to the build.

The Ant Script

We will now develop the Ant script that controls how our project is built and what artifacts are generated. One of the nice things about having two separate tools, each focused on achieving different goals, is that we can use them separately. We will be able to use Ant and the build script we will develop to build the project independently of Anthill. This will allow the developers to build the project locally (on their development environment) using the same script. That's a good thing because the developers should make sure that the project builds and passes all the unit tests locally before committing any source code to the VCS.

Let's begin writing the Ant script to build this project (in a file called build.xml). The first step in writing the script is to define the <project> element as shown below:

```
<?xml version="1.0"?>

<project name="JavaEdge" basedir="../" default="all">
```

The name attribute defines the name of the project, that is JavaEdge. The value of the basedir attribute may be surprising, but this build script is in the build subdirectory, and we want all of our paths in the build script to be relative to the project root directory. Hence we specify that the project base directory as "../".

Next, we define a set of properties. The first two are used to identify the project as shown below:

```
<property name="name"     value="${ant.project.name}"/>
<property name="version"  value="dev"/>
```

The name property is given a value equal to ant.project.name, which points to the value of the name attribute in the <project> (that is, JavaEdge). This property is just a shortcut because instead of writing ${ant.project.name}, we can now write ${name}. The version property is used to uniquely identify each and every build of the software once we start using Anthill to do controlled builds.

The next three properties are used to configure the compiler when we compile our code:

```
<property name="debug"        value="true"/>
<property name="deprecation"  value="false"/>
<property name="optimize"     value="false"/>
```

The next group of property declarations models the layout of our project directory tree. These properties tell Ant about the location of each of the directories holding our source code, library JAR files, etc.:

```
<!-- Properties related to the directory tree used for the build -->

<property name="src.java.dir"  location="src/java"/>
<property name="src.tests.dir" location="src/test"/>
<property name="src.ojb.dir"   location="src/ojb"/>
<property name="src.web.dir"   location="src/web"/>
<property name="src.sql.dir"   location="src/sql"/>
<property name="lib.dir"       location="lib"/>
<property name="doc.dir"       location="doc"/>
```

We also define the properties that tell Ant where to put intermediate products that it generates during the build. We keep all of these intermediate products in the \build\temp directory and its subdirectories. As a result, it becomes easy for us to clean them up later:

```
<!-- Properties related to the temporary directories used for the build -->

<property name="build.dir"         location="build/temp"/>
<property name="build.classes.dir" location="${build.dir}/classes"/>
<property name="tests.dir"         location="${build.dir}/tests"/>
<property name="tests.classes.dir" location="${tests.dir}/classes"/>
<property name="tests.data.dir"    location="${tests.dir}/data"/>
```

The next set of properties identifies the locations where Ant should put the results of our build. Any JAR or WAR files created by the build will be placed into the location pointed to by ${dist.dir}, which corresponds to the \dist directory by default. For example, the generated Javadocs are placed in the location pointed to by ${dist.api.dir}:

```
<!-- Locations of generated artifacts -->

<property name="deployDir"    location="dist"/>
<property name="dist.dir"     location="${deployDir}"/>
<property name="dist.api.dir" location="${dist.dir}/api"/>
```

```xml
<property name="dist.download.dir" location="${dist.dir}/download"/>
<property name="dist.todo.dir"     location="${dist.dir}/todo"/>
<property name="dist.tests.dir"    location="${dist.dir}/tests"/>
<property name="dist.metrics.dir"  location="${dist.dir}/metrics"/>
<property name="dist.java2html.dir" location="${dist.dir}/java2html"/>
```

Next, we define a group of properties that identifies the database-related properties, which will be used when we create the database tables for testing. Generally, it is a good idea to use property values instead of strings within you tasks. This makes it easier to modify your Ant scripts in the future, since everything is in one place and you need to make the change only once rather than searching the entire Ant script for strings. Another advantage of using properties, rather than hard-coded values, is that properties can be overridden. This allows your script to be used in different environments without making any changes in it:

```xml
<!-- database properties -->

<property name="db.driver" value="org.gjt.mm.mysql.Driver"/>
<property name="db.url"    value="jdbc:mysql://localhost/waf"/>
<property name="db.user"   value="root"/>
<property name="db.pass"   value="password"/>
```

Our last set of properties define the classpaths that should be used to compile our project:

```xml
<!-- classpaths -->

<property name="build.sysclasspath" value="last"/>
<path id="compile.classpath">
  <fileset dir="${lib.dir}">
    <include name="**/*.jar"/>
    <include name="**/*.zip"/>
  </fileset>
  <fileset dir="${lib.dir}/build">
    <include name="**/*.jar"/>
    <include name="**/*.zip"/>
  </fileset>
</path>

<path id="tests.classpath">
  <path refid="compile.classpath"/>
  <pathelement location="${build.classes.dir}"/>
  <pathelement location="${tests.classes.dir}"/>
</path>
```

Main Targets

Build files can get quite complex with many targets and interdependencies between them. One strategy that we would suggest to use in the build files for dealing with the complexity is to create a set of **main targets**. These main targets then are responsible for calling all the dependent targets that work together. We would suggest creating the following main targets:

❑ dev
   Used to create an incremental build of the project. This is probably the most often used target during development. Every time you make a change and want to test it, you would run this target.

❑ dev-clean
   After your changes pass all the tests, you would typically run this target, which does a clean build. It's a good idea to run a clean build before you complete or commit a change to the version control system because a clean build can reveal dependencies on the outdated and deleted files.

❑ doc
   This target is run every time we want to regenerate the documentation for the project.

❑ all
   An all encompassing target, which does a complete build of the project and produces all the documentation and project artifacts.

A good tool that can help you visualize the targets present in your build script and the dependencies between them is Vizant (available at http://vizant.sourceforge.net/).

The following graph shows the targets and the dependencies that exist in the build script for the JavaEdge project:

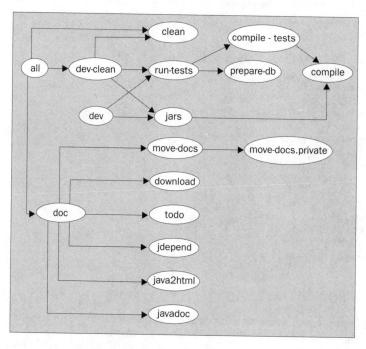

Here are those main targets defined in the build file:

```xml
<!-- Main Targets -->

<!-- default target calls all other targets -->
<target name="all">
  <antcall target="dev-clean"/>
  <antcall target="doc"/>
  <antcall target="clean"/>
</target>

<!-- Do an incremental development build-->
<target name="dev">
  <antcall target="JARs"/>
  <antcall target="report-on-tests"/>
</target>

<!-- Do a clean development builds-->
<target name="dev-clean">
  <property name="dev.clean" value="yes"/>
  <antcall target="clean"/>
  <antcall target="jars"/>
  <antcall target="run-tests"/>
</target>

<!-- Generate all the documentation -->
<target name="doc">
  <antcall target="javadoc"/>
  <antcall target="todo"/>
  <antcall target="move-docs"/>
  <antcall target="download"/>
  <antcall target="jdepend"/>
  <antcall target="java2html"/>
</target>
```

Compiling

The most fundamental piece of the entire build script is the compilation target. This target is created using three steps:

- Creating the required directories
- Calling the compiler to compile the source code
- Copying any non-code resources that need to be available in the classpath

```xml
<!-- Compile the code -->

<target name="compile">
  <mkdir dir="${build.dir}"/>
  <mkdir dir="${build.classes.dir}"/>

  <javac destdir="${build.classes.dir}"
         debug="${debug}"
         deprecation="${deprecation}"
         optimize="${optimize}" >
    <classpath refid="compile.classpath"/>
    <src path="${src.java.dir}"/>
```

```
    </javac>

    <copy todir="${build.classes.dir}">
      <fileset dir="${src.java.dir}">
        <include name="**/*.properties"/>
        <include name="**/*.version"/>
      </fileset>
    </copy>

  </target>
```

The `javac` task takes care of compiling Java code. The `destdir` attribute identifies the output directory for the compiled classes. The `classpath` tag identifies the classpath to be used for this compilation. The `src` tag provides the location path for the Java source files.

Compiling the sources places the compiled class files in a different location from the source Java files. Also, we want to ensure that any resources to be made available via a classloader also get moved. Therefore, we use the `copy` task. This task uses a `fileset` to define the files that will get copied. In the above code, we have copied all the property and version files.

Packaging for Deployment

The next target packages our project into a WAR file and a JAR file. To deploy our project application, we just need a WAR file. However, we are creating the JAR file so that we can run unit tests separately from the build, and all the code that we need on the classpath is included in the JAR file:

```
<!-- Create the WAR and JAR file(s) -->

<target name="jars" depends="compile">
  <mkdir dir="${dist.dir}"/>

  <war warfile="${dist.dir}/${name}.war"
       webXML="${src.web.dir}/WEB-INF/web.xml">
    <lib dir="${lib.dir}">
      <exclude name="ejb_2_0.jar"/>
      <exclude name="servlet_2_2b.jar"/>
    </lib>
    <classes dir="${build.classes.dir}">
      <include name="**/*.class"/>
      <exclude name="**/ejb/*.class"/>
    </classes>
    <classes dir="${src.ojb.dir}">
      <include name="**/*"/>
    </classes>
    <fileset dir="${src.web.dir}">
      <exclude name="**/*.#*"/>
    </fileset>
  </war>

  <!-- create JAR file for running unit tests from command line -->
  <jar jarfile="${dist.dir}/${name}-${version}.jar"
       basedir="${build.classes.dir}">
  </jar>
</target>
```

The war task has special way of handling the files that end up in the WEB-INF, WEB-INF/lib, and WEB-INF/classes directories. The contents of each of these special locations can be specified using a fileset element. In our example, the fileset called lib places all JAR files found in the lib directory of the project in the WAR files in the WEB-INF/lib directory. This ensures that the classpath that we need for compiling is included in the WAR file. The classes fileset ensures that all of the compiled application classes get placed in the WEB-INF/classes location in the WAR file.

We can have multiple filesets of the same type within our task, that is, we can grab files from different source locations and place them in the same destination location in a WAR file. In our application, we have separate source locations for our Java source code and the OJB configuration files. But at run time, we want the OJB configuration files to be accessible via a classloader. Hence, they need to be in the same location as our class files. We use two distinct classes filesets for this purpose. The first classes element includes our compiled class files (located in ${build.classes.dir}) in the WEB-INF/classes location of the WAR file. The second classes fileset includes our OJB configuration files (located in ${src.ojb.dir}) in the same location as the classes in the WAR file.

Creating a JAR file is even easier. We use the jar task to specify the name and location of the resulting JAR file and the base directory. Every file found in the specified base directory (or any of its subdirectories), will be included in the resulting JAR file. If you need more flexibility than that or if you need to filter out some files and include files from multiple locations, the jar task also supports nested filesets that provide all those capabilities.

Compiling Test Code

Compiling the test code is almost identical to compiling the main project code. Instead of placing the compiled class files in the ${build.classes.dir}, we place them in the ${tests.classes.dir}. The classpath used for compilation is the tests.classpath, which includes the compiled project code:

```
<!-- Compile Test Code -->
<target name="compile-tests" depends="compile">
  <mkdir dir="${build.dir}"/>
  <mkdir dir="${tests.classes.dir}"/>

  <javac destdir="${tests.classes.dir}"
         debug="${debug}"
         deprecation="${deprecation}"
         optimize="${optimize}">
    <classpath refid="tests.classpath"/>
    <src path="${src.tests.dir}"/>
  </javac>

  <jar jarfile="${dist.dir}/${name}-tests-${version}.jar"
       basedir="${tests.classes.dir}">
  </jar>

  <copy todir="${tests.classes.dir}">
    <fileset dir="${src.ojb.dir}">
      <include name="**/*"/>
    </fileset >
    <filterset>
      <filter token="OJB_DB_URL" value="${db.url.ojb.test}"/>
```

```
      </filterset>
      <fileset dir="${src.tests.dir}">
        <include name="**/*.properties"/>
        <include name="**/*.version"/>
      </fileset>
    </copy>
  </target>
```

One interesting thing to note in the `copy` task is that, when we copy the OJB configuration files to make them accessible by the test code, via a classloader, we apply a replacement filter. This filter changes the value of the `subprotocol` attribute in the `jdbc-connection-descriptor` element of the `repository.xml` file (refer to Chapter 5 for the discussion on the `repository.xml` file). This allows us to use a potentially different database URL for automated testing during the build than for production.

Preparing the Database

The JavaEdge project requires a database for most of the tests. While we could have the requirement that a database with all the required tables and users is going to be available to run all the tests, that would be a broken link in the chain of testing. This is because if the database schema changes (that is, if we add a column to one table and remove it from another table), and we try running the tests that require the new database schema against an old database, they will fail. Equally, what if some developer inadvertently makes a change to the database schema? If we do not rebuild the database every time we do a build, we may not catch that inadvertent change for a long time (maybe until we try to put the application into production). So, we should have the option of creating the database required for our application from scratch with every build. This is actually quite easy since we already have all the database scripts in our source tree. All we need to do is execute the scripts against a database, and Ant provides us with a task to do this. Look at the following code:

```
<!-- Prepare test database - creaete tables and user-->

<target name="prepare-db" if="dev.clean">
  <sql driver="${db.driver}"
       url="${db.url}"
       userid="${db.user}"
       password="${db.pass}"
       classpathref="compile.classpath">
    <transaction src="${src.sql.dir}/create_java_edge.sql"/>
    <transaction src="${src.sql.dir}/mysql_user_setup.sql"/>
  </sql>
</target>
```

The `sql` task allows us to execute SQL statements against a database via a JDBC connection. This task requires the name of the driver to be used, the URL of the database, the user name, and the password for establishing the database connection, as well as a classpath containing the driver. The `<transaction>` element allows us to execute multiple SQL commands on the same database connection. The `src` attribute of this element points to the location of the file containing the SQL to be executed. In our project, we are going to first execute the `create_java_edge.sql` script. This script drops the existing database (if it exists) and then recreates the entire required database from scratch. Then, we are going to run the `mysql_user_setup.sql`, which creates the user account required by our project.

Note that this target includes an `if` attribute. This target will run only if the `dev.clean` property exists. As we declare the `dev.clean` property in the `dev-clean` target, the database will get rebuilt only if we run the `dev-clean` target (or any other target that calls `dev-clean`, such as the `all` target).

Using Ant properties to hold the value of the database URL, user name, and password (instead of hardcoded strings) will allow us to integrate this build script with the Anthill build server as a continuous integration tool.

Running the Unit Tests

Running our tests as part of every build is quite easy, given that we can use the JUnit framework. Ant contains a pair of optional tasks called `junit` and `junitreport`. The `junit` task can be used to run a single JUnit test for a whole series of tests. It can produce XML-formatted test results as well as plain text results. The `junitreport` task basically applies an XSLT stylesheet to the XML-formatted test results. The use of these tasks is demonstrated in the following snippet:

```
<!-- Run JUnit test cases -->

<target name="run-tests" depends="compile-tests, prepare-db">
  <mkdir dir="${tests.data.dir}"/>
  <mkdir dir="${dist.tests.dir}"/>

  <junit printsummary="on" haltonfailure="false" fork="true">
    <classpath refid="tests.classpath"/>
    <formatter type="brief" usefile="false"/>
    <formatter type="xml"/>
    <batchtest todir="${tests.data.dir}">
      <fileset dir="${tests.classes.dir}" includes="**/Test*.class"/>
    </batchtest>
  </junit>

  <junitreport todir="${dist.tests.dir}">
    <fileset dir="${tests.data.dir}">
      <include name="TEST-*.xml"/>
    </fileset>
    <report format="frames" todir="${dist.tests.dir}"/>
  </junitreport>
</target>
```

The `haltonfailure` attribute controls whether the build should end when a unit test fails. We set this attribute to `false` because the build does not consist only of running the tests, and we want all the other components to run regardless of whether all the tests are successful. The `fork` attribute tells the task that all unit tests should run in their own JVM rather than inside the JVM running the Ant script. The `classpath` element allows us to specify the classpath to be used for running the tests. In our example, we are referring to the classpath that we created at the beginning of this build script. The `tests.classpath` contains the classpath we used for compilation plus the compiled classes and test cases in our project (the OJB property files are included in the test cases classpath, copied over during the compilation target).

The two `formatter` elements tell the `junit` task about the kind of output to be generated. The `brief` formatter produces text-based output similar to `junit.textui.TestRunner`. The `xml` formatter ensures that all test results are saved in an XML format so that we can apply a stylesheet to them later. The `batchtest` element can contain a number of `fileset` elements, which are used to identify the unit tests to be run. The `junit` task then runs all the unit tests identified by these elements.

289

Formatting the JUnit results is accomplished using the `junitreport` task. This task accepts an attribute `todir` that identifies the location where the formatted report should be placed. A `fileset` element within this task identifies the XML files containing test results to be formatted, and the `report` element identifies the stylesheet to be applied, which is either `frames` or `noframes`.

There are a couple of points that you should remember when you're using `junit` and `junitreport` tasks with Ant. The first is that `junit.jar` needs to be in the classpath available to Ant; so, it needs to be in either the `lib` directory under your Ant installation or added to your system classpath. The second is that if you are using `junitreport` with JDK 1.3, you need to download Xalan (from **http://xml.apache.org/xalan-j/**) and make sure the **xalan.jar** file is available to Ant's classpath (the same as with `junit.jar`).

Generating Javadocs

Ant allows you to generate Javadocs with every build. The `javadoc` task is probably one of the larger Ant tasks with a large number of options. Most of these options map directly to options available in `javadoc.exe` that come with the JDK, and you need to use only a few of the options to generate a simple set of Javadocs:

```
<!-- Generate javadocs -->

<target name="javadoc">
  <mkdir dir="${dist.api.dir}"/>

  <javadoc packagenames="*"
           sourcepath="${src.java.dir}"
           classpathref="compile.classpath"
           destdir="${dist.api.dir}"
           author="true"
           version="false"
           use="true"
           windowtitle="${name}"
        doctitle="&lt;h1&gt;${name}&lt;/h1&gt;">
  </javadoc>
</target>
```

XDoclet-Generated To-Do List

XDoclet is a powerful code-generation tool that uses Javadoc comments as its input metadata. Based on this input, XDoclet can generate EJBs and Data Transfer Objects, or portions of a web application. In our application, we are going to use XDoclet to generate something very simple, but still very useful. We are going to generate a to-do list based on the to-do items left in our code in the form of Javadoc comments:

```
<!-- Create ToDo List -->
<target name="todo">
  <mkdir dir="${dist.todo.dir}"/>

  <taskdef name="document" classname="xdoclet.doc.DocumentDocletTask"
```

```
                              classpathref="compile.classpath"/>

    <document sourcepath="${src.java.dir}"
              destdir="${dist.todo.dir}"
              classpathref="compile.classpath">
      <fileset dir="${src.java.dir}">
        <include name="**/*.java"/>
      </fileset>
      <info header="To-do list"
            projectName="${name}"
            tag="todo"/>
    </document>

  </target>
```

Publishing Project Documentation

The `move-docs` target illustrated below is not very interesting but it provides one little trick. Some tasks support an `if` attribute, which determines whether the task gets executed or not. If the property pointed to by the `if` attribute exists, the task gets executed, otherwise, it does not. We are going to use this attribute in the following `move-docs` example:

```
<!-- Move documentation directory to the deployment directory -->
<target name="move-docs">
  <available file="${doc.dir}" property="doc.dir.present"/>
  <antcall target="move-docs.private"/>
</target>

<target name="move-docs.private" if="doc.dir.present">
  <move todir="${dist.dir}">
    <fileset dir="${doc.dir}"/>
  </move>
</target>
```

If the `${doc.dir}` exists, which indicates the directory holding the project documentation exists, we would move it to its publish location, otherwise, we would like not to do anything. But the move task does not support the `if` attribute. Hence, it's not going to be very easy. The trick is that we can produce the same behavior as if the move task did support the `if` attribute by wrapping the move task in its own target. Since targets now support the `if` attribute, the move task will be executed only if its wrapping target gets executed, and the target will get executed only if our condition is met.

Packaging for Distribution

The `download` target, illustrated in the following code snippet, creates two `tar.gz` files, one that includes only the project binaries and one that includes the binaries as well as the source code. Creating `tar.gz` files in Ant consists of two steps: first the `.tar` file needs to be created, and second it needs to be zipped. We use the `tar` task to create the TAR file. This task accepts a `fileset` called `tarfileset`. These `filesets` allows us to specify which files should be included in the TAR file, as well as some useful attributes, such as `prefix`, which allows us to prefix the path of every file in the `fileset` with the specified value. This is very handy if you want the `.tar.gz` file to be unarchived into a directory identifying the project name and version (as shown in the code):

```xml
<!-- Create the binary and source distributions -->
<target name="download">
  <mkdir dir="${dist.download.dir}"/>

  <!-- .tar.gz all the source code to the deploy directory -->
  <tar tarfile="${dist.dir}/${name}-${version}-src.tar">
    <tarfileset dir="${basedir}" prefix="${name}-${version}">
      <include name="${build.dir}/*"/>
      <include name="conf/*.*"/>
      <include name="${dist.dir}/*.?ar"/>
      <include name="${lib.dir}/*.?ar"/>
      <include name="${src.dir}/**/*"/>
      <exclude name="**/CVS/*"/>
      <exclude name="${src.dir}/**/*.*~"/>
    </tarfileset>
  </tar>
  <gzip zipfile="${dist.download.dir}/${name}-${version}-src.tar.gz"
        src="${dist.dir}/${name}-${version}-src.tar"/>
  <delete file="${dist.dir}/${name}-${version}-src.tar"/>

  <!-- .tar.gz the dist directory -->
  <tar tarfile="${dist.dir}/${name}-${version}.tar">
    <tarfileset dir="${basedir}">
      <include name="conf/*.*"/>
      <include name="dist/*.?ar"/>
      <include name="lib/*.?ar"/>
    </tarfileset>
  </tar>
  <gzip zipfile="${dist.download.dir}/${name}-${version}.tar.gz"
        src="${dist.dir}/${name}-${version}.tar"/>
  <delete file="${dist.dir}/${name}-${version}.tar"/>
</target>
```

Once we've created the .tar file, we use the gzip task to gzip it and we get a .tar.gz file. We then delete the .tar file, since it is no longer needed. In our example, we create two .tar.gz files, one for the source distribution and one for the binary distribution. The only difference between the two is the files that are included in the tarfileset. The source distribution includes all the binary files included in the binary distribution, in addition to the build directory containing the Ant build scripts and the source directory. The exclusion rules ensure that the .tar.gz files do not contain any of the CVS directories or any old versions of files (old files having the name format *.*~).

Source Code Metrics

For the JavaEdge projects we used a tool called JDepend (available at http://www.clarkware.com/software/JDepend.html) to calculate the project source code metrics. JDepend has an Ant task that is distributed with Ant in the optional.jar file, but you still need to download the jdepend.jar file and add it to Ant's classpath.

JDepend generates an XML file that holds the computed metrics for the source code identified by the <sourcespath> element. We can then apply an XSLT stylesheet to transform the XML report to HTML. For this purpose, we use the style task as shown in the following code:

```
<!-- Create metrics of the source code-->
<target name="jdepend">
  <mkdir dir="${build.dir}"/>
  <mkdir dir="${dist.metrics.dir}"/>

  <jdepend outputfile="${build.dir}/jdepend-report.xml"
           format="xml"
           fork="yes"
           classpathref="compile.classpath">
    <sourcespath>
      <pathelement location="${src.java.dir}"/>
    </sourcespath>
  </jdepend>
  <style basedir="${build.dir}" destdir="${dist.metrics.dir}"
         includes="jdepend-report.xml"
         style="${ant.home}/etc/jdepend.xsl"/>

</target>
```

Converting Source Code to HTML

An HTML version of all the source code for a project makes it really simple to take a quick look at how things are implemented. We use the java2html target for this purpose as shown in the following code snippet:

```
<!-- Create java2html for the source code -->
<target name="java2html">
  <mkdir dir="${dist.java2html.dir}"/>

  <java classname="j2h"
        fork="yes"
        dir="${basedir}"
        classpathref="compile.classpath">
    <arg value="-js"/>
    <arg value="${src.java.dir}"/>
    <arg value="-d"/>
    <arg value="${dist.java2html.dir}"/>
    <arg value="-n"/>
    <arg value="${name}"/>
    <arg value="-m"/>
    <arg value="4"/>
  </java>
</target>
```

This target uses a tool called java2html (available at http://www.java2html.com) to do the heavy lifting. Since the tool does not have an Ant task, we have to call it as we would from the command line. We use the java task, which can be used to execute a Java class, to invoke the java2html tool. The classname attribute allows us to specify the name of the class whose main() method should be executed. In our example, we are calling the j2h class (it is a helper entry class in the default package). The fork attribute is used to specify whether the j2h class should be executed within the same JVM as is running the Ant script (the default setting), or within a new JVM (the option we chose). If we are going to fork this task, the dir attribute allows us to specify the directory from which the forked JVM should be started. This is important because it serves as a base for any relative paths. The last attribute of this task is the classpathref. This attribute tells Ant where to find the class to be executed. Since we included the j2h.jar file in the lib/build directory of the JavaEdge project, we can use the compile.classpath here.

The java task has a number of elements including arg, jvmarg, sysproperty, classpath, and env. For the purpose of this chapter, we are going to use only the arg element. Using these elements, we are going to pass startup arguments to the j2h class. From the documentation of the java2html software, we know that the -js option allows us to specify the directory holding the Java source files. So we configure our task with one arg element whose value is -js and another element whose value is ${src.java.dir}. We do the same for the other options accepted by the j2h class.

Cleaning up Temporary Files

Cleaning up temporary files is necessary if we want to do a clean build. A clean build starts from scratch, compiling every source file and not relying on any of the previously compiled classes. A clean build should be run every time you are about to finish a change and commit your work to your Version Control System. Doing a clean build ensures that there are no dependencies on files or classes that may have been deleted.

In our build script, we can run a clean development build by running the dev-clean target. As we've seen in the Vizant-generated plot of the targets in our build script, the dev-clean target calls the clean target, which actually does the cleanup work. The clean target is not very complex. We are only deleting the directories that hold our intermediate build artifacts:

```xml
<!-- Clean up Targets -->
<target name="clean">
    <delete dir="${build.dir}"/>
    <delete dir="${tests.dir}"/>
</target>

</project> <!-- The end of the file -->
```

Running the Build

Now that we have created our build script, it is a simple matter to run it. Assuming you have included the Ant installation's bin directory in your path then it's simply a matter of selecting which of the main targets to execute:

- ❏ ant all
- ❏ ant dev
- ❏ ant dev-clean
- ❏ ant doc

Using Anthill for JavaEdge

In this section we will go over the installation and setup of Anthill. We will then illustrate how the JavaEdge project is configured in Anthill.

Installing and Setting up Anthill

One of the advantages of Anthill over other build server-type tools is its ease of installation.

1. You can download the latest Anthill distribution from http://www.urbancode.com/projects/anthill/. Note there are in fact two version of Anthill: AnthillPro and an open source version of Anthill. To maintain the open source theme of the book we'll be using this version.

2. Now, unzip the downloaded archive into an installation directory (in our example, it is `c:\Anthill-1.5`).

3. Copy the `ANTHILL.war` file from Anthill's `dist` directory (`c:\Anthill-1.5\dist\`) to the deployment directory of your web application server (the `webapps` directory if you are using Tomcat).

4. Start your web application server.

5. Point your browser to the address http://localhost:8080/anthill/. You should see the Anthill configuration page as shown in the following screenshot. This page requires you to provide the Anthill installation directory (`c:\Anthill-1.5` in our example). You need to provide this information only the first time you run Anthill, and every subsequent time you will be taken directly to the main page of Anthill.

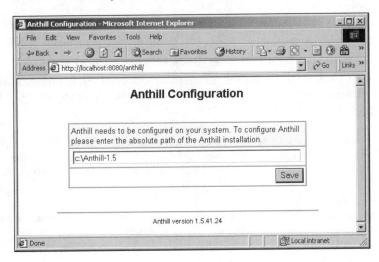

Anthill's main page contains five different sections: Anthill Properties, a list of Projects managed by Anthill, a list of Dependency Groups managed by Anthill, a list of available Schedules, and the Build Queue:

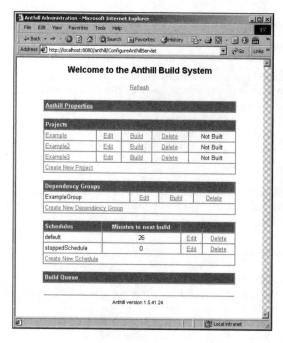

❑ **Anthill Properties:**
This link takes you to a page where you can configure the following properties:

❑ The mail server Anthill should use to send out notification e-mails.

❑ The "from" e-mail address Anthill should use when it sends out e-mails.

❑ Anthill's URL. The e-mails Anthill sends out with build results include links to the project build logs; Anthill needs to know its URL so that it can properly construct the links included in the e-mails.

❑ **Projects**
This section displays a list of all projects currently managed by Anthill. For each project there is a link to the project's properties page, and the project intranet site. A green or red bar in its row indicates the success or failure of the project's last build. You can create new projects by following the link at the bottom of this section.

❑ **Dependency Groups**
This section allows you to create dependency groups. Dependency groups are made up of multiple projects that have relationships among themselves. It is a great way to start practicing software reuse.

❑ **Schedules**
This section lists the schedule available within Anthill. Each schedule also displays the number of minutes till it fires next.

❑ **Build Queue**
The build queue shows which projects (if any) are currently being built or have been scheduled to be built. Most of the time the build queue is empty unless a schedule has just fired or a project has been told to build.

Setting up a New Project

To set up a new project in Anthill, click on the Create New Project link on the main page of Anthill. This will open up the project properties page. This page allows you to configure all the project-specific properties that Anthill needs to build you project:

_temp Properties

The name of this project.	
anthill.project.name	_temp
The class name of the version adapter. Right now only the UrbanCodeVersionAdapter is implemented so do not change this value.	
anthill.version.adapter	com.urbancode.anthill.adapter.UrbanCodeVersionAdapter Configure com.urbancode.anthill.adapter.UrbanCodeVersionAdapter
The class name of the repository adapter. The repository adapter is responsible for interaction with the source control repository.	
anthill.repository.adapter	com.urbancode.anthill.adapter.CVSRepositoryAdapter Configure com.urbancode.anthill.adapter.CVSRepositoryAdapter
The paths to the build script relative to the project root directory.	
anthill.build.script	
Build tagging policy.	
anthill.build.tag	Always ⦿ Successful only ○ Never ○
This is an optional property. The paths to the publish script relative to the project root directory. (In the near future, we are going to get rid of the publish script. Publishing of the projects will still be possible but will need to take place in the main build script.)	
anthill.publish.script	
The path to which the build artifacts are to be moved. Most of the time you can leave this empty. Anthill will then place all publish artifacts in the publishDir/${project.name} directory under the Anthill root. This will by default allow Anthill to make the project artifacts available via a browser at the url: <anthill.server>/anthill/projects/${project.name}.	
anthill.publish.dir	
The url at which the build artifacts are available. Most of the time you can leave this empty. See description of anthill.publish.dir.	
anthill.publish.url	
The email address(es) to send build logs to. The first input field is the user's name and the second is their email address.	
anthill.users	
Email send policy.	
anthill.mail.policy	Always ⦿ Failed builds only ○
Parameters to be passed to Ant during the build process.	
anthill.build.ant.params	
Parameters to be passed to Ant during the publish process.	
anthill.publish.ant.params	
anthill.java.extra.options	
anthill.schedule	default ▾
	Update

Let's cover some of the key properties.

- ❏ **anthill.project.name**

    This property serves as an identifier for the project. The project name should not include any spaces.

- ❏ **anthill.version.adapter**

    The version adapter controls how the version number assigned to the project gets calculated and incremented on every build. This property allows the user to specify the concrete implementation of version adapter that is to be used for the project. In the screenshot the `com.urbancode.anthill.adapter.UrbanCodeVersionAdapter` is used. This default version adapter supports versions in the following format:

    ```
    <prefix><build><postfix>
    ```

    Here, `prefix` can be any alphanumeric string, `build` has to be a numeric string, and `postfix` has to be an alpha string. So you can have a version number such as "1.1.5 Beta" that gets incremented to "1.1.6 Beta" for the next build. Another example of a version number could be "1.2.3 build 432" which would be incremented to "1.2.3 build 433."

- ❏ **anthill.repository.adapter**

    This property identifies the name of the concrete repository adapter that is to be used for this project. In the screenshot the `com.urbancode.anthill.adapter.CVSRepositoryAdapter` is used. Anthill supports CVS, Perforce, PVCS, VSS, MKS, and StarTeam. Support for ClearCase should be available by the time this book comes out. We will discuss the repository adapter properties in more detail in the section on *Configuring the Repository Adapter*.

- ❏ **anthill.build.script**

    This property tells Anthill where to find the project build script relative to the project root. This is a key property; Anthill would not know how to invoke Ant to build the project without this property. Since Anthill knows the location where it put the project sources checked out from VCS, and with the help of the build script property it knows the location of the build script relative to the check out location of the project, it can calculate the absolute path to the build script and use that to invoke Ant.

- ❏ **anthill.build.tag**

    This property determines whether and when Anthill applies a label to the project in the VCS. When set to **Always**, Anthill labels the project in the VCS with the current version number in every build. Setting it to **Successful only** causes Anthill to apply a label only if the build is successful. Setting it to **Never** lets Anthill know that it should not apply a label to VCS under any circumstances.

- ❏ **anthill.users**

    This property allows you to configure the e-mail addresses of the people who will receive the notification e-mails on every build. To add a new person, enter the name or initials in the first text field and the e-mail address in the second text field (the two text fields are located just below the list of the existing user names and their e-mail addresses). To stop sending build status e-mails to a person, just check the box next to that person's name and press the **Update** button.

❏ **anthill.build.ant.params**

As discussed earlier in the chapter, one of the benefits of using properties in your Ant build scripts (instead of hardcoded string values) is that we can override them while calling Ant. This property is used for the same purpose. This property allows us to override property values in our build script with the values specified. As you can see, we are overriding quite a few of the database properties. This is because we do not have a MySQL database installed on the same machine as Anthill; as a result, the default localhost URL used in the build script will not work. But it's not a problem; we can pass the property values that will work in our environment.

With this discussion of all the major property settings that are required to get your project up and running within Anthill completed, now, let's discuss the repository adapter properties.

Configuring the Repository Adapter

The repository adapter is responsible for communicating with the Version Control system (VCS). Anthill supports six different Version Control Systems (CVS, Perforce, PVCS, VSS, MKS, and StarTeam) via a repository adapter specific to each VCS. During the development of the JavaEdge application, we used CVS, a popular open source VCS. Hence, we are going to cover this repository adapter. Anthill needs to know several pieces of information while interacting with CVS, such as how to connect to CVS, which module to work with, where to check out that module, and which branch is to be checked out:

com.urbancode.anthill.adapter.CVSRepositoryAdapter Properties

The name of the directory to which CVS will checkout the project. This must be a relative directory path. The path will be relative anthill's home directory.
repository.cvs.work.dir `work`
The name of the CVS module that stores this project. The paths of the version file, build script, and publish script, are all relative to the CVS module. For example, if the CVS module is Anthill and the build script is Anthill/build/build.xml, then the location of the build script is build/build.xml.
repository.cvs.module ` `
The CVS ROOT used to log in to CVS. Please keep in mind that if you are using pserver authentication, then the user must log in manually from the machine running Anthill into the CVS. (Logging in manually will allow the CVS client to store the CVS password for future use).
repository.cvs.root `:pserver:username@ipOrHost:/usr/local/cvs`
The name of the CVS user account used by Anthill.
repository.cvs.anthill.user `anthill`
The name of the CVS branch that Anthill is to build. (Most of the time this will be blank.)
repository.cvs.branch ` `
Update

❏ **repository.cvs.root**

This property provides the information on how to connect to CVS. The value of this property is in the standard format used by CVS and it identifies the method used to connect to CVS (pserver – password server – in this case), the user connecting (anthill in our example), and the location of the CVS repository (cvs2.urbancode.com:/usr/local/cvs in our case).

❑ repository.cvs.module
The module Anthill needs to work with is identified via this property. For the JavaEdge application, our source code was stored in the waf module.

❑ repository.cvs.work.dir
This property identifies the work directory used by Anthill. This is the directory to which the project source code will be checked out. This directory is relative to the root directory of Anthill. Probably, you will not need to change this default value of work.

❑ repository.cvs.branch
Anthill also support branches and can build software located on a branch. However, the discussion of how to work with branches is beyond the scope of this book. To tell Anthill to build a specific branch, just enter the branch name in this property.

❑ repository.cvs.anthill.user
The value of this property identifies the VCS user account used by Anthill. Using this information, Anthill filters out any revisions made by this user from the list of revisions, which it gets from the VCS. If Anthill did not filter out the changes that it made, it would rebuild the project every time the schedule fired. This is because there would always be at least one revision – the revision of Anthill applying a label to the project in VCS.

Once you've got Anthill properly configured, nothing further is required to let it manage the build process. Every time there is a change in the repository Anthill will automatically trigger a build.

Team Development with Anthill

During a major part of the development of the JavaEdge application, the authors used Anthill to manage builds of the project. Every time one of the authors checked in code changes, Anthill rebuilt the application, ran unit tests, generated Javadocs and source code metrics, and did all those other goodies we put in the build script, then sent an e-mail out to the authors letting them know that a new build of the application was ready. This made it very easy to keep up on the changes being made by other authors. Each e-mail sent out by Anthill announcing a new build included a revision log that listed all the source files changed since the last build as well as the name of the person making the change and a comment describing the change for each source file.

Having the builds take place at a central location ensured that all the dependencies required to build the application were included in the project. Communication about the project was also greatly simplified because the unique build numbers assigned to each build provided a sure way to identify a particular version of the software. If one of the team members was having problems running a particular build of the software, communicating the problem build to others was very explicit. This way, one of the other developers could quickly give the same build a try and identify whether the problem was with the build or with the environment used by the original developer.

Summary

In this chapter, we got acquainted with the Ant build tool, which has become the standard for building Java-based software and is gaining momentum even in non-Java environments. We put together a build script for our JavaEdge application. Our build script produces a whole range of artifacts that are very useful during team-based development. In addition to compiling and packaging the software, our build script creates JavaDocs and to-do lists, calculates code metrics, converts the code to HTML, creates the database, and runs unit tests; and it can do all of this when we issue a single command.

We also looked at how Anthill fits into our build process adding repeatability and consistency. Using Anthill we were able to accomplish our goals of ensuring that only source code that is present in the VCS is included in the build, assigning a unique and traceable version number to every build of the software, and automatically applying a label to the VCS upon every build. Achieving these goals is critical to successful team-oriented development.

Index

A Guide to the Index

The index is arranged hierarchically, in alphabetical order, with symbols preceding the letter A. Most second-level entries and many third-level entries also occur as first-level entries. This is to ensure that users will find the information they require however they choose to search for it.

G

O

W

X

Got more Wrox books than you can carry around?

Wroxbase is the new online service from Wrox Press. Dedicated to providing online access to books published by Wrox Press, helping you and your team find solutions and guidance for all your programming needs.

The key features of this service will be:

- Different libraries based on technologies that you use everyday (ASP 3.0, XML, SQL 2000, etc.). The initial set of libraries will be focused on Microsoft-related technologies.
- You can subscribe to as few or as many libraries as you require, and access all books within those libraries as and when you need to.
- You can add notes (either just for yourself or for anyone to view) and your own bookmarks that will all be stored within your account online, and so will be accessible from any computer.
- You can download the code of any book in your library directly from Wroxbase.

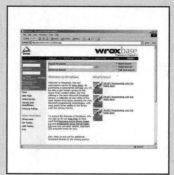

Visit the site at: www.wroxbase.com